Distributed UNIX System Administration

Team Procedures for the Enterprise

John R. Wetsch, Ph. D.

R&D Books
Lawrence, KS 66046

R&D Books
an imprint of Miller Freeman, Inc.
1601 West 23rd Street, Suite 200
Lawrence, KS 66046
USA

Cover art created by Robert Ward.

Distributed in the U.S. and Canada by:
Publishers Group West
1700 Fourth Street
Berkeley, CA 94710
ISBN: 0-87930-540-1

 Miller Freeman
A United News & Media company

Table of Contents

Hardware Administration Module

Network Administration Module

Security Administration Module

Operations Administration Module

Appendices

Introduction

UNIX is an operating system which has evolved from the time of the mainframe and emerged as a useful and reliable multitasking operating system. It began as part of the Multics project, a joint effort between Bell Labs, Massachusetts Institute of Technology, and General Electric. Two Bell Lab computer scientists, Dennis Ritchie and Ken Thompson, combined their knowledge of Multics and the C language (including C's predecessor B) and derived the beginnings of the first UNIX system in the early 1970s.

The emerging technology of the mid-1980s was distributed computing. Networks consisting of personal computers running network and distributed operating systems have become a dominant method of business processing replacing many functions formerly reserved for the mainframe. *Distributed UNIX System Administration: Team Procedures for the Enterprise* focuses on the use of such UNIX systems in the enterprise. It divides the system administration process of an enterprise into modules of software, hardware, network, security, and operations administration and also provides SAmatrix, an automated program written in C++ for managing the tasks of all administration modules. The customizable framework provided by SAmatrix can help an administrator assess a distributed environment to identify weaknesses and organize improvements.

UNIX has proven itself as an operating system capable of running on a wide range of systems that span microcomputers, midrange systems, mainframes, and even supercomputers. UNIX has also become a very open system. Today, there are many variants or flavors of UNIX that include BSD (Berkeley Software Distribution) and its variants (such as Solaris, SunOS, netBSD, freeBSD, and Linux) and System V and its various implementations (such as Xenix, AIX, and HP-UX).

All the UNIX flavors have a lot in common. Nearly all of UNIX is written in C, with only a small part of the kernel coded in assembly language. The part of the kernel written in assembly and the parts specific to a computer architecture are unique to each UNIX environment. The main environment explored in this book is System V UNIX. Variations are noted, but obviously not all variations can be included. However, if your UNIX environment differs from those discussed in the text, the methodology presented here can still form a dynamic foundation that allows you to adapt tasks by categorizing them into administration modules and synthesizing them into operations administration. It can also serve as a stepping stone to learning more about the ever-widening world of UNIX and other computer systems environments.

Features of this Book

Audience

Distributed UNIX System Administration addresses both technical and managerial needs. It assumes at least a user-level knowledge of UNIX.

Conventions

To illustrate commands, output, etc., certain symbols and commands are given special treatment using a system of font types, styles, and symbols as follows:

Symbol description	*Example/illustration*
Commands are Courier bold	**chown**
Nonliteral arguments are Courier italic	**mkdir** *directory*
Input, output, code, parameters, and filenames are Courier	/usr/adm/messages
[] (Brackets) present optional input parameters	**ls** [-l]
~ (Tilde) is the home directory of a user	~*username*
* (Star) is a wildcard for 0 or more characters	*
? (Question mark) matches one character	?
{} (Curly braces) contain parameters, with | for OR selections	{yes|no}
^ or Cntl indicate control key combinations, such as Control-d	^d or Cntl-d

Objectives

As the provider of computing services today, the system administrator must be able to take the broad view of enterprise-wide systems and maintain a local environment. In essence, not unlike the Internet, technical support personnel work in a specified domain of expertise that must go out and connect to other domains. *Distributed UNIX System Administration* seeks to give you an understanding of the domain of the UNIX system administrator and introduces the key areas of UNIX system administration.

Often, system administration and system management tasks can be the same thing. However, as organizations grow, a system manager usually oversees a group of system administrators and other technical personnel and is responsible for setting and enforcing the implementation of IS policies and procedures. But because this book classifies the management of systems into the administrator's domain, it can serve as a means for a systems manager to understand what is required to incorporate a UNIX system into the environment by understanding the general tasks of the manager and other administrators.

Content

The software, hardware, network, and security modules provide the foundation for understanding the tasks required for successful operations administration. You must understand the system before you can properly assess the system. After understanding and assessing the system, only then can you develop an operations management design.

The software module organizes basic kernel and shell programming, file systems, and application management. The hardware module provides the knowledge to manage device drivers and peripheral hardware installation and continuing hardware maintenance. The network module explains how networks are set up on UNIX machines, provides a performance test kit, and presents the options for Internet access.

The security module provides shell scripts and explains procedures for security, system accounting, and monitoring. A layered security environment manages network, system, application, data, and physical security. Utilities to support security procedures are provided for each of these layers.

The operations module brings together each of the previous modules for providing services to users and management information throughout the enterprise. The system administrator must manage a wide range of tasks: kernel rebuilds, troubleshooting, performance monitoring, security, system configuration, programming, etc. The operations administration module offers a methodology for quantifying these tasks. This module establishes a process of measuring operations administration to improve the quality and reliability of a UNIX environment. This methodology can be applied to one or many systems and can provide users with the statistical analysis necessary for an overview of distributed systems that make up an enterprise. The more distributed the system, the more complex the system becomes and the more statistical analysis is needed to understand how the system behaves as a whole. The information obtained from such an analysis gives the UNIX staff the means to establish sound policies and procedures for managing the enterprise and dealing with specific strengths and weaknesses of the system.

Using this methodology, you can adapt any environment into the operations administration module providing a means to address heterogeneous environments in terms of hardware, software, networks, and security. The more thoroughly you can address these environments, the better your assessment results will be.

What this Book Can Do

This book can become a dynamic reference that provides pointers to system level solutions. Inside you will find references that may give you exactly what you are looking for or that may serve as a pointer to additional reference material for more information pertinent to your environment.

What this Book Cannot Do

This book cannot answer all your questions about distributed systems. No single book can do that because the problems that can arise are too numerous and varied.

As a system administrator, you are exposed directly to information glut, endless tasks, and thankless long hours. Working in a technology field, you are constantly barraged with system modifications, updates, configuration changes, and integration of both old and new technology. Your normal routine must be fast moving and provide reliable service to your users, addressing their needs and concerns from just running an application to setting up production and development environments. As your operation progresses from a department or workgroup to an enterprise-wide system, your field of expertise extends beyond the operating system and user support to networks, database administration, security concerns, and overall system management. In an enterprise system, you are no longer the sole system administrator of a UNIX system, but part of a team of technologists that addresses hardware, software, networking, security, and operations issues.

In addition, any distributed system consists of heterogeneous components such as LANs, server platforms, and user interfaces. That translates into Novell networks, TCP/IP, multiple flavors of UNIX, Microsoft NT, mainframe legacy systems, middleware, DOS, Windows, OS/2, etc. — basically a very complicated mix that cannot be managed by one person or understood by reading one book.

A Dynamic Reference for a Dynamic Job

Components of the system administrator's job include supplying information systems (IS) support, providing technical infrastructure, and making sense of the systems so they work. Although the headaches of system management and security for information systems have vastly increased for distributed systems, there are a considerable number of benefits too. Those benefits have given the user a wider variety of applications ranging from development tools to word processing. Overall, a remarkable level of system integration has occurred, such that it is rare to see an office worker without a computer sitting on his or her desktop.

I hope that this book will help support your system administration duties and enable you to manage systems, from large to small, by broadening your knowledge of the UNIX environment and guiding you through the process of developing an enterprise-wide system administration plan. As an administrator or systems manager, understanding your system makes it possible for you to make decisions that affect your system hardware, software, network, security, or operational tasks. Thus, knowledge of your system and the capability to build an effective operations plan are key to enterprise-wide system administration for any environment.

Though complex, UNIX offers advantages to the enterprise that can be enjoyed to their maximum through sound system administration policies and procedures. To that end, *Distributed UNIX System Administration: Team Procedures for the Enterprise* can provide value in supporting and understanding the important UNIX system administration modules.

Software Administration Module

Chapter 1

The Basics

The fundamentals of learning UNIX system administration are understanding the operating system, knowing the key components, and developing an understanding of file organization. The UNIX operating system is a combination of processes, files, and tools, all controlled by the kernel, the UNIX component responsible for managing system tasks. These components give UNIX its strength as an enterprise-wide operating system capable of functioning in nearly every computer environment and platform.

Operating System Overview

UNIX is a set of software programs that allows the computer and the user to interact. This man–machine interface is key to the successful operation of any UNIX system and allows control of the computer, provides packages of tools to facilitate customization of the environment, and is the actual interpreter between you and the machine.

A UNIX system has three basic layers, as depicted in Figure 1.1: the kernel, the shell, and programs.

The top layer contains the environment that the user interacts with directly. The programs and tools used by the system include utility programs that come with the system or were developed by an administrator; programs, tools, and data files for networking and communications; and database, word processing, programming, and other user applications.

To use the top layer, an intermediary is required to interpret and execute instructions and responses between the user and the bottom layer. This intermediary is the shell. A system program, the shell acts as a language interpreter, a customizer of the operating environment, and a translator of all requests submitted to the computer. Multiple shells are able to run on top of the kernel, giving each user a working environment with the ability to run multiple tasks with multiple users. Variants include the C and Korn shells (to be discussed in more detail later) among others.

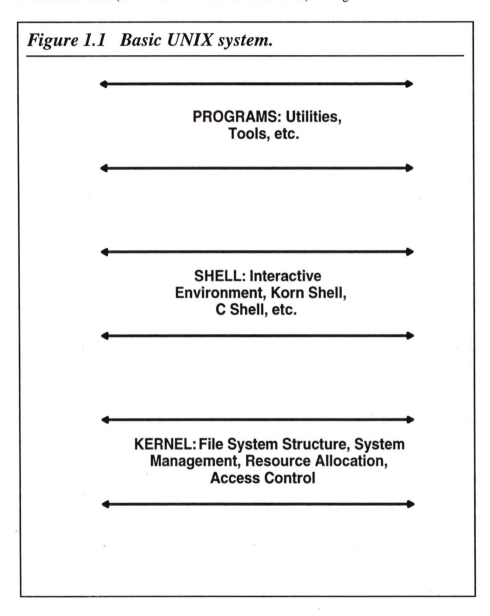

Figure 1.1   Basic UNIX system.

PROGRAMS: Utilities,
Tools, etc.

SHELL: Interactive
Environment, Korn Shell,
C Shell, etc.

KERNEL: File System Structure, System
Management, Resource Allocation,
Access Control

The heart of the UNIX operating system is the kernel or bottom layer as shown in Figure 1.1. The kernel is loaded into memory and stays operational for as long as the computer is on. It is through the kernel that you have access to your machine. It is responsible for computer access control, system resource allocation, file system maintenance, and memory management. Without the kernel the user would not be able to access or use files, interface with the computer, or have an operational UNIX environment.

Shells

A shell is an interactive program executed either automatically when the user logs in, or else by the user from another shell. A shell determines the operating environment and can sometimes be distinguished by its prompt. The executable shell name, descriptive name, and prompt for some shells are:

Shell	*Name*	*Prompt*
sh	Bourne shell	$
bash	Bourne again shell	$
ksh	Korn shell	$
csh	C shell	%
jsh	Job Control shell	$
zsh	Z shell	%

The most common shells are the Bourne shell (**sh**), the C shell (**csh**), and the Korn shell (**ksh**). These common shells come with commercial UNIX OS products, whereas other shells like the Bourne Again shell (**bash**) and the Z shell (**zsh**) are in the public domain and can be obtained from public sites like GNU. Shells are case sensitive and are much like any other program. Your working shell becomes active when you log onto the system and does not terminate until you have logged off. It is the heart of the man–machine interface as it translates your requests and puts needed programs in memory and executes them.

The power of UNIX is in the shell, and it is through the shell that the system administrator controls the system. Acting not just as an interpreter, the shell also provides scripting capabilities that allow you to build your own tools. Skillful shell programming also can become a cornerstone for the success of the system administrator. Being able to write shell programs will allow the administrator to interact with all layers of the UNIX environment from applications and security to networking and system management.

The shell programs are found in the /bin directory. The Bourne shell is the original shell and it can be executed as /bin/sh. The C shell, with a syntax that resembles C, can be found at /bin/csh. The Korn shell, written to merge the best features of the Bourne shell and C shell, can be found at /bin/ksh.

Shell scripts developed in one shell may not seamlessly transfer to another shell, but you can learn their differences through reading and experience. Programs written for this book will be either in the C or Korn shell. I will leave it up to the budding system administrator to run various shells to find differences. It should be noted that a C shell script that begins with a # (pound) character calls a Bourne shell to interpret the shell program. In Bourne shell scripts, programmers may use the : (colon) symbol as an interpreted null. In addition, C shell and newer Bourne shell scripts use the syntax #![*path*], where *path* denotes the shell in which the script should be executed (i.e., #!/bin/sh).

Processes

When interacting with the kernel, a user sends a request through a program, command, or utility expecting a response from the kernel. The kernel responds by executing a special program called a *process*. A process is an executed program that will be managed by the kernel to allow the program to properly execute. During this execution, the kernel also manages file creation and deletion; manages data movement outside of memory; and separates the initiators, or owners, of the process for process management. Processes are started by the kernel through system calls, although the kernel calls the init process directly. In turn, processes are removed from memory by the kernel when completed or killed by an owner or administrator.

The parent process of a user is the shell process, including its environment in which the user works. When the user enters a command, the shell makes a system call, called fork, to the kernel to create a new process. With fork, the kernel creates an exact duplicate of the parent process, called a child process, which includes the program text and data loaded into a different area of memory. (Any process that generates a new process is the parent and the new process generated is known as the child process.) The exec system call is also made to the kernel to allow the process to run. Each process is assigned a process ID (PID). When a process completes, or exits, it lets the parent know and the kernel is notified to free up the resources used by the child. If the parent does not acknowledge the demise of its child, the PID of the child remains, resources are freed, but the result is a process that will not die, known as a "zombie" process. (The administrator sees a zombie as a <defunct> process.) Zombie processes can be a nuisance but are cleared when the system reboots.

Special types of processes are known as *daemon* processes, or just daemons. Once initiated, usually at system startup, daemons provide user services and run without user supervision. They also can be requested by users, a timer, or system occurrences such as errors, which activate errdaemon. As another example, the printer daemon is invoked with the **lp** command. The printer daemon, lpsched, stays in memory in an inactive state until awakened by **lp** to send something to the printer. Other daemons are vigilant such as cron, the UNIX timer program. The cron daemon, used for scheduling, executes programs and commands as defined by the administrator or any user with cron privileges.

Passwords and IDs

The system administrator and all system users begin their interaction with the system by logging in. The user enters a case-sensitive log-in ID and password. [Setting up user log-in IDs and passwords is discussed in the Security Administration module (Chapters 8 and 9)]. Once connected, the system displays a shell prompt, such as $ or %, depending on the shell in use and whether any system-specific customization has been done. A special user ID called root, along with a closely guarded password, allows the user to access the system as a *superuser.* When successfully logged in, the superuser, or root user, will have a distinctive pound sign prompt (#).

The administrator logging in as a superuser carries the responsibility of global privileges; that is, privileges that allow the administrator to do anything permissible to all files, programs, and processes within the UNIX universe. Only the administrator should log in as a superuser. Never give the superuser password to personnel who are not system administrators. In addition, for general system usage, the administrator should not use the superuser password. It is best to log in with your regular user ID, and if superuser privileges are needed in your system travels, use the **su** command to get superuser privileges.

Pathnames and Directories

The # shown in the examples below indicates the system is in superuser mode. For general usage of the commands in the example, superuser privileges are not required. To start, you may want to find the current working directory by executing the **pwd** (print working directory) command:

```
# pwd
# /usr/root
```

If executed right after logging in, **pwd** displays the user's home directory. If you have been moving around in the system and are sure where your home directory is, enter the change directory (**cd**) command without arguments. This action resets the current working directory to your home directory then automatically executes the **pwd** command to print the current working directory.

```
# cd
# pwd
# /usr/root
```

Next, execute a list command to see a directory listing.

```
# ls
bin
c_files
john
list.c
```

So far, these are general user commands, but for the system administrator, the **ls** command can be quite beneficial. When executed with the –a option (for "all"), **ls** provides a complete listing:

```
# ls -a
.
..
.profile
bin
c_files
john
list.c
mbox
```

First, note that . and .. stand for the relative path of the directory. The . (dot) represents the current directory, and the .. (dot dot) represents the parent directory. Files that begin with a . (e.g., .profile) are not displayed using **ls**, whereas **ls** –a does display these hidden files.

User Environments

Note the .profile file, which is used to configure the user environment. A simple .profile file for a user may look like this:

```
$ cat .profile
#
# User profile
#
umask 077
PATH=.:$HOME/bin:$PATH
export PATH
TERM=vt100
export TERM
exec /usr/local/bin/usermenu2
```

Users each have their own profile in their home directories. The user profile can be customized for a particular user or class of users. Therefore, it is possible to set up a profile type for each user type across enterprise systems. This allows users to have access privileges and the appropriate environment for their needs. Also, a system profile is generally kept at /etc/profile that provides system-level configurations persistent for all users.

In the example user .profile, the # sign indicates a standard comment statement for shell programming and C programs. The capitalized words are environment variables. The line PATH=.:$HOME/bin:$PATH assigns the current directory (.) to the PATH variable. A $HOME directory, for example /usr, is assigned to $HOME as well as to the variable $PATH, which may already have an assignment. This line assigns the user's personal path to the PATH variable in the profile. Each path assigned to PATH is separated by a colon (:).

After assigning a variable, complete the configuration by placing the variable in the environment so it is recognized as the correct variable assignment. After assigning PATH, export the PATH variable using the **export** command. The same is done for a proper terminal assignment; that is, the terminal type (vt100) is assigned to the variable TERM, then TERM is exported. Finally, this .profile kicks off a specified user menu with the line **exec** /usr/local/bin/usermenu2. This menu may contain whatever applications and system access the system administrator wants to grant that particular user. For instance, a general system user will have different needs than a software developer, so the system administrator might configure standardized environments for user types.

Classifying the types of users on your system and properly setting up environments is of utmost importance. What really controls the user interaction and access to the system is the shell environment. A user who can access the shell directly can change environment variables. In some cases you may want this, but in others the ability to change shell variables would be undesirable, and the user's shell usage must be restricted. For instance, accessing a Web page through the Internet does not give you access to the system OS but may give you read and write privileges through a Common Gateway Interface (CGI), in which case, going to a Web page and being able to drop to a shell environment would cause security problems.

By setting and exporting variables, it is possible for a user or administrator to change an environment. To see what variables are set for a shell, use the **env** command.

```
$ env

MENU_DIR=/usr/local/menu
LOGNAME=wetsch
MAIL=/var/mail/wetsch
TERM=vt100
```

```
PATH=.:/adm/wetsch/bin:/usr/sbin:/usr/bin:/usr/local/bin
HOME=usr/adm/wetsch
SHELL=/usr/bin/ksh
HZ=100
MANPATH=/usr/share/man:/usr/local/man
EDITOR=/usr/local/bin/vi
TZ=US/Eastern
```

When checking out a user's shell, whether to inspect the variables or solve a problem, a system administrator should never begin by logging in as root, in order to avoid any possible Trojan horses or duplication of the user's problem(s) at the superuser level. It is best to have the user log in first and see what the problem is. If this cannot be done, the superuser can to do a *switch user* using the **su** command to enter the user's environment. However, to go into a user's environment without a password by simulating a login for the user and the user's shell, you must (1) be the superuser and (2) use a dash (–) with the user's log-in ID. If the dash is not used, the current environment you are in will stay the same. For example, # **su** –wetsch switches to the user's environment, and # **su** wetsch keeps the current environment.

Using the dash is crucial. If you keep your environment the same by not using the hyphen option, you may not be able to duplicate the user's problem. Or, if you are able to duplicate the user's problem, the effect of the problem may be increased because variables such as PATH could easily extend to your directory, system directories, etc. Remember, if you set up different .profile for different classes of users, your user class is different than the user you are assisting.

Note that if you know the password of a user and you are not root, you can change your identity to that user by using **su** and entering the password.

Permissions

Execute the **ls** command with the –la option to get a "long format all" listing:

```
total 70
drwx--x--x   5 wetsch    other      512      Aug  9 00:09 .
drwxrwxr-x  36 root      sys       1024      Jul 27 03:01 ..
-rw-------   1 wetsch    other      151      Dec 26 19:95 .profile
-rw-------   1 wetsch    other      512      Aug  9 00:09 .sh_history
drwx------   2 wetsch    other      512      Nov 28 19:95 bin
drwx------   2 wetsch    other      512      Apr  3 19:39 mail
-rw-------   1 wetsch    other 15659        Feb 19 11:32 kermit.man
drwx--x--x   2 wetsch    other      512      Apr  3 19:39 johns_html
```

This list contains, starting at the rightmost column, the name of the file, the date and time the file was created or last modified, and the file size in bytes. The remaining four columns contain information regarding permissions related to the file.

UNIX files have basically three types of owner permission groups. These permissions are the user, a specified group, or root. The fourth column from the right in the long format listing lists the groups with access to each file. A group is defined as a group of users (such as *other* or *sys* in the example), all of whom are given the same permissions, as opposed to the permissions granted to individual users or the permissions given to the world. Groups can be defined by the system administrator to accommodate groups of users at all levels, from managers to developers.

To the left of the group name is the owner of the file. The number to the left of the owner is the number of links to the file. A link is a symbolic reference to a file allowing more than one name to be used to reference the same file. In the leftmost column is a 10-bit descriptor of the file type as well as the permissions available to root, group, or owner. The leftmost bit begins with:

– (dash)	ordinary file
d	directory
b	a device file, block type
c	a device file, character type
s	a domain socket file
l	a symbolic link to a file
p	a named pipe

The next nine bits refer to the permissions allowed for the file. These bits are broken up into three groups of three as shown in Figure 1.2.

From left to right, the first three bits set permissions for the file owner, the next three bits set permissions for the group, and the last three bits set permissions for all other users. The superuser of the system has the ability to set and maintain all nine permission bits so that the integrity and availability of the system can be maintained.

Three types of permissions are available: read (r), write (w), and execute (x). Read permission allows the user to look at the file while preventing the user from making changes. The write permission allows the privileged user to read and make changes to

---

Figure 1.2 File system permissions.

l user permissions   l group permissions   l other permissionsl the file. If the file is a shell script or some other executable program, the execute option allows the owner to run the program. So a file with the designation

```
-rw-------
```

indicates that it is an ordinary file with read and write privileges available to root and the owner. If the permissions are

```
-r-----r--
```

owner and other, only, have read privileges and the group is excluded. Setting the ownership on *other* means global or world read access to the file; that is, anybody, including the group, which appears excluded, can read it.

chmod is the command to change permissions. You can use **chmod** two ways. The first method is more symbolic and uses the designators

u	the User
g	the Group
o	Other users
a	All users

In addition, a plus sign (+) is used to add permissions, and the minus sign (−) is used to remove permissions. The syntax of **chmod** in this format is

```
# chmod [ugo] [+|-] [rwx] file(s)
```

To add a write permission to the kermit.man file for the world (other), enter:

```
# chmod o+w kermit.man
```

The long list (**ls** -l) before and after is

Before

```
-rw-------  1 wetsch    other    15659 Feb 19 11:32    kermit.man
```

After

```
-rw-----w-  1 wetsch    other    15659 Feb 19 11:32    kermit.man
```

To remove the write permissions altogether, enter

```
# chmod uo-w kermit.man
```

and `ls` –l returns

```
-r--------   1 wetsch    other    15659 Feb 19 11:32    kermit.man
```

This symbolic method has a numeric counterpart based on octal numbers. Experienced system administrators prefer the numeric method because it gives brevity to the **chmod** command and greater control with the shortened syntax. In the numeric method, the permissions for each bit group area can be populated with a number from 0 to 7. That means a single octal number defines permissions for user, group, or other, as shown in Table 1.1.

To set permissions on `kermit.man` to write-only for the user or owner of the file and read-only for the world, enter

```
# chmod 204 kermit.man
```

`ls` –l now returns

```
--w----r--   1 wetsch    other    15659 Feb 19 11:32    kermit.man
```

From **chmod** 204, note that w is set for the owner with octal 2. The first number thus sets the three permission bits of the user/owner group. The second number, 0, sets the permission values for the group bits. In this case, no permissions were set. The last three permission bits, for the world or other, are set in this example with octal 4, which sets only the read permission bit.

The nine permission bits are not the only bits in town. In addition to r, w, and x permissions, there are also the s, t, and l permissions. These permissions describe the complete *mode* of a file. The s permission sets the user ID (setuid), t sets the

Table 1.1	**chmod** *octal permission description.*	
Octal	*Permission Bits*	*Description*
0	---	No permissions set
1	--x	Execute permission set
2	-w-	Write permission set
3	-wx	Write and execute permissions set
4	r--	Read permission set
5	r-x	Read and execute permissions set
6	rw-	Read and write permissions set
7	rwx	Read, write, and execute permissions set

sticky bit, and l sets mandatory locking. A file mode can be described as the state a file is in by its bit settings. For instance, changing the permission bits changes the security or protection mode of the file. All files can have their mode set, but it is most important for the operation of executable files.

Setting a sticky bit on an executable file allows an image of text from the program to be placed in the swap area so that the program loads faster at execution. It is not used as often today as it was in the early history of UNIX, but it is sometimes reserved for use on large executable files that include system deliverables, such as editors, compilers, and shells. Therefore,

```
# chmod +t filename
```

sets the sticky bit, and **ls** -l before and after shows

Before

```
-rwxr-xr-x  2 root bin     156059 Feb 12 11:32   filename
```

After

```
-rwxr-xr-t  2 root bin     156059 Feb 12 11:32   filename
```

Caution: If you like making programs sticky, remember not to overdo it. Each sticky program uses swap space. Therefore, with many sticky programs and many users executing those programs on the system, your swap space will overrun and a noticeable degradation of your system will occur. Sticky programs should be limited to less than one-third of your available swap space.

When setting the sticky bit on a directory, it is possible to set up the directory to give only root and the owner of a file in the directory the ability to delete the file. Setting the sticky bit on files located in public directories prevents nonowners of a file and nonsuperusers from cleaning out the files of others. For example, the public directory /tmp may appear as

```
drwxrwxrwx  1 bin  bin      512 Feb 12 11:32   tmp
```

By setting the sticky bit with **chmod** +t /tmp, the listing appears as

```
drwxrwxrwt  1 bin  bin      512 Feb 12 11:32   tmp
```

With this setting, the file owner now has some protection for files located in public places. Note that this setting can be applied to any directory, but it makes sense primarily for public directories because private directories should have the permission bits set properly.

You can also use octal numeric representation with **chmod** to set additional bits; hence, four octal numbers instead of three are used to set file permissions. Use Octal 1000 to turn on a sticky bit. Additional control is achieved with the set user ID (**setuid**) and the set group ID (**setgid**) commands. By setting these bits, you can pass owner permissions to the group. Octal 2000 and 4000 represent **setuid** and **setgid**, respectively. When these bits are set, an s replaces one of the bits in the permission lineup of r, w, or x.

Passing the permission of the owner can cause a security concern. **setuid** and **setgid** are discussed more fully in the Security module (Chapters 8 and 9). Other items of note concern setting SUID and getting a permission listing like -rwSr-xr-x, meaning that SUID is set but the execute bit is not. Also, when copies of a file are made, the permission bit settings are not preserved and will default to the privileges of the owner making the copy.

Two more methods can be used to assign permissions: the = symbol and the **umask** command. To assign read and write permissions to all, use

```
# chmod a=rw filename
```

in addition to the previous methods of

```
# chmod ugo+r+w-x filename
```

or

```
# chmod 555 filename
```

or

```
# chmod +rw-z filename
```

Finally, the **umask** command allows the permission mode to be set automatically. In the output of the .profile file shown previously, **umask** 077 is the first command in the file. The 077 does not set the permissions bit to 077 as **chmod** 077 does by setting permissions to read, write, and execute for everyone and the group and turning them off for the user, the owner of the file. Rather, **umask** 077 masks out the read, write, and execute bits for the *group* and *other* but not for the user. **umask** 077 effectively turns the read, write, and execute permissions on for the user and turns off all other permission bits. The resultant file, when created by the user, is

```
-rwx------  1 user1   other    15659 Feb 19 11:32   filename
```

```
# umask 000 results in
```

```
-rwxrwxrwx  1 user1    other      15659 Feb 19 11:32    filename
```

You must be cautious when applying **umask** to directories. When the permissions of a directory are set, they apply to all files in the directory. That is, if you set a directory through **umask** to be read-only, any file in that directory, regardless of its assigned permissions, will be read-only. Thus, by setting the system umask, you are effectively setting the parameters on how others can access their files. To find out what the umask value is for your system, just enter **umask** at the prompt.

In addition to the topics covered in this overview of the UNIX system, five other areas are basic to UNIX: logins, system startup/shutdown, where to find files, scheduling, and using an editor.

Logins

Logging in, one of the most important features of a system, allows a user access to the system and validates that user as someone authorized to use the system. The system administrator must not only assign user log-in IDs and passwords but must also manage users and help them to successfully log on to the system, a challenging task when dealing with new system users.

At login, the screen displays a banner of some sort that welcomes you to the system. Some systems use disclaimers or warnings as a banner to inform you of the system's intended use. Along with a banner, the system displays a log-in prompt, such as

```
Welcome to the Enterprise UNIX system

login: wetschj
```

After entering a user ID, such as wetschj, the system prompts you for a password:

```
password:
```

The system does not display the password you enter in order to prevent others from seeing it on the screen. If you type your password incorrectly, you receive an error message. The system administrator may also limit the number of incorrect login tries you can make on the system before you are logged off.

Once logged in, you may be asked to enter your terminal type with

```
TERM=(vt100)
```

Your default terminal type is displayed in parentheses. Pressing the Return key accepts the default. To change the terminal type, type a new one in before pressing Enter. For example:

TERM=(vt100) vt320

The system then looks in the terminal configuration files for a valid terminal type that can be assigned to the TERM variable. If the system finds a valid type it returns the response

Terminal is vt320

If an invalid terminal type is entered, the response is

Terminal unknown

Having the wrong terminal type assigned to TERM causes predictable but peculiar results. Characters to the screen may be doubly echoed, line wraps may not work properly, backspaces and control codes may not be interpreted properly, uppercase and lowercase output to the screen may be reversed, or keyboard keys may not be properly enabled. These problems should first be addressed by checking the TERM variable using the **env** command. In addition, you may want to check to see if the terminal default matches the terminal actually being used. If you get meaningless characters on your screen after a successful login, it is also possible that the terminal is communicating at the wrong speed. Pressing the Break or Return key can sometimes rectify this problem. If not, try logging in again and check for the correct terminal type.

The only time a user does not need to log in to a system is when the system login is already established and a session is open. Also, some log-in procedures may be transparent between systems after an initial login. This allows users to move between systems that belong to the same network while logging in to only one system on the network. Getting out of a working session can vary, but usually entering **exit** or Cntl-d (^d) works.

Shutdown

Important to operating any UNIX system is properly shutting it down and starting it up. Unlike a PC running DOS, a UNIX system cannot just be powered off. An arbitrary poweroff runs a risk of damaging system files and directories and possibly even the drive. Only in emergencies, such as an evacuation where a quick shutdown is needed or when power is to be shutdown to your facility and you have no time to perform the shutdown procedure, should a poweroff be attempted. When you return to resurrect the system, be prepared to do some work to get everything back in shape.

If you want to see what run level your system is at, execute the **who** -r command:

```
run-level 3   Feb 8   22:12   3   0   S
```

In this example, the current run level of the system is 3 and the information to the right states that on February 8th at 10:12 PM, the system was moved from run level S to run level 0. Some UNIX systems, such as BSD and XENIX, only recognize multi-user and single-user modes, in which case the results of **who** -r will vary from this example.

The **shutdown** command is located in a system directory, usually the /etc directory for System V UNIX systems or the /sbin or other system file storehouse directory in other systems. **shutdown** is used to put the system in an assigned state and can only be run by root. The general states, modes of operation, or init levels (i.e., the same as run levels) are shown in Table 1.2.

Init levels above 3 exist, including an init level 4, which may be defined by the user; init level 5, which is another shutdown mode; and init level 6, for an immediate shutdown.

As shown in Table 1.2, init levels S and 1 appear to be duplicates. However, there are some discrete differences between these seemingly identical modes. With init level S, the system administrator brings the system into a maintenance mode and removes any background processes. Init level 1 keeps the background processes running. Thus, at init level 1, all daemon processes are running, whereas init level S only maintains the required daemons. Init levels 2 and 3 are both multi-user run levels and can be used on network systems. However, init level 3 allows for remote file sharing and networked systems, whereas init level 2 is expected for non-networked systems.

An init level can be called in two ways, and permission to set an init level should be restricted to the superuser. First, the **init** command can be used to shut down the system.

```
# init 0
```

Table 1.2   Primary shutdown init levels.

Init level	Description
S	Single-user mode
0	Prepare system for a power down
1	Single-user mode
2	Multi-user mode
3	Network multi-user mode

However, the **shutdown** command is considered better because it gives the system administrator more options. In the command line

shutdown -i0 -g60 -y

the -i option sets the init level to 0; -g sets a grace period before shutdown of 60 seconds, although some systems may define this as 60 minutes; and -y sets a yes response to any system prompts. Without -y, the system administrator is prompted to confirm shutdown. Shutdown takes a system down gracefully. It sends shutdown messages that warn users to get off the system (this is why a grace period is important), and it may even perform a file system check (fsck) when the system is rebooted. An fsck during maintenance is prudent but not always needed during shutdown. It prolongs the process; that is, a **shutdown** command requires changing the system to a different run level when returning the system to regular user mode. When rebooting the system after the shutdown, the reboot startsthe fsck process. For a faster boot on BSD systems with **shutdown**, bypass fsck at startup with the -f option. However, in most cases the regular reboot using fsck should be used to provide necessary file system checks at startup.

On BSD systems, the syntax for the **shutdown** command varies. Basically, execute the command with the time of shutdown specified as now, in minutes, or by clock time with a supplied message to be broadcast to all users. For example, enter

shutdown 23:00 "System will shutdown at 11:00 PM"

or

shutdown +30 "System will shutdown in 30 minutes"

or

shutdown now "System will shutdown now"

Shutting the system down to maintenance mode will be discussed in the next chapter. A recommended procedure to prepare for a normal System V UNIX powerdown is:

1. Whenever possible, warn users with the system news motd file when the system will be down and for how long. (motd is used to store messages that are read by users at login.)
2. Log in to the system as the superuser.
3. Use the **wall** command to send a message to all users that the system will be going down. Usually 10–15 minutes prior to shutdown is enough warning. I usually give enough time to allow a call just in case a user is in the middle of an important process that may extend beyond the scheduled shutdown time by a few minutes.

4. Check to see how many users are on the system with **who** -u or **ps** -ef (alone or with an appropriate pipe to **grep** *processtype*).

5. Execute the **sync** command. In UNIX this is a traditional shutdown step, although on some machines it may not be needed. When invoking sync, the buffers are flushed and a correct system image is written to disk. In some **shutdown** commands, sync is embedded and executes automatically. Nonetheless, running sync is good practice.

6. Finally, execute the **shutdown** command to init level 0. A grace period should be called, and the -y option should be used (i.e., **shutdown** -i0 -g60 -y). Caution: Once a shutdown is in progress, do not attempt to interrupt it. It is better to let the system come down gracefully, then you can restart it.

When the shutdown process is complete, the system sends a message saying it is safe to powerdown or restart the system. You may be prompted to Press any key to reboot when a shutdown is complete. Watch your screen and note any system prompts that appear. Also note that outputs to the screen tell you what daemons are being turned off. During shutdown, observing output messages can give you an excellent sense of what is happening during the shutdown process.

During the shutdown process, the system runs an init level script, which in turn invokes utilities to bring the system down gracefully. On a System V UNIX box, the /etc/rc0 script invokes UNIX utilities and commands to bring the system down. (Note: the /etc/rc[0-6] scripts are used to set up the proper init level during init level changes, shutdowns, and system startups.) The /etc/rc0 script invokes the killall utility, which cleans up daemons and other processes that are running by issuing **sync** commands as needed, unmounting file systems using **umountall**, and issuing the **uadmin** command to halt the processor.

In a BSD system, you have a different array of shutdown options available. For instance, if you are going to shut the system down for a poweroff, using the -h option will completely halt UNIX.

```
# shutdown -h +10 "Down for Maintenance in 10 Minutes"
```

Here, the time option of 10 minutes is set and the shutdown message Down for Maintenance in 10 Minutes is broadcast to the users. Another BSD shutdown parameter is r with the same syntax as -h. The -r option causes an immediate reboot when the system reaches maintenance mode. This option should be used to warm boot your system.

Startup

System startup is as important as shutdown. You can begin a startup when shutdown is complete. As with a shutdown, observing what happens can give you insight into the startup process: watch your screen and note any system prompts and outputs that appear.

Unless you are booting up to a maintenance level after a shutdown, some UNIX systems give you this option by way of ^d (Cntl-d). That is, after shutdown you will receive a prompt for the root user ID, which when entered, places the system at init level 1.

When booting the system, the BIOS boots from your hardware followed by a boot of the UNIX operating system. If your system has multiple operating systems, you may be prompted for a particular one; if you do nothing, the system may boot to a default. When booting is complete, the log-in prompt should appear.

Note that some UNIX systems may have customized boot scripts that run after the normal boot to bring a special peripheral online, do some automatic function, or perform some other task. In this case, the boot script should be allowed to run after the initial login appears. When it is finished, the login should reappear or be accessible.

Starting from scratch, the first order of business to get UNIX operational is for the read-only memory (ROM) in the hardware to start. The instructions in ROM do some initial checking and internal configuration to your system and send instructions to the CPU to start loading the kernel through a program called the loader, accessible from the first block on the hard disk. The loader loads into random access memory (RAM) and prepares to load the kernel. The kernel may load automatically, or you may be presented with a colon (:) prompt, whereby you need to press Enter to begin the load.

The kernel is located in the root file system and may be called unix. When loaded, the kernel performs a self-initialization and loads a swapper program used for scheduling UNIX processes. Once the swapper is in place, the system must recognize the devices attached to it. This is done through the init process, which reads the /etc/inittab file and brings up the system configuration. When this is complete, you are prompted to enter the date.

Next, the system checks the file systems; then you are prompted to run fsck. After fsck is complete or omitted (it is best to let fsck run at this time), the commands in the /etc/rc file, the run commands file, are run. The rc file contains the necessary information to run the system at the specified init level, which includes cleaning the /tmp directory, mounting file systems, making sure system daemons and other required services are started, and doing other necessary startup and system cleanup tasks.

Now the kernel needs to connect to a terminal to let the administrator log in. This is done with the getty process, which reads the gettydefs file and configures the TTYs for user access (more on gettydefs to follow). The system should now be up at the proper run level, with an active terminal and a log-in prompt displayed. From this point on users can access the shell and execute commands.

Finding Files

The traditional method for displaying the basic UNIX file layout is the tree structure. This hierarchical structure is illustrated in Figure 1.3, which shows the top level (root) of the tree structure and subsequent directories under root, with the blocks under each directory representing files.

UNIX systems have special directories that specify the locations of important files. Files exist at the root directory, but four of the main directories underneath root are bin, tmp, etc, and usr. Depending on the flavor of UNIX you are using, you may have other key subdirectories such as var, adm, lib, and others.

The bin directory contains the UNIX files required for the fundamental operation of the system. This allows the administrator to use UNIX utilities when only the root file system is mounted. Other utilities are stored in /usr/bin. The /tmp directory is where temporary files are stored. The /etc directory has utilities geared for the system administrator as well as a significant number of subdirectories for program defaults (/etc/default), the init level scripts (/etc/rc.d), and kernel and device driver configuration files (/etc/conf). Additional locations for compilers, mail, printing, user home directories, temporary storage, and more is located in /usr subdirectories. The /dev directory is an important file directory for device files for UNIX system peripherals.

A listing of the /root directory may look like this:

```
# ls -l
total 8534
-r--------   1 root   auth        0 Aug 20   20:11  .lastlogin
-rw-------   1 root   root       15 Dec 14   1995   .mailrc
-rw-------   1 root   root      885 Sep 15   1996   .profile
-rw-------   1 root   other    4868 Feb 02   1995   .sh_history
```

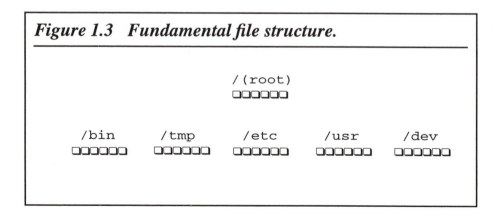

Figure 1.3   Fundamental file structure.

```
-rw-r--r--    1 root   root       833 Jan 04   1995   .utillist2
drwxr-xr-x    2 bin    bin       2416 Jul 17   1995   bin
-r--------    1 bin    bin      78725 Jan 22   1995   boot
-rw-r--r--    1 root   other       28 Oct 27   1995   con
drwxr-xr-x    9 bin    bin       9024 Jan 17   1995   dev
-r--------    1 bin    bin        584 Dec 15   1995   dos
-rw-r--r--    1 root   other      508 Oct 13   1995   error.sh
drwxrwxr-x   19 bin    auth      3664 Aug 20   20:11  etc
drwxrwxr-x    5 bin    bin       2640 Aug 07   1995   lib
drwxr-xr-x    2 root   root      1024 Dec 29   1995   lost+found
-rw-------    1 root   other     4554 Mar 12   11:53  mbox
drwxrwxrwx    2 root   root        32 Jan 22   1995   mnt
drwxr-xr-x    2 bin    bin        128 Jan 22   1995   shlib
d--x--x--x    6 bin    bin         96 Jan 22   1995   tcb
drwxrwxrwt    4 sys    sys       2288 Aug 20   20:15  tmp
drwxrwxrwx    8 root   other      224 Sep 23   1995   tmpsend
-r--r-----    1 bin    mem    1023411 Apr 17   1995   unix
-r--r-----    1 bin    mem    1008672 Jan 17   1994   unix.old
-r--r-----    1 root   other  1025248 Apr 17   1995   unix.sav
drwxrwxr-x   42 root   auth       720 Mar 01   1995   usr
drwxr-xr-x    3 root   sys         48 Jan 22   1995   var
drwxr-xr-x    3 root   other      128 Oct 28   1995   vfind
#
```

The kernel or core of your operating system is the file labeled `unix`. Notice two additional files, `unix.old` and `unix.sav`. System administrators keep old kernels that they know are stable on their system for emergencies. This is especially important when a new kernel is built and then found not suitable because the kernel became corrupted or a device was configured incorrectly. It is imperative to get the system back up and running. By booting from an old kernel, such as `unix.sav` or even an older one, `unix.old`, the system can be brought up, and a new kernel can be configured. Other directories, subdirectories, and files are discussed later in this book.

Scheduling

In nearly every computing environment it is necessary to automatically schedule tasks. In UNIX, this is accomplished using `cron`, the UNIX timer. The `cron` daemon runs in multi-user mode, is time responsive, and reads the `/etc/spool/cron/crontabs` directory. Files created to run a cron can be generated easily with an editor. To list the contents of the cron file, enter **crontab** -l. To unload, or remove, the cron file, enter **crontab** -r.

Cron continues to operate after a user has logged off the system and can be used for any automated function a user deems necessary. Because of the sensitivity of cron to time, it is recommended that date changes to the system be done when the system is in single-user mode, during which cron is inactive and cron processes cannot be inadvertently started or ignored. A cron file can be given any name and may appear as:

```
0 5 * * * echo "Time for System Maintenance" > /dev/ttyaA
0 4 1 ** /usr/lib/monitor
0 4 1 * * /usr/lib/syschk
#15 14 3 2 1 //bin/date>/dev/console
```

The above example is short but illustrates the point. First, an * (asterisk) is used as a wildcard, and the # (pound) is used to provide a comment or to comment out a line so it is not executed. Of the numbers from left to right in the line

```
0 5 * * * echo "Time for System Maintenance" > /dev/ttyaA
```

0 refers to minutes, 5 refers to hours, and the next place holders are the day of the month, the month, and the day of the week. The asterisks in the day of the month, month, and day of the week locations refer to any day of any month. Sunday is considered as the first day of the week, and it is numerically labeled 0. Therefore, to kick off a backup routine at 10:00 PM every Sunday, enter into a cron file

```
0 22 * * 0 /bin/cpio -ocvB > /dev/tape
```

To run a different backup procedure every day of the week except Sunday at 10:00 PM, enter

```
0 22 * * 1-6 /usr/adm/backup1
```

As shown in the line above, you can enter a range by using a – (dash) and match all values for a particular field using an * (asterisk). You can also select multiple parameters for a specific field by using a , (comma). For instance, to list all processes running on a system every 15 minutes and save them to a log file, enter

```
0,15,30,45 * * * * /bin/ps -ef >>/usr/adm/process.log
```

In the example above, the file process.log would get unbearably large if not maintained. But to gather a sample of processes running unattended for a brief period of time, such a statement could be useful. When finished, the line could be removed from crontab or commented out with the comment symbol (#) for use at a later time. In practice, the cron file may be long and should be well written. Comments should be used to section off the file in order to display administrative functions, system functions, security functions, etc., for better maintenance of the file.

To activate a cron file, use the **crontab** command. For example, you could start a cron file with the name admcron with

#**crontab** admcron

This will load the file and activate admcron. If it does not load and you receive an error message, you probably already have a cron file running. This active cron file can be unloaded using the -r option with crontab as noted above (e.g., **crontab** -r). Then the crontab file must be reloaded. It is best to check to see if you have a cron file active using the **crontab** -l command before trying to load a new file.

The system administrator can control cron access and record cron activity. In the /usr/lib/cron directory, you can create the files cron.allow and cron.deny. In these files, you can place log-in names of users who are allowed cron access in the allow file and those restricted in the deny file. To cut down on having to maintain these files, the administrator can simplify matters by entering only users allowed in cron.allow and not use the cron.deny file. It should be noted that cron.allow and cron.deny are not necessary, nor are they dependent on each other. The absence of both of these files will allow only root to access cron, or if cron.allow is absent and an empty cron.deny is present, all users may have access to cron.

For cron to log cron activity to a file, change directory to /etc/default and create a log file called cron by entering the variable CRONLOG=yes in the file and then saving it. If the cron log file already exists, edit the existing file using the vi editor. You will have to reboot your system, but your /usr/lib/cron/log will now be active. With a lot of cron activity, this file can get quite large, so it is imperative that it is monitored. When it gets too large, you can zero out the file by entering

> /usr/lib/cron/log

Note that the > (greater than) symbol is a redirection operator. In this case, you are redirecting nothing to the file, and it will be overwritten by a file with the same name (i.e., log). If you use the >> symbol, you append to the file. For example, the command line

cat log.old >> log

would append the file log.old to the file log. Of course, the first time this is done log is empty, and when the operation is complete, the files are equivalent in content. Note: Redirection is a very powerful means to move and save data and manipulate files. For additional information, see Appendix E, *UNIX Shell Script Construction.*

Using an Editor

An editor is a much-needed tool that gives the system administrator the ability to write and modify tools and utilities as needed. This section focuses solely on vi.

To open an existing file or to create a new file, the **vi** command is invoked:

```
# vi filename
```

In UNIX, everything is file based and files can be open in different modes. In the line

```
# vi +n filename
```

the letter *n* specifies the line number to go to in the file you are opening. The line

```
# vi + filename
```

opens a file at the last line of the file. The line

```
# vi +/{x} filename
```

opens to a specified character string {*x*} in the file. The line

```
# vi -r filename
```

opens the last changes made to a file. Finally, the –R option, as in

```
# vi -R filename
```

opens the file for read-only mode. Read-only mode is also accomplished by

```
# view filename
```

To learn more about the vi editor, see Appendix D, *Using the vi Editor.*

Summary

This chapter presented many of the fundamentals of beginning UNIX administration. A system overview discussed how the shell controls all user access to the system, introduced the concept of a process and how it differs from a program, and discussed methods of controlling access through the use of passwords and IDs.

The system overview introduced the concepts of paths and directories and discussed how an understanding of file organization and file permissions can help you keep your system organized and user access maintained with processes such as chmod and umask. System organization is defined first and foremost by the directory hierarchy, with root at the top followed by the subsequent key system directories.

Finally, the system overview discussed how permissions and environment variables define how an administrator or user uses the system. The ability to grant permissions and configure environment variables affords an administrator considerable authority in the system, which directly affects the man–machine interface for all users.

This chapter also discussed how to gracefully bring the system down to perform maintenance and how to set up scheduling. Maintenance allows the administrator to keep the system in top shape. While in maintenance mode, the administrator also can accomplish tasks, such as setting permissions, scheduling, loading drivers, etc., without adversely affecting a user — except that users other than the administrator cannot access the system when it is in maintenance mode.

This chapter shows how to get a better view of your system — by determining what is in it, what runs on it, and what is required to run on the system — with the use of the **ls**, **pwd**, **ps**, and **env** commands.

## Chapter 2

File Systems

The backbone of a UNIX system is its file system. As such, this system must be maintained to ensure optimal performance, security, and functionality of the system.

Logical and Physical Structure

The Directory Tree

The system itself can be interpreted as both a logical and physical structure. To better understand the UNIX file system, the previous chapter introduced the hierarchical tree structure, a logical representation of the system that looks at the file structure from the top down with the root file system at the top. A file system is a directory and all its associated subdirectories and files. Figure 2.1 shows the hierarchy of the UNIX file system with all directories stemming from root.

In addition to the key directories stemming from root, Figure 2.1 shows two additional file systems, /usr1 and /usr2. You can assume that the system administrator has added these two additional directories to root.

Directory /usr1 contains three additional subdirectories: /bin, /data, and /utils. Theoretically, you can add logical subdirectories and files up to infinity to both /usr1 and /usr2. Figure 2.2 shows file systems (dashed lines) stemming either from root or another subdirectory. A directory that resides above another in the hierarchical scheme is known as the parent directory.

The physical view of the UNIX file system shows its uniqueness. A physical structure representation is depicted in Figure 2.2. Note the dashed lines connecting / usr1 and /usr2 to root. The dashed lines indicate that these file systems can be attached to or detached from root, a mechanism known as *mounting* and *unmounting* the file system. Figure 2.2 also depicts the key directories (i.e., /bin, /dev, /usr, etc., mentioned in Chapter 1) as attached to root by a solid line, meaning these are subdirectories of the root file system and cannot be unmounted. Mountable directories, such as /usr1 and /usr2, can be detached.

A physical file system is a directory structure of additional subdirectories and files that can be physically separated from the root directory. The root directory is also a physical file system, but as long as UNIX is running, it cannot be unmounted. Important directories are actually subdirectories of root that can be accessed as long as UNIX is running. If these directories were in a mountable file system other than root, the utilities and tools located in them would not be accessible until their parent directory was mounted.

For mounted file systems, root is the top level of the file hierarchy followed by the mounted file system. If the file system is not mounted, it should not appear as a directory listing with the **ls** -li command. In addition, the **ls** -li command verifies that the mounted file system appears as a directory under root.

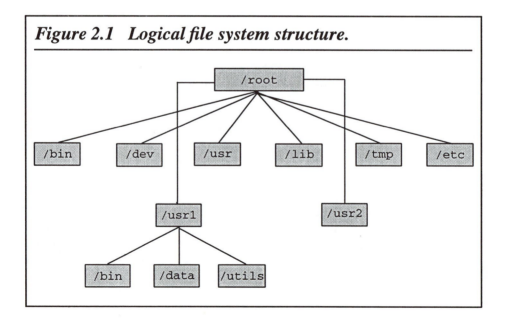

Figure 2.1   Logical file system structure.

Navigating the File System

The directory structure provides the road map to a UNIX system. If you were inside the UNIX kernel trying to find the file /usr1/data/appdb, you would begin by stepping out of the kernel into the electronic stream on stepping stones called nodes. The first node would be the root (/) node. Root would point to /usr1, /usr1 would point to the node /data, which in turn would point to the destination file appdb. These nodes are information nodes and are referred to as *inodes*.

Block Structure

A file system is partitioned into 1,024 bytes/block. Some UNIX systems may have a variant to the block size, but it will always be a multiple of 512; thus, the minimum block size could be 512 bytes/block.

A file system block structure is depicted in Figure 2.3.

The very first block is block 0, also known as the *boot block*. The boot block is followed by the *superblock*. Following the boot block and superblock are a variable number of blocks known as the *i-list*. The i-list stores a list of numbers known as the inodes. Once a boot block, superblock, and i-list have been defined, the remaining blocks, up to the amount of free disk space, are allocated as data blocks to store data, programs, additional directories, etc.

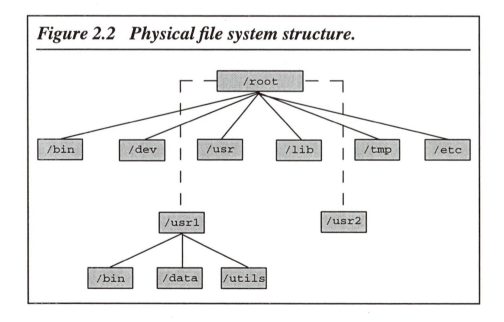

Figure 2.2   Physical file system structure.

Superblocks

Mounting a file system creates two superblocks per file system: one stored in memory, the other kept on the disk. When a file system is changed, such as when a file or directory is added or deleted, the memory copy is updated. When shutting down a system, it is important to maintain the superblock so that changes to a file system are maintained. When the file system is unmounted or the **sync** command is run, the superblock on the disk is changed to reflect the superblock in memory. If this is not done, then your system may think it has files available that were deleted, or worse, files that were loaded onto the system may appear missing.

The information in the superblock is critical to a file system. The superblock contains:

- size of the file system
- total number of inodes and blocks available
- location of blocks and inodes
- blocks allocated to inodes
- free blocks available
- how the file system has been mounted
- other information, including the type of UNIX system you are using

---

Figure 2.3 Basic UNIX block structure.

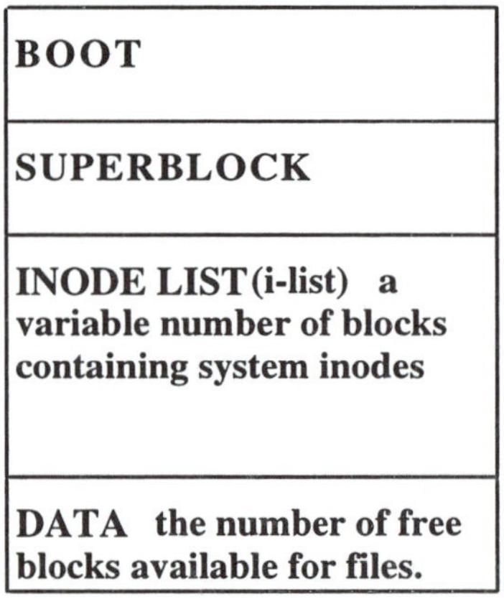

BOOT

SUPERBLOCK

INODE LIST (i-list) **a variable number of blocks containing system inodes**

DATA **the number of free blocks available for files.**

Inodes

The inodes stored in the file system not only contain road map information on a file, but discrete descriptive information, too. This information is interpreted when you run the **ls** command. Inode information includes:

* number of file links
* dates of file creation, modification, and access
* an inode change date
* user and group ownership
* permissions of the file, including an execution flag
* file type (i.e., directory, ordinary file, special file, named pipes)
* file size
* starting block address

Whenever you change permissions, create a file, etc., you are changing and generating inode information. An **ls** -1 printout from an assortment of directories shows the information the inode stores:

```
drwxr-xr-x    9 bin    bin      6870    Feb 5    11:18 dev
-r--------    1 bin    bin     78725    Mar 22   1995  boot
crw--w--w-    1 root   root   19,135    Mar 22   1995  /dev/ttyA
brw-rw-rw-    5 bin    bin     2,  4    Mar 22   1992  fd10
```

To actually see the inode number of the file, execute **ls** -1i:

```
12543    drwxr-xr-x 9 bin    bin      6870    Feb 5   11:18 dev
23451    -r-------- 1 bin    bin     78725    Mar 22 1995  boot
345211   crw--w--w- 1 root   root   19,135    Mar 22 1995  /dev/ttyA
45633    brw-rw-rw- 5 bin    bin     2,  4    Mar 22 1992  fd10
```

The new number to the far left in each line is the inode number for the file.

Linking Files to the Same Inode

It is possible to associate files to the same inode; that is, associate one or more filenames to the same file. This is done using the link, or **ln**, command. The **ls** -1 command displays the link count for a file in the listing. The link count tells how many links there are to that file; that is, how many references or symbolic names are available for a file.

The link command is sometimes likened to the copy command. That is, with one copy of a file on the disk, you are able to use multiple names to access it. However, link and copy have the obvious difference that a copy is a complete copy of a file, but the link is only a reference to a file. The syntax for the link command is

```
# ln /path/path/source-filename /path/path/dest-filename
```

which allows the source file (*source-filename*) to be accessed by the destination file (*dest-filename*).

The link created using **ln** is sometimes referred to as a hard link to distinguish it from links created using **ln** –s, which are soft or symbolic links. Both types of links are removed with the **rm** command. A hard link created by **ln** differs from a soft link created by **ln** –s. A hard link becomes permanently attached to the chosen inode in contrast to a soft link, which can be moved to a different directory and still remain valid. It should be noted that hard links are confined to links within the file system because inodes are shared. A soft link can cross file system boundaries because it is a pointer reference and specifies the pathname of the file being linked to.

Building a File System

The **mkdir** command creates a directory and the **rmdir** command removes it. However, to create a mountable file system requires the **mkfs** command, or the more user-friendly interface to **mkfs**, the **newfs** command. These commands physically put a file system on the disk. In the process of creating a file system, you can specify the number of inodes available and the number of blocks allocated. Be aware that creating a new file system eliminates any existing files that may reside within the block space made available to the new file system.

Planning for the New File System

Creating a file system begins with planning. Before creating a new file system, gather the following information:

• Number of blocks needed for the file system. These are the physical disk blocks that are used by the file system. To determine the number of blocks to allocate to the file system, you need to know what will be kept in the file system, such as a database application, a storage location, or possibly workspace for a development team. Planning for enough space and proper administration of that space reduces the frequency of redoing file systems. Your only limitation is the amount of available free space you have on your disk.

- Number of inodes needed for the file system. Each file requires an inode regardless of the size of the file. If many files are to be stored in the new file system, such as in a software development environment, a large number of inodes would need to be allocated.

- Whether the file system needs to be a block device or a character device. For information on device files, see the Hardware Administration module (Chapters 4 and 5).

- Block size required. Necessary if your block size differs from the default of 1,024 bytes.

- Bytes per inode. Necessary if you need a specific number of bytes per inode.

- Amount of free space to be reserved.

- Whether you need a particular type of file system, such as BSD fast file or old System V.

As noted, some of these parameters have defaults. To determine the defaults and minimum requirements needed, check the file system installation/configuration documentation provided with your operating system.

Creating the File System

To create an example file system called `/dev/c1d2` in which to store several large data files, enter

```
# mkfs /dev/c1d2 10000
```

This creates the file system as a block device, a special file type necessary if the disk drive where the file device is stored is also a block device (type b). The creation of the special block device file is done using the **mknod** command, which is discussed in further detail in the Hardware Administration module.

In the above usage of the **mkfs** command, the number `10000` specifies the number of blocks; specifying the number of inodes is optional. When just the blocks are specified, mkfs creates one inode for about every 2Kb of a 1,024-byte block. So, for a 10,000-block file system, mkfs creates 5,000 inodes, which should be plenty. To specify the exact number of desired inodes, 2,500 for example, enter

```
# mkfs /dev/data01 10000:2500
```

To change the block size to a different multiple of 512 bytes for the file system, such as 2,048 bytes/block, add the −b option

```
# mkfs -b 2048 /dev/c1d2 10000
```

The default to the –b option is 8,192 bytes, which is the logical block size of the file system.

Other options are available to the **mkfs** user to increase compatibility with applications and other versions of UNIX. In addition to the –b option that specifies block size, the –I option specifies the bytes per inode, and the –m option specifies the amount of free space to be reserved. Some mkfs utilities, such as in System V UNIX, also have the –F option, which allows you to specify a particular file system such as the BSD fast file (**ufs**) or old System V (**s5**) system. An example usage of **mkfs** with several parameters is

```
# mkfs -F s5 -b 2048 /dev/rdsk/c1t0d0s1 102400
```

When a new file system is created, any existing file in the file system is destroyed. Therefore, always make a backup before creating a new file system.

Here, mkfs creates an older System V file system on the second partition of the first disk (i.e., from /dev/rdsk/c1t0d0s1). This is discussed in the Hardware Administration module.

The key attributes of your file system are stored in the files /etc/fstab or /etc/vfstab, your system configuration files. A system configuration file, read by the system at startup, determines what files are to be mounted at startup as well as a directory of information for your UNIX system on the available file systems. A new file system must be added to your system configuration file (fstab or vfstab). An fstab file may resemble the following:

```
/dev/0s1 /usr
/dev/0s3 /usr2
/dev/1s1 /usr3
```

/dev/0s1 refers to the physical device. /usr refers to the file system name. The fstab file is used by the various mount commands, such as **mountall**, **rmountall**, and **mount**. During bootup, this file is read to automatically mount your file systems.

Mounting and Unmounting a File System

When a file system is created, check it out right away. Before you can check a file system, you must know how to mount and unmount it. The command for mounting the file system is **mount**, and the command to dismount the file system is **umount**.

Follow these steps to modify an existing file system. Assume /data01 is a user-defined file system for data storage and you need to increase its size.

1. Notify your users that you are taking the system down for maintenance.

2. Shutdown your system to single-user mode.

3. Enter single-user or maintenance mode, logging in as the superuser.

4. Check to see that the file system is mounted. Run either # **df** /data01 or # **mount** (with no arguments) to see mounted file systems.

5. Backup your file system to tape and verify that it is OK.

6. Enter # **umount** /data01

7. Enter # **mkfs** /dev/c0t0s0 data01 819200 (to remake the file system)

8. Enter # **fsck** /dev/c0t0s0 (to check out the new file system)

9. Enter # **mount** /data01 (to mount the new file system)

10. Go to the new file system (# **cd** /data01) and restore your files from tape.

11. Once everything is OK and you have no further maintenance to do, bring the system back up into multi-user mode. In this instance, you may want to check your file system configuration file to make sure it has been updated properly; if not, make the appropriate changes to the file.

Before beginning with the above procedure, make sure you are familiar with how to do each step, such as shutdown, backup, and restore.

Using fsck

fsck is the foundation for maintaining a healthy file system in a UNIX environment. This file system checking utility must be run on a UNIX system on a routine basis. Running fsck regularly helps you to recover your system in case of a hard shutdown and keeps your file systems from degenerating into unrecoverable messes. Most UNIX systems today run it automatically at startup.

Running fsck

To run fsck you should always be in single-user mode. Enter the command by itself with no arguments, as in

fsck

or with arguments and a specific file system, as in

fsck -D -y /dev/dsk/c0t0s0

This line tells fsck to specifically check the /dev/dsk/c0t0s0 file system, do some extra checking with the -D option, and answer *yes* automatically to all prompts with the -y option. A list of fsck options is shown in Table 2.1. These options provide considerable flexibility to the **fsck** command.

When fsck runs, it goes through several steps including up to six phases (some versions have five phases). Table 2.2 describes all six phases including the operation of the utility.

Responding to fsck Messages

Step 1 may return an error such as:

```
CAN NOT READ: BLK 1044
CONTINUE?
```

Because this could be a hardware error, your first response should be to record the reported block and answer with a y for *yes*. If block reads continue with these errors, answer n for *no*. Too many failed block reads probably mean disk problems, such as a bad controller. Do not proceed further with fsck and get your hardware checked.

When an error message occurs in fsck, an n to a query usually causes termination. It is usually better to let fsck run to completion, then rerun it until the errors have been cleared.

Table 2.1	*Key fsck options.*
Option	***Description***
y	Answers yes to all fsck queries
n	Answers no to all fsck queries
s	Rebuilds the free list (unconditional)
S	Rebuilds the free list only if fsck phases 1–4 show no errors
f	Does a fast check, ignoring fsck phases 2–4. Checks only block and sizes during phases 1 and 5 and may rebuild the free list during Phase 6
b	Forces an automatic boot if the root file system is changed and a boot is considered necessary
q	fsck works quietly and may not report all problems
D	Additional checks on directories including the . (dot) and . . (dot dot) directory inodes

Table 2.2 Steps for `fsck`

Step	Name	Description
1	Read, write, and seek errors	Indicates a hardware error has occurred while checking the file system. When trying to access a block and the utility is prevented from reaching it, a seek error occurs. If the utility is unable to read from or write to a block, a read/write error occurs.
2	Initialization	The superblock of the file system is checked to see if it is valid. The inode list is compared with the size allocated to the file system. An error occurs if the inode list is reported as larger than the file system, indicating that the super-block no longer is reliable, hence corrupted.
3	Phase 1	Checks blocks and sizes. The inode information on links, size, type, and addresses are checked.
4	Phase 1b	An additional pass through the inodes to check for duplicate blocks. Done if more than 10 duplicate or bad blocks are found.
5	Phase 2	Checks directories and pathnames and compares data with information obtained from Phase 1.
6	Phase 3	Checks connections to directories and creates inodes for directories that could not be located during Phase 2. The utility will try to connect these directories to the `lost+found` directory, and if successful, this phase calls Phase 2 again to check the connected directory.

fsck reports Step 2 errors during the initialization. If you get a Size check output showing a file size less than the inode size, your file system is corrupted — specifically, the superblock is corrupt. You will want to run fsck again to recheck this error. The System V file system debugger fsdb is also used to check on the superblock with a syntax similar to fsck, such as:

```
# fsdb /dev/0s1
```

where the command is used with the file system. If you are unsure of the physical name of the file system, check the fstab file. The output from fsdb can be cryptic, and manipulating the inodes reported by fsdb is risky. It is best to thoroughly check your user manual on the use of and options available with the **fsdb** command. When a size check error is consistent and the superblock cannot be repaired, it is best to re-create the file system and restore it from your backups.

Step 2 also checks other important initialization areas that are required for fsck to run successfully. This includes a memory check, finding the root inode, ascertaining that the file system is a block or character device, and more. A common error reported during this step is that the file system is mounted. In order for fsck to run on a file system, it must be unmounted — the only exception is the root directory.

Step 3 gives an error that needs a response if data was inadvertently written to an unallocated inode or if the inode was damaged. Errors such as UNKNOWN FILE TYPE or PARTIALLY ALLOCATED INODE appear along with the inode number. You will be asked for a {y|n} response to CLEAR these inodes. When in doubt, answer y.

Table 2.2 (continued)

Step	Name	Description
7	Phase 4	Checks references to the link count with the inodes found during phases 2 and 3. This phase allows duplicate blocks and bad inodes to be cleared and updates inode link counts if incorrect.
8	Phase 5	This phase checks the free list, which includes checking block addresses and making sure the allocated blocks to the file system are there and the integrity of the blocks are intact.
9	Phase 6	During Phase 6, the free list is rebuilt.

Step 3 may also provide misleading information. Sometimes, when checking a large database file, `fsck` returns an erroneous report on block number and size. The way a large database file is written to disk may occasionally cause `fsck` to skip blocks during its test. In addition, newly installed data files report no problems with `fsck`, but as they grow, `fsck` returns the message POSSIBLE FILE SIZE ERROR I=1422. When it is normal for `fsck` to report this error, as in this situation, an attempt to correct the supposed problem could damage the data. To find if the file is truly bad, use the **ncheck** command with the inode number to locate the file. Once the file is located, you can replace it with a good copy, if necessary.

Step 3 may also report other problems such as:

- 6500 BAD I=564 showing a bad block with an out of range address

- DIRECTORY MISALIGNED I=67, a directory error similar to POSSIBLE FILE SIZE ERROR. The **ncheck** command can be used to find a genuinely bad directory

- EXCESSIVE BAD BLOCKS

- EXCESSIVE DUP BLOCKS

EXCESSIVE BAD BLOCKS and EXCESSIVE DUP BLOCKS indicate a damaged inode. In either case, you should respond with y to let `fsck` assess the condition of the inode and continue. If the error is persistent, you may be faced with another hardware problem. However, it is best to let `fsck` fix the problem for you if it can.

If Phase 1 reports any table overflow errors enter y to continue. When a Phase 1 errors occur, `fsck` may be able to run to completion. However, it is important to rerun `fsck` as many times as needed until zero errors are reported, unless of course you receive an expected POSSIBLE FILE SIZE ERROR report. If errors such as 4565 DUP I=96 are reported in Step 4, `fsck` should be run again, too.

Phase 2 can generate an error that is near catastrophic for your file system. The error ROOT INODE UNALLOCATED, TERMINATING terminates `fsck` and means that the root inode of the file system in question cannot be allocated. You will have to restore the contents of the file system from backup media. Another error Phase 2 can give is

```
ROOT INODE NOT DIRECTORY,
FIX?
```

A y response is your best answer here, but be prepared for more errors down the road. A response of n terminates the utility. The next error Phase 2 can generate is

```
DUPS/BAD IN ROOT MODE,
CONTINUE?
```

This is a response to data collected in Phase 1 indicating that duplicate inodes exist. A
y response allows the utility to continue with no action taken, and an n terminates
fsck. If Phase 2 finds an inode out of range — that is, it is an inode number greater
than the inodes allocated — you receive:

```
I OUT OF RANGE I=6789
NAME=/dump
REMOVE?
```

Because this is an inode that does not exist, answer y and get rid of it. Other errors
such as

```
UNALLOCATED I=5454  OWNER=root MODE=0 ..... (additional info follows)
```

or

```
DUP/BAD I=4367 OWNER=wetsch  MODE=666 .....
```

ask you to remove the file. Because in nearly all cases these are unallocated inodes or
bad or duplicate blocks, it is best to answer y and have it removed when the REMOVE?
presents itself. On files with duplicate blocks, it is best to run fsck and remove them.
Phase 3, depicted in Step 6, checks connectivity. This makes sure that your inodes are
connected to a directory. If a disconnected inode is found, it will be connected to the
lost+found directory. You will receive errors indicating unreferenced directories
with the output

```
UNREF DIR    OWNER=root    MODE=666 ...
RECONNECT?
```

If you are successful with a y response, then the unreferenced directory is attached to
lost+found. If unsuccessful, you receive a SORRY with

```
NO SPACE IN lost+found DIRECTORY
```

or

```
NO lost+found DIRECTORY
```

It is good practice to see if a file system has a lost+found directory. If not, you want
to create one using the **mkdir** command. Then you must slot or notch the directory so
there is room for inode storage. The procedure is:

```
# mkdir lost+found
# cd lost+found
# touch fa fb fc fd fe ff [........nn]
# rm f*
```

You can create as many files in lost+found as you like, but you must also delete them to create notches — usually 20–30 notches are enough. When fsck returns lost+found errors, your lost+found directory is either full or missing, so you want to be sure to create a directory that is large enough. Note that when files are placed in lost+found, they are referenced by their inodes and lose their filename. It is up to the system administrator to investigate these files and find their rightful owner. If not traced to an owner, they can be moved for further research or deleted. However, it is recommended that they not be allowed to remain in lost+found because they take away from the number of notches supplied in the directory. Also, an n response to a Phase 3 reconnect just ignores the error and continue.

Phase 4 checks reference counts. During this step (7) you could receive UNREF FILE errors. This message is the file equivalent to the unreferenced directory errors in Phase 3. Respond y to try to connect the file inode to the lost+found directory. If you should receive the same lost+found directory errors mentioned in Phase 3, you are given an option to respond {y|n} to CLEAR? the file. If inode link counts do not match up, you receive a LINK COUNT report on a file or directory. The {y|n} query you receive from this message is ADJUST? A y adjusts the link count to its proper setting and an n ignores the problem. If unreferenced files are not cleared up, you are not allowed to mount the file system.

Phase 4 is the time during the run of fsck that the bad blocks and duplicates reported in Phase 1 can be cleared. BAD/DUP file and directory errors are reported, and a y is required to clear them at the query prompt. Phase 4 also checks the superblock free inode count and compares it to the fsck count of the free inodes. If a discrepancy is found, you get the error

```
FREE INODE COUNT IN SUPERBLK
FIX?
```

A y corrects the count and an n leaves it in the error state. The inode count checks the count of the links to files and directories in the file system.

Phase 5 takes us to Step 8 of the fsck run. This phase checks the free list. The free list is the list of empty blocks maintained by the file system so that it has the correct number of free blocks available. This step keeps the size of the file system intact. It reports on the number of bad blocks in the free list, number of duplicate blocks in the free list, a bad free block count, or the number of blocks that were discovered but are missing from either the allocated or free block list.

Queries you respond {y|n} to are

- FREE BLK COUNT WRONG IN SUPERBLK
  FIX?

  This fixes the block count in the superblock with an obvious y response to FIX?

- EXCESSIVE BAD BLOCKS IN FREE LIST
  CONTINUE?

  This reports that you still have too many unacceptable blocks in the free list. You
  can terminate fsck with an n, but to finish fsck you need to answer y. The y
  response causes no action to be taken against the blocks, but you undoubtedly will
  need to run fsck again.

- EXCESSIVE DUP BLOCKS IN FREE LIST
  CONTINUE?

  A {y|n} response here generates the same action as the previous error message
  but may also cause the next error.

- BAD FREE LIST
  SALVAGE?

  Although more than one type of free list error could be referenced by this message, you still want to have a good free list. Responding with an n will not fix it. A
  refresh of the free list block is accomplished with a y response as a new correct
  list replaces the old one.

Because of the importance of your free list, Step 9 of the fsck process calls Phase
6 to SALVAGE FREE LIST. During Phase 5, fsck attempts to fix this list, but just in
case, the free list is rebuilt in Phase 6. This is particularly beneficial if the salvage
operation during Phase 5 had a problem.

Now that fsck has completed all of its steps, it terminates, but not without leaving a few possible parting messages. If changes were made to a file system by fsck,
you will see

***** FILE SYSTEM WAS MODIFIED *****,

The more cryptic response

***** BOOT UNIX (NO SYNC) *****

is also possible if the root file system or the root superblock was modified. It is important to note that fsck has modified the root file system on disk but the "bad" root file
system information is still in memory. Therefore, do not run the **sync** command
because you will copy the bad memory copy over the good disk copy. Any other

option of running sync now does the same. So, as noted in Chapter 1, the **shutdown** command also performs a sync, and your system is also capable of doing an automatic sync if you just leave it sitting there. The solution is to do a hard boot (hit reset) to your system. Because you should be in single-user mode and your file systems would generally be unmounted, you probably do not have to worry about creating additional problems. Reboot the system back to single-user mode and run fsck again until you can cleanly proceed through the steps of this important file system utility.

Run fsck regularly to keep your file systems from degenerating into an unrecoverable mess. Remember to mount your file systems after running fsck. On System V, usually the best thing to do when you have finished your maintenance work in single-user mode is shutdown the system to init level 0. When it is ready to poweroff, shut it off and let it reboot back up into its normal multi-user mode.

Other Useful File System Commands

Some additional UNIX commands are useful for checking on a file system and doing other file system work. For instance, you may want to see how much space is used and how much space is free for a file system, how many inodes there are, or how many blocks are available.

The **df** command is a good monitoring tool. It displays the amount of free space available on your disk. Use the -t option to see the total allocated size of the file system and the -v option to see the percentage of free blocks. The output of a **df** command entered at the prompt may look like

```
# df
//dev/0s0       3401 blocks    761 i-nodes
/usr/dev/0s1 156722 blocks 10455 i-nodes
/tmp/dev/0s3  65433 blocks  1523 i-nodes
```

As a general rule of thumb, you should work to maintain your file systems below 90 percent full. You should take action to keep your file systems from getting full when they approach 80 percent of capacity. This is particularly true for your root file system. If you do not maintain your file systems, the system degrades. When your root file system is full, your system either crashes or reports a multitude of errors that require immediate action to maintain the system.

The **du** command displays information being used by a specific directory. You can also display individual files with their sizes using the -a option. Using **du** as follows:

```
# du /appusr
```

gives the block size of the directories in the file system as well as the total blocks used by the file system:

```
855     /appusr/prgs
430     /appusr/prgs/src
8677    /appusr/data
5746    /appusr/data/old
6       /appusr/spool/app
764     /appusr/test
16478   /appusr
```

Here, note that the block size at the bottom of the list is the total number of blocks used by the file system /appuser.

Note that size-reporting commands such as **du** and **df** report in 512-byte block sizes and that your native UNIX might use a different default block size, such as 1,024 bytes/block. Hence, two blocks of 512 bytes may equate to one 1,024-byte block (native).

The creation and maintenance of file systems is an extremely important task for the UNIX system administrator. Files and directories are removed using the **rm** command, but when the system administrator is logged into the system as the superuser, the **rm** command must be used with caution. For instance, an inadvertent **rm** -rf * run from the root directory will completely wipe out your UNIX system. More on this in the Security Administration module (Chapters 8 and 9).

Cleaning up file systems is also part of the maintenance function. This can be accomplished by manually executing commands or setting up commands to run automatically through cron. Cleanup involves removing unneeded old files — files called *core,* created when a process inadvertently terminates, and zero-byte files. In some cases, you may want to retain these files, but generally old files not used should be backed up and deleted, and core and zero-byte files should be removed. Other files important to the administrator are log files. These files should be monitored so they do not grow too large; when necessary they should be zeroed out and allowed to grow again.

This shell script checks file and directory sizes and takes the appropriate actions.

```
# cleanup -- a script to check on file sizes
PATH=/bin:/usr/bin
CLEANLOG=/tmp/cleanup.tmp
rm -rf $CLEANLOG
# Report on file sizes of key files. Customize block sizes to
# reflect what is considered too large for your system. This
# will be primarily dependent on available disk space.
echo "Today's Cleanup date is `date`"
echo "-------------------------------------"
/usr/adm/messages      25000
/usr/adm/pacct         25000
/usr/adm/sulog         25000
```

By routinely running tools to maintain your system, you can reduce some of the time it takes to run an extensive suite of scripts automatically. It is also necessary to monitor your scripts and modify them to ensure that they are doing the job you want them to do. From a security perspective, make sure your maintenance programs are only accessible and executable to the superuser. If you are liberal in your privileges, you can open the door to modification or replacement of your maintenance programs by a potentially malevolent user.

Software

Maintaining Access to Applications

Applications are programs that make your system usable. They can range from UNIX daemons, which provide system services, to shell scripts. In many instances, the primary application may be a database system, such as Oracle, Informix, or Sybase, used to provide enterprise-wide solutions. These applications need maintenance. Depending on your organization and the role of the system administrator, you may have a separate database administrator, or the system administrator may also be expected to perform the database administrator function. In all circumstances, the roles of system administrator and database administrator require a close level of cooperation.

The system administrator is the human component of the man–machine interface (MMI). As such, the system administrator's ability to maintain any application on a system by providing a working system to the end-user is crucial to fulfilling the role of the MMI. To contribute to the success of the MMI, the system administrator must make sure that the system is functional, reliable, and complete. That is, the system administrator makes sure that the system provides the tools to help users do their jobs, that the system does not routinely crash, and that the users have access to their tools and programs in a consistent manner.

This chapter focuses on UNIX system administration from the perspective of software administration. It discusses the concept of process introduced in Chapter 1 in more detail, how to set up a UNIX environment, and how to optimize your UNIX system through the kernel. Finally, it briefly touches on database administration, which can be a key focus of a UNIX system.

Processes

Applications begin as a single process — a program, such as a shell, that runs in memory on your system. When a command is invoked or a request is made of the initial process, it creates a new process. For example, the shell process creates the shell interface between UNIX and the user.

A new process is created by the original or parent process using the **fork** command and so is considered "forked." The forked process is also known as a child process. Forked processes, concurrent child processes, or processes in general may also be referred to as threads. However technically, a thread is a running process that can interact with other processes in memory.

Identifying a Process

The **ps** command is used to report the status of processes running in memory. The columnar report displayed provides data on

- PID, the process ID,
- PPID, the parent process ID,
- TTY, the associated terminal,
- TIME, the CPU time spent running the process, and
- CMD, the name of the process.

    Explore the **ps** command and its parameters, some of which are:

-e	display the status of every process
-f	provide a full listing
-u *username*	provide a process list for a specific user

A snapshot and partial listing of **ps** -ef follows.

```
$ ps -ef
  UID   PID  PPID C  STIME TTY       TIME  COMD
  root   0    0   80 Jul 15 ?        0:06 sched
  root   1    0   80 Jul 15 ?        6:13 /etc/init -
  root   2    0   80 Jul 15 ?        2:31 pageout
  root   3    0   80 Jul 15 ?      564:22 fsflush
  root 544    1   80 Jul 15 ?        0:03 /usr/lib/saf/sac -t 300
  root 545    1   60 Jul 15 console 0:01 -sh
  root 238    1   80 Jul 15 ?       10:44 /usr/sbin/in.routed -s
  root 240    1   80 Jul 15 ?       10:53 /usr/sbin/in.rdisc -r
```

```
root 224    1  8   Jul 15 ?        0:00 /usr/sbin/aspppd -d 1
root 18439 1  80  Aug 16 ?        4:40 /usr/sbin/in.named
root 272    1  80  Jul 15 ?        9:30 /usr/sbin/inetd -s
```

ps -ef produces a very long list. To filter the list for specific information, such as any process that is a ttymon, execute the following:

```
# ps -ef | grep ttymon*
  UID   PID  PPID  C    STIME TTY    TIME COMD
  root   598   548  1   Jul 20 ?      0:00 /usr/lib/saf/ttymon
  root   599   548  2   Jul 20 ?      0:00 /usr/lib/saf/ttymon
  root   600   548  1   Jul 20 ?      0:00 /usr/lib/saf/ttymon
  root   603   548  1   Jul 20 ?      0:00 /usr/lib/saf/ttymon
  root   604   548  1   Jul 20 ?      0:00 /usr/lib/saf/ttymon
  root   605   548  1   Jul 20 ?      0:00 /usr/lib/saf/ttymon
  root   606   548  1   Jul 20 ?      0:00 /usr/lib/saf/ttymon
  root   607   548  2   Jul 20 ?      0:00 /usr/lib/saf/ttymon
  root   608   548  1   Jul 20 ?      0:00 /usr/lib/saf/ttymon
  root   609   548  2   Jul 20 ?      0:00 /usr/lib/saf/ttymon
```

The UID gives the username, the PID is the process number, the PPID is the PID of the parent process that spawned or forked this process, and C tells how this process is scheduled. You can find the priority (PRI) of a process using the -l parameter, which returns a long list that also includes process status, address of the process, and more.

In this listing, notice that often not everything lines up with the header, due to the variable length of many of the output fields, which are delimited by a space. A **ps** output for a specific user is:

```
$ ps -fu wetsch
   UID    PID  PPID  C    STIME TTY     TIME COMD
 wetsch  6906  6824 40  00:09:40 pts/15   0:00 /bin/ksh
 wetsch  6980  6906 80  00:10:49 pts/15   0:01 ps -fu
```

This example demonstrates the UNIX parent–child relationship at work. The interactive Korn shell (/bin/ksh) is used and given a PID of 6906. The user started **ps** -fu, which became a forked process with its own PID of 6980, but it is attached to the user's shell as noted by PPID 6906:

```
 wetsch  6906  6824 40  00:09:40 pts/15   0:00 /bin/ksh
 wetsch  6980  6906 80  00:10:49 pts/15   0:01 ps -fu
```

Interrupting a Process

At times, processes do not behave as expected. They may run forever and appear stuck. They may appear to be running but may not be doing anything, as with a defunct process. They may be doing something the administrator does not like, such as filling up the root file system with a continuous write to the /temp directory. The **ps** command allows you to find the process ID of an errant process so you can get rid of it. For instance, **ps** -ef | more produces a page-by-page listing of all your processes. You can exit this listing at any time by pressing the q (for quit) key. If you see a defunct process

```
mollyb 7950 5006 80 00:10:49 pts/15 0:01 <defunct>
```

wait a few seconds and run **ps** again to see if the process is still defunct. (Defunct processes are also known as zombie processes.) If the process persists, run the **kill** command to terminate it.

The **kill** command sends an interrupt signal to the currently running process. Table 3.1 lists the various signals available to the kill function. These signal interrupts are used in shell programming to provide specific actions to your program for a specified event.

To kill the process for UID mollyb without regard to consequences, use:

```
# kill -9 7950
```

To get rid of UID mollyb and all related child processes enter

```
# kill -9 5006
```

When signal 9, the SIGKILL parameter, is passed to a process, it causes an abrupt halt to the process. This option does no cleanup to the zombie process and may even cause other processes connected to it to become zombies. You will have to manually clean them up. For instance, if the zombie process is related to a database application, the -9 option coming from the superuser may cause damage to other related database processes, such as stored procedures that were executed, possibly leading to database corruption. Therefore, although the -9 option can be useful, it is best to reserve it for removing processes that cannot be removed with other options. Also, if your **kill** command does not remove the zombie process, you have to search for the parent process and remove it. If the parent process is a zombie and cannot be terminated, you then need to reboot the system to remove the zombie.

Zombies usually do not adversely affect your system but can be a nuisance. Therefore, do not react immediately to reboot your system if you cannot remove the zombie. Assess the situation first, it may not be as severe as you think. If possible, wait to reboot during a regular maintenance cycle. If your zombies are frequent and filling up the process table, you need to determine what is causing the problem and try to eliminate the cause to remove the symptom.

For processes that are the back end of a database, **kill** –13 or **kill** –15 are better because the signal sent (i.e., the option specified) allows for a more graceful shutdown of the process. The –13 or –15 signals take a little bit of time to take effect, so be patient. Note that when SIGQUIT (–3) interrupts a process, it creates a dump file called core. The core file is created when a signal is sent to the kernel. Unless you want to use core files for debugging, they should be erased because they can be large and consume a lot of disk space.

The kill procedure can vary by application. Just jumping in with a **kill** –9, or in some cases a **kill** –13, can set error conditions. If you are dealing with a commercial application, the manufacturer may have a recommended kill procedure to follow in order to avoid causing additional problems. If unknown, the administrator should start with a –15. If this fails, a succession of –1, –3, and then –13 signals can be applied before trying a –9.

Table 3.1 Signal interrupts available to kill.

Signal interrupt	*Description*
0	Normal termination (SIGEXIT)
1	Hang up (SIGHUP)
2	Break signal (^d) (SIGINT)
3	Quit the process (SIGQUIT)
4	Illegal instruction (SIGILL)
5	Put a trace on trap (SIGTRAP)
6	IOT instruction (SIGIOT)
7	EMT instruction (SIGEMT)
8	Arithmetic/floating point exception (SIGFPE)
9	Kill all — no exceptions (SIGKILL)
10	Bus error (SIGBUS)
11	Segmentation error (SIGSEGV)
12	Error from a system call (SUGSYS)
13	Pipe error (SIGPIPE)
14	Alarm clock (SIGALARM)
15	Kill or terminate signal (SIGTERM)
16	User-defined signal (SIGUSR1)

Changing Process Priority

When your system is working with a high load against the CPU, you can lower the scheduling priority of tasks to give other processes a better chance of getting a slice of CPU time. To increase the priority of a task, you must lower its *nice* number — variable NI in the **ps** output. To display the nice number of a process, run **ps** with the −l option. In the output of **ps** −l, NI heads the nice number column and PRI heads the priority column. Nice numbers usually range from −19 to +19 on BSD-type systems. Check your system documentation to determine what the actual range is for your system.

To increase the priority of a process, decrease the nice number. Process owners can decrease the priority of their own processes, but only the root user can increase the priority of a process. This prevents the regular users of a system from increasing the priority of their commands without the assistance of the superuser. The syntax of the **nice** command is **nice** −/+*n command.* To set a process to run at the highest priority, enter

```
# nice -19 myprocess
```

where *myprocess* is whatever program you want to execute.

To increase the scheduling priority of a process, you need to know its PID and NI variables. If a process has a PID of 5500 and its NI number is 0, you can move it up in priority by entering **renice** 5 5500. This increases the priority of the process by five steps. Execute **ps** −l −p 5500 to see if the action to increase the priority had any effect. If your UNIX implementation does not have renice, then adjusting niceness for a process in progress may not be possible.

Configuring the User Interface

Control of the man–machine interface (MMI) begins with the system environment, which is established by variables that can be set and maintained by the superuser — and the user, if permitted. Variables such as HOME, PROMPT, PATH, TERM, and SHELL are frequently used to define user control. If you want to control user access to the shell, set the user variables and provide a user interface, which could be a character-based menu process or a graphical user interface (GUI).

The following example demonstrates setting up a user process following user logon. First, a user logs on and his .profile executes. A simple user profile may be:

```
$cat .profile
#
# This is your personal profile file - do not delete!
#
```

```
umask 077
PATH=.:$HOME/bin:$PATH
export PATH
TERM=vt100
export TERM
exec /usr/local/bin/menux
```

The last command in the profile executes the program menux (in this case, a shell script). This program could be anything, but for our purposes it is a character-based menu implemented to provide some control to the user environment (Listing 3.1).

When executed, the following screen is displayed rather than the normal shell prompt:

```
              MENUX SHELL MENU

                  MAIN MENU

          1.) Access Database
          2.) Go to Report Menu
          3.) Who is logged on
          4.) Exit

          Please enter your choice:

---------------------------------------------------------
```

Be careful when setting up user interfaces. It is possible for a user to drop to the shell from a shell script by entering the ! (exclamation mark, also known as the bang). To prevent this security hazard, use the **trap** command to capture the signals specified as arguments from being relayed outside of the shell (i.e., **trap** " " 1 2 3 14 15).

The signals **trap** can capture are the same as those **kill** can send (see Table 3.1). Not all signals need to be trapped. The menux shell program traps the interrupts needed

---

Listing 3.1 **menux** *— A character-based menu.*

```
#Set up any other environment parameters you may need that are
#important to your system for applications that are accessible
#through this menu

trap "" 1 2 3 14 15
```

to prevent the user from inappropriately exiting the shell. The user must use the menu option to properly exit the program, which will also perform a logoff. By customizing the interface, it is possible to display a set of user applications without allowing full access to the system. Also, privileges can be granted or restricted with file permission settings, and privileges can be arranged through the security supplied with other applications, such as databases that give access rights based on user logins to specific tables, down to the field level.

Tuning the Operating System

An important part of maintaining access to applications is maintaining optimal performance of the system. Tuning an operating system isn't something to be taken lightly, and unless you know or have the time to determine the optimal settings for your system, it is best to stay with the system defaults. However, you may be required to fix a UNIX system that has been operating poorly. If you cannot find an obvious problem, look into the kernel parameters. They may have been changed and it would probably be to your advantage to rebuild the kernel and return it to the system defaults. Overall, you serve your system best by making sure there is plenty of disk space, properly maintaining your file systems, and using the proper hardware before messing with the kernel variables.

Reconfiguring the Kernel

Not unlike the user environment that can be configured with variables, the UNIX system also has a number of parameters that can be set. You may start receiving error messages like `too many processes -- cannot fork`, `inode table overflow` or system error messages that tell you the operating system is not working properly. When these messages become frequent, consider reconfiguring your kernel. You may have to look at the parameters of your existing kernel and analyze where changes should be made. The user interface to rebuild a kernel has been made friendlier by vendors, but it is system specific and consequently may differ from what appears here.

The range of parameters for your system are in the file `mtune` located in `/etc/conf/cf.d/mtune`. The actual parameters you need to tune are in the `stune` directory found in `/etc/conf/cf.d/stune`. You can analyze the files in `stune` and determine the values available to you in `mtune`. When you are ready to proceed with a rebuild, make sure you

- do not exceed the range of values specified,
- keep a copy of `stune` so that you can reverse your changes, and
- make legitimate changes that do not throw your system out of balance, making it unstable.

Listing 3.1 (continued)

```
#Note, you can reset the environment variables from your pro-
file#in the script.

PATH=$PATH:/etc:/binDBPATH=/usr1/database/binTERM = vt100

export PATH DBPATH TERM        #Setting your environment parameters

while true
do
clear
echo "
                    MENUX SHELL MENU

                        MAIN MENU

            1.) Access Database
            2.) Go to Report Menu
            3.) Who is logged on
            4.) Exit


            Please enter your choice:        "
read selection
case $selection in
    1) dbms       #Enter Command or shell script here to run
       ;;         #database application
    2) clear
       rpt.sh     #Shell script to bring up a reports submenu
       ;;
    3) clear
       user.sh    #Another example of executing a shell script
       ;;
    4) exit       #Exit from the menu
       ;;
#Note: Continue menu as necessary

esac
done
```

The mtune file looks like the sample shown in Table 3.2. A complete listing is rather large so the illustration here is only to give you a feel for what the file looks like.

In essence, performance is a balancing act and parameters are not consistent across UNIX systems. Performance is directly affected by the amount of RAM memory available and the number of processes running on the system. Software applications can also affect performance. An enterprise-wide database system will be configured differently than a system dedicated to network traffic. Parameter changes should not be taken lightly, and the system defaults should be maintained unless system usage dictates otherwise.

> Remember this simple rule when changing kernel parameters — when you increase the performance in one area of the system you will affect and probably decrease the performance in another area.

The stune file contains the same variables as **mtune** but has only one setting that shows the current system settings. Thus to change a value, specify a valid value by changing the stune parameter.

After changing the stune file create a new kernel. Remember, you must be in maintenance or single-user mode before starting your actual work on the kernel, and make sure you have your native system documentation available to help dissect the variables. When you finish making the changes to stune, run kconfig from the root directory. You may also have a system administrator interface program, such as sysadm, that also allows you to build a kernel. Once again, be sure to check your native system documentation for the proper interface to build a kernel. This interface will keep you from having to do much, if any, manual intervention because it allows you not only to configure your system but to save changes and install the new kernel, too.

Table 3.2 mtune — Kernel parameters.

Variable	Default	Minimum	Maximum
NBUF	250	200	1000
NCALL	30	30	250
NINODE	150	100	600
NFILE	150	100	600
NMOUNT	25	25	25
NPROC	100	50	400
ULIMIT	3072	2048	12288
*******	AND THE LIST GOES ON		

After it starts, do not attempt to stop the kernel build process from running. Even if you find an error, it is better to let the build run to completion and then reset your system to run from the old kernel. When the build is complete, you will have a new file called unix in your root directory. You should reboot the system and make sure all devices, file systems, and new parameters come up and online. If so, your kernel rebuild was a success. Because you run the risk of creating an unstable system when modifying kernel variables, run a process or perform a regular maintenance check to your system to make sure that all is in good order. It is also important to monitor the system, especially in a production environment, to make sure everything is running smoothly.

If you encounter any system problems, return to the old kernel and attempt another build. Depending on the severity of the problem you may want to wait to do this until you have set aside some maintenance time that will not adversely affect your users.

Establishing a Performance Baseline

Monitoring the performance of your UNIX system can be a big task, yet necessary to provide the best system available. By monitoring your system, you can determine its norm and create a baseline. Then when something unknown occurs, you can better estimate its effect on your system. As stated previously, no two UNIX systems are alike. Each UNIX system is configured by the system administrator to provide specific services. In UNIX there really is no such thing as a homogeneous environment, and it would be rare to even find backup or "hot" sites set up to perfectly emulate their production counterparts.

To monitor UNIX performance, you can obviously go out and buy performance monitoring tools. However, it is also possible to use your own system resources to monitor system performance. You have the ability to monitor command usage, page swapping, CPU usage, and more. System V UNIX uses the **sar** command. Other UNIX platforms use **vmstat**. On some systems, such as AIX or Solaris, both **sar** and **vmstat** are available. I will focus on **sar** and System V monitoring.

The System Activity Reporter, sar, allows the administrator to get a sampling of the system for a specified period of time. sar measures buffer activity, CPU utilization, caching, memory swapping, paging, queuing, and process status. System documentation on the **sar** command provides the necessary options and descriptions of sample output that you can expect from your system. Some **sar** options are –u for CPU utilization, –b for buffer activity, –p for paging activity, and –n for cache statistics. Many more **sar** options are available. To see output for CPU utilization, enter

```
# sar -u 5 10
```

Here, the parameters 5 and 10 tell `sar` to report every five seconds 10 times:

10:44:05	*%usr*	*%sys*	*%wio*	*%idle*
10:44:10	8	47	33	12
10:44:15	5	65	11	19
10:44:20	10	74	16	0
10:44:25	10	70	20	0
10:44:25	5	30	10	55
10:44:30	0	0	0	100
10:44:35	0	0	0	100
10:44:40	6	73	13	11
10:44:45	3	42	8	47
10:44:50	0	0	0	100

Having established how closely `sar` needs to monitor system activity, the real work begins in understanding what the sar data mean.

Begin by collecting sar data relevant to typical workloads of your system, such as minimum, average, and peak loads. If you are unsure when these loads occur, `sar` can provide the data by observing system performance over time. Your observations of typical activity become your system performance baseline. Your initial views should look into system CPU utilization, caching, swapping, and paging, although to be thorough, you may want to collect data on all system components. Be prepared to spend considerable time analyzing this data in order to spot trends. You may want to monitor areas dealing with semaphore activity, inode status, and queue status, especially if you are experiencing problems with them or if other activity does not provide any clues.

Only when system behavior is fully understood should any attempt be made to start adjusting system parameters. For instance, if you notice that caching and paging is heavily used and slowing system performance, look at the processes causing this activity. If it is an application, check your application parameters first to determine if they are set properly. When new application parameters are set, use **sar** to see if there is an improvement, making sure to correlate revised parameters with your baseline; reestablish a new baseline if you keep the new parameters. If your application tuning is not effective and there appears to be no other cause, look at your tunable parameters, make adjustments, and recheck the system performance against your baseline.

Remember that no two UNIX systems are going to be alike and that if you are dealing with a production-level system, you should not take adjusting parameters lightly. The best case is to have a test system that can be created to mirror a production machine and the load on the production machine. You should try to replicate problems encountered in production. This allows you to play with the system parameters without affecting a production-level system.

This type of work is very tedious because it is best to change only one variable at a time and then retest. Consequently, you should choose the parameters that need to be changed wisely, take scrupulous notes, and be prepared to set parameters back to original configurations. These tasks are complex and require a full-time effort. Experience is the best guide. If necessary, bring in an expert on kernel performance. Do not ever believe that just changing a kernel parameter will make your system better. Be sure you can test it and then prove it.

Process Accounting

Setting up and using a native accounting system can provide a wealth of information for analyzing your system. Different from a sar report, system accounting gives you information on who is using your system and how they are using it. This type of usage can have an important effect on system performance. For instance, if you have software developers working on a system, they may be compiling programs at a time when other users are using an application. For small organizations this may be a problem; larger organizations usually have a separate development system. If such usage is causing your problem, you may want to consider breaking up the workload to run on separate UNIX machines. Then your organization is on its way to providing distributed UNIX services.

For software administration, you can provide accounting reports ranging from which commands were used to how many bytes were actually transferred and accessed during a specified accounting period. The wtmp, utmp, and pacct files hold system accounting information. wtmp and utmp are located in the /etc directory; pacct is located in /usr/adm (this directory may also contain wtmp on some UNIX releases such as BSD).

The wtmp (for "who temp") file stores log-in processes. Remove this file if you do not want this information stored, then check your init scripts (i.e., /etc/rc) and any other procedures you may have that reference this file. Process information is captured in the pacct (for process accounting) file. This file records information that includes the name of the command used, the start and stop times, processing times, and memory used. This is, of course, a lot of information, and it quickly builds up in the pacct file.

The procedure to record processing information is not automatic. You must start the accton program to turn on the ability to write process information to your accounting files. You can invoke the accounting process from your startup script (/etc/rc) by issuing the **startup** command from the accounting library, usually /usr/lib/acct. This command writes to wtmp and runs accton. If you do not want to run **startup**, then you must comment out the command in the /etc/rc file. The common setup for **startup** is from your init level 2 startup script, and the line `/bin/su -adm -c /usr/lib/acct/startup` is entered in this file. Also, `shutacct` is used to stop accounting when **shutdown** is invoked.

With this background information on the accounting process, look at an overview of the accounting system. User `adm` has an `acct` subdirectory, in which the additional directories `fiscal`, `nite`, and `sum` are found. Just remember that the accounting utilities are at `/usr/lib/acct` (Figure 3.1).

The `fiscal` directory is used to set up your reporting periods, which can be specified, but the default is monthly. The `fee` file is used to enter any specific charges assigned to a user in addition to what you incorporate into your accounting system. Using the **chargefee** command, enter

chargefee wetsch 15

to charge an additional 15 units to user `wetsch`.

The `nite` subdirectory keeps accounting records that are processed daily, records on system status, and disk accounting records. Within the `nite` subdirectory is the `diskacct` file, which contains disk usage data. Collective reports and records from system accounting are kept in the `sum` directory.

The complexity of the System V accounting process is in the placement of the files in the user `adm` directory, the accounting utility files, and the `wtmp` and `pacct` files. But the ease of use of this system is in reporting the accounting data. As noted above, reports are stored in the `sum` subdirectory and contain the month and day of the report generated. Three basic account commands are used to generate reports, and you can activate these automatically using `cron` or manually as needed. These utilities are:

- `/usr/lib/acct/ckpacct`
- `/usr/lib/acct/runacct`
- `/usr/lib/acct/monacct`

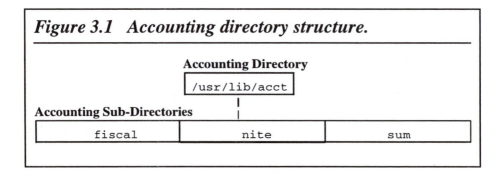

Figure 3.1 Accounting directory structure.

The **ckpacct** command checks the size of the pacct file and lets you know if there is enough space available in the /usr/adm directory. When the file system is nearly full, the utility stops writing process records and, as the pacct file gets large, starts a new pacct file and labels the old files sequentially (i.e., pacct1, pacct2, pacct3, pacct4, ...). Process accounting stops when fewer than 500 blocks are available. You can start the accounting process again by freeing up the space and running ckpacct again.

The runacct utility is designed to create reports from the accounting information by integrating the account records. You can specify the output of the utility in a filename of your choosing. It is recommended that prior to kicking off runacct you also run the dodisk utility also found at /usr/lib/acct/. The importance of this is to compile file metrics before runacct is executed. It should also be noted at this point that the report files are in ASCII format.

To condense your reports further into a monthly summary, use the **monacct** command on a monthly basis. This utility creates summary files in the fiscal directory and restarts them in the sum subdirectory. **monacct** is extremely useful for summarizing your monthly system usage, and if you are billing for services, it serves as a means of generating your billing. This summary gives you a good measure of how your system is being used and provides important information on processes that consume the most resources and those that execute with little effect. For example, you can document specific loads on your system, identify processes that are a substantial burden, and modify the times those processes are run. This obviously allows you to distribute your available resources better and make more resources available to your users when they need them. It is preferable to run the accounting utilities on a regular basis at a time when system usage is at a minimum.

Managing the accounting files is your next priority, once you get the feel for using the accounting procedures for your system. You must keep strong accounting information and manage the growth of the accounting files. You should archive these files and eventually move them to tape. There really is not a rule of thumb as to how often you should archive the files, what you should keep on your hard disk, when to move the files to tape, when files are no longer needed, and so forth. Your guide should be what your organization requires, factoring in the rate of growth of the files, which depends on system usage and the amount of disk space you have available. A general method used to maintain these files is to copy them to an archive directory that you create and use the **nulladm** command to recreate a filename with the proper permissions of 664, assigning both user and group to adm, such as /usr/lib/acct/nulladm.

There are many variations on the accounting process. One primary difference is in which directories the files are kept. Some System V flavors use the /var/adm instead of the /usr/adm directory to store accounting files and associated subdirectories. In addition, you may have a set of options available to you in one UNIX version that are not available in another. Therefore, it is always good to check the native documentation to see what is available and where your accounting files and utilities are stored.

An accounting report containing headers and typical information is shown in Table 3.3. Table 3.4 contains a summary of the accounting files, directories, and utilities. This table can give you a better overall view of the accounting system to supplement the descriptive usage of this valuable accounting tool. Using process accounting efficiently can assist the system administrator in enhancing performance and charging fees for the amount of system usage.

Table 3.3   Description of accounting report headers.

UID	User ID (numeric)
LOGIN NAME	Username
CPU	Cumulative amount of user CPU time in minutes.
KCORE-MINS PRIME NPRIME	A prime time and nonprime time measure of memory usage over the entire accounting period.*
CONNECT	The amount of time the user was connected during the account period.
DISK BLOCKS	The total amount of disk space used by the user. Note: this total is an average that includes all disk I/O
# PROCS	Total number of processes run that were owned by the user.
# SESS	A count of the number of user logins.
# DISK SAMPLES	This field is 0 if dodisk has not been run. It tells the number of times dodisk was run and is the number the DISK BLOCKS metric is averaged over.
FEE	The total fees entered with the chargefee utility.

*Prime and nonprime times are determined by the settings in the /etc/acct/ holidays file. These settings are defined by the administrator.

Table 3.4   Summary of system accounting files, directories, and utilities.

Full pathname	Type	Brief description
/usr/adm/acct/fiscal	Directory	The fiscal reports directory
/usr/adm/acct/nite	Directory	The accounting working directory
/usr/adm/acct/sum	Directory	Summary directory with information for monacct
/usr/adm/acct/sun/ loginlog	File	File that is updated with each login to the system.

Table 3.4 (continued)

Full pathname	Type	Brief description
/usr/adm/fee	Directory	Collects fee information
/usr/adm/pacct	File	Accounting file that maintains information of each process run in the system.
/usr/adm/wtmp	File	The "who is" file providing a summary of log-in and log-off data.
/usr/lib/acct/dodisk	File/utility	Processes disk I/O information. Recommended to be executed before runacct.
/usr/lib/acct/ckpacct	File/utility	Checks the status of pacct and stops accounting processing when the /usr/adm directory is within 500 blocks of being full.
/usr/lib/acct/runacct	File/utility	A daily utility to gather process, disk, connect, command usage, and fee information. Report files have a month/day indicator in the mmdd format.
/usr/lib/acct/monacct	File/utility	Creates a monthly summary report.
/usr/lib/acct/startup	File/utility	Required to start the accounting process.
/usr/lib/acct/shutacct	File/utility	Shuts down the accounting process.
/usr/lib/acct/chargefee	File/utility	Allows a number of units to be charged to a specific log-in ID.
/usr/lib/acct/holidays	File	Sets prime and nonprime hours. Holidays must be reset each year. An * in this file is equivalent to a comment marker.
/usr/lib/acct/nulladm	File/utility	Creates a filename with 664 permissions and assigns user and group to adm.

The acctcom utility will be the last word on accounting in this chapter. This utility reports on specific usage for a specific user (-u), specific time (-s), specific group (-g), or a combination of these and other options available. The report comes from information stored in pacct and is in the format shown in Table 3.5. Table 3.6 shows optional displays that can be obtained with the acctcom utility.

These outputs give you an excellent understanding of how your system is performing, who is using it, and when. For instance, to look up my own usage for any processes run after 6:00 PM with a hog factor, I enter

```
$ acctcom -s 18:00 -u wetsch -h
END AFTER:     Mon July 7 11:00:00 1997
COMMAND                  START     END       REAL      CPU      HOG
NAME    USER   TTYNAME TIME       TIME      (SECS)    (SECS)   FACTOR
vi      wetsch tty10   11:33:47 10:47:22   1415.15   1247.92  0.88
lp      wetsch tty10   11:49:13 10:49:33     20.43      3.21  0.22
```

The -s option specifies the request time in 24-hour time format (00:00–23:59). This means that any process running from 18:00 to the current system time is displayed in the output. The -u option selects the specific user, and the -h option requests the hog factor. In the output, the HOG FACTOR heading replaces the MEAN SIZE heading usually displayed. The hog factor tells you how much CPU time was used for a specific process. A hog factor of 1.0 means the process consumed 100 percent of the CPU resources when it was run. A 0.90 hog factor indicates 90 percent utilization. The balance between high CPU utilization and the amount of time it takes to completely run the process must be considered. For instance, a process with a hog factor of 1.0 that only takes a fraction of a second to run probably will not adversely affect your system and users will remain happy.

Table 3.5   acctcom output description.

Command name	Name of measured process
USER	Log-in ID
TTYNAME	Name of the TTY in use for the process (i.e., tty1a)
STARTTIME	System clock time the process started
ENDTIME	System clock time the process ended
REAL(SECS)	Actual processing time in seconds
CPU(SECS)	CPU usage time in seconds
MEAN SIZE (K)	Mean memory size

Software

If you have a process that is really "hogging" your system, you may want to make sure the process is running at a time that does not adversely affect your system process or users. You can minimize the impact of high hog factor processes with the **nice** command to change the priority of a command when it is executed. This allows processes that are not as hoggish to execute prior to commands that are high on the hog factor. Overall, it is a judgement call that must be made to keep system performance optimal without adversely affecting the integrity or reliability of your system.

Table 3.6	*Optional* **acctcom** *output.*
F	Indicates the fork or exec flag.
STAT	Indicates the system exit status.
HOG FACTOR	Percentage of CPU time consumed by a process.
KCORE MIN	Memory usage in terms of kcore-minutes.
CPU FACTOR	Factor computed as (user time)/(system time + user time).
CHARS TRNSFD	Total number of characters transferred during I/O.
BLOCKS READ	Total number of blocks used during block I/O.

Hardware Administration Module

Chapter 4

Communicating With Peripheral Devices

The physical layer of a computer system is the actual hardware your system uses. Peripherals that a UNIX system must communicate with and control include devices such as hard drives, floppy drives, tape drives, printers, network connections, and RAM.

Device Files and Drivers

Device Files

The UNIX kernel communicates with peripheral devices using a type of file known as a special file or device file. The system uses the device file as the interface to the device. All devices with which the system communicates require a device file. Located in the /dev directory, device files consume no disk space and have no disk blocks allocated to them.

The /dev directory can contain literally hundreds of files required by a system. These files are of three basic types: regular files (a normal UNIX file), directory files (directories and subdirectories), and special files (device files). UNIX interacts with special files the same as it does with ordinary files. File permissions on special files are read the same as with any other file, and user and owner privileges can be set as needed. I/O to these files is handled in the same way I/O is handled by other files in a UNIX system. In addition, the inodes for a special device file provide the usual file type information, which includes a means to identify whether the inode is a block or character type. Consequently, the operating system always believes it is communicating to a file, even though these files are of a special type.

Other advantages of UNIX I/O with device files, which is basically how UNIX handles all I/O, include:

- I/O can be redirected to another file.

- I/O can be redirected to other peripherals.

- Device driver I/O is handled the same way as I/O to other files.

Device files are of two types: character and block. Character files allow I/O to be transferred a single character or byte at a time, whereas block files allow I/O to be buffered, usually in increments of 512 bytes/block, before transferring the block.

Device Drivers

To complete the interface between the device file and the kernel is the device driver — the code in the kernel that implements the interface with the peripheral device. For device drivers to be recognized by the system, they must be loaded into your kernel. Early UNIX systems required that a user manually enter the device, shutdown the machine, and restart the system to make the driver active and to bring the device online for the first time. Now, loading a new device driver manually is less frequent. Many vendor-supplied devices can be recognized by the operating system. Also, SCSI (Small Computer System Interface) drivers in a system can be configured for SCSI devices. In addition, many devices come with setup scripts to get the device up and running on a system.

Understanding the interaction between the operating system, drivers, special files, and hardware can prepare you to fix and isolate problems and manually load a device driver. The operating system communicates with a device driver using a device file in /dev or an associated subdirectory. The device file identifies the type of device and the specific hardware component the system will be communicating with, using a numbering convention referred to as major and minor numbers.

Naming and Numbering Conventions

Understanding what the name of a special file means and to what the major and minor numbers refer can get confusing. A listing of /dev might look something like:

brw-r-----	1 root	other	45,143	Jan 15	1993	5s1
brw-r-----	1 root	other	45,175	Jan 16	1994	5sa
crw-rw-rw-	3 bin	bin	52, 2	Feb 22	1994	cga
crw-r--r--	1 root	other	8, 0	Mar 13	12:21	clock
crw-r--r--	1 root	other	7, 0	Feb 22	1994	cmos
crw-------	3 bin	terminal	3, 1	Aug 19	02:31	console
drwxr-xr-x	2 root	backup	2544	Apr 15	1994	dsk
crw-rw-rw-	1 root	other	19, 120	Apr 15	1994	tty000
crw-rw-rw-	1 root	other	19, 121	Apr 15	1994	tty001
crw-rw-rw-	1 root	other	19, 122	Apr 15	1994	tty002
crw-rw-rw-	1 root	other	19, 123	Apr 15	1994	tty003
crw-rw-rw-	1 root	other	19, 124	Apr 15	1994	tty004
crw-rw-rw-	1 root	other	19, 125	Apr 15	1994	tty005
crw-rw-rw-	1 root	other	19, 126	Apr 15	1994	tty006
crw-rw-rw-	1 root	other	19, 127	Apr 15	1994	tty007
crw-rw-rw-	1 root	other	19, 128	Apr 15	1994	tty008
crw-rw-rw-	1 root	other	19, 129	Apr 15	1994	tty009
crw-rw-rw-	1 root	other	19, 130	Apr 15	1994	tty010
crw-rw-rw-	1 root	other	40, 24	Apr 15	1994	e3B0
crw-rw-rw-	1 bin	bin	52, 4	Feb 22	1994	ega
cr--r--r--	1 root	adm	64, 0	Apr 15	1994	eisa0
cr--r--r--	1 root	adm	32, 0	Feb 28	1994	error
brw-rw-rw-	5 bin	bin	2, 60	May 08	1993	fd0
brw-rw-rw-	5 bin	bin	2, 60	May 08	1993	fd0135ds18
brw-rw-rw-	4 bin	bin	2, 36	Feb 28	1994	fd0135ds9
brw-rw-rw-	5 bin	bin	2, 4	Feb 28	1994	fd048
brw-rw-rw-	6 bin	bin	2, 52	Feb 28	1994	fd096
brw-rw-rw-	6 bin	bin	2, 52	Feb 28	1994	fd096ds15
brw-rw-rw-	5 bin	bin	2, 60	May 08	1993	fd096ds18
brw-rw-rw-	4 bin	bin	2, 36	Feb 28	1994	fd096ds9
brw-rw-rw-	7 bin	bin	2, 53	Feb 28	1994	fd1
brw-------	2 root	adm	1, 0	Feb 28	1994	hd00
brw-------	2 root	adm	1, 15	Feb 28	1994	hd01
brw-------	2 root	adm	1, 23	Feb 28	1994	hd02
cr--r-----	1 root	mem	4, 1	Feb 28	1994	kmem

File permissions that start with a b refer to devices that are block type, and file permissions that start with a c are of character type. The device numbers of the special files are always listed in pairs. As shown, a listing of these files does not display the file size parameter. Instead, the listing displays something like 19, 121, designating the major number (19) and the minor number (121), respectively. The major number provides the connection to the kernel by pointing to the driver loaded into the kernel, allowing the kernel to communicate with that type of device. The minor number specifies which particular piece of hardware this special file accesses, such as a disk controller. In the case of serial devices, the minor number specifies the port of the device.

The major number allows you to group devices. Devices with a major number of 1 refer to hard disks (hd), and major numbers of 2 are floppy disks (fd). TTYs have a major number of 19, and their minor number refers to the actual port of the device, so

```
crw-rw-rw-   1 root      other      19, 124 Apr 15  1994 tty004
```

means that this TTY's special file is a character file, not unlike other TTYs with a major number of 19; has read and write permissions for all; and connects to serial port 124. Be aware that major/minor numbers are highly system specific.

The variants of UNIX derived from System V use naming conventions to specify hard disks and their associated special files; for example, c*controller number*d*drive number*s*segment* (or *partition*) *number*. The naming convention depends on the UNIX implementation. A device with the name /dev/dsk/c0d1s1 is a special block file for the second partition on the second disk of the first controller. (Note: numbering starts at 0 and not 1.)

Partition numbers (s) have a defined convention, as shown in the table below. In some UNIX flavors the partition number is replaced with a lowercase letter, such as, a, b, c, d. Some partitions may not be used.

Partition description	s
swap partition	1
user file systems	2
kernel file system mount	3
the entire disk	6
boot partition	7
for the /var file system	8
for the /var file system	9

The swap partition listed above is used for virtual memory; that is, holding information from memory on a disk when the memory available is insufficient. The user file systems partition is used to make space available for user files and directories.

Special-Purpose Device Files

Certain special files in the /dev directory have a specific purpose and meaning. Some of the files you may encounter are /dev/console, /dev/mem, /dev/kmem, and /dev/null. /dev/console, usually a monitor, is a character device with write permissions for the main system console. The files /dev/syscon and /dev/systty are associated with /dev/console. All three files have the same major and minor numbers and consequently refer to the same device driver. Permissions to syscon and systty are both read and write for root and a superuser group such as adm, but read-only for other users. The special file /dev/systty points to the actual hardware port of the console, whereas syscon refers to a virtual console. (Note: syscon and systty are not present in all systems.)

The /dev/mem and /dev/kmem files are special files that contain memory maps. /dev/mem maps the physical memory and /dev/kmem maps the kernel virtual memory. Driver programs can be written to access and use these memory areas, but they are few, limited, and beyond the scope of this book.

The special file /dev/null, a very useful character device, serves as a bucket to dump unwanted bits. By directing output to this file, you can get rid of unwanted bits and still be able to use the file. For instance, if you want to verify a tape but do not want to write the contents of the tape to your disk, direct the output to /dev/null.

Other special-purpose file types in /dev are listed in Table 4.1. /dev may also contain symbolic links to devices that aid the system administrator and user in connecting to the proper device. A symbolic link is created using the **link** command, allowing the administrator to give a device any name desired in order to make the use of a device more manageable. For instance, if /dev/rt0p0 refers to a tape device and you create a link and call the file tape, that link points to the special file of the real tape device.

Table 4.1   Other device filenames and descriptions.

Special filename (/dev)	Description
mtn	Tape device
pts/[number]	Also used for virtual terminals
win[number]	Window device (SunOS)
mouse	Mouse device
ram[number]	RAM disk
swap	Swap device
[*]stn	SCSI tape device (SunOS)

Special-Purpose /dev Subdirectories

In addition to special device files, /dev usually contains some special subdirectories. The hard disks on a system require both block device files, which allow the kernel to buffer the data passed by their device drivers, and character device files, which allow the device file to pass data a byte at a time. Therefore, two important special-purpose subdirectories are /dev/dsk, which contains the block device files for the hard disks on the system, and /dev/rdsk, which contains the character device files for those same hard disks.

A listing of /dev/dsk may look like

```
brw------- 2 root sys 0,0 Feb 28 1994 0s0
```

or

```
brw-r--r-- 1 root sys 0,18 Jul 4 1994 1s0
```

In the first line above, note that the device filename is 0s0, naming the first disk on the first controller. Other file systems on this disk would be labeled 0s1 (second partition on the first controller), 0s2 (third partition on the first controller), and so on. In the second line, the filename is 1s0, the first partition on the second controller. Because the special block files here are going to a hardware device, they are not pointing directly to the hard disk, but rather to the controller.

/dev/rdsk (r stands for raw) houses the character device files that allow the hard disks on the system to communicate with devices and programs that require character-based, or raw, I/O for best performance. UNIX maintains a file system, creates inodes for each file, and handles I/O in blocks. Removing this overhead by creating a gateway that allows UNIX to pass data directly to the executing program without processing improves performance.

For example, many of the major database engines require raw I/O and recommend that raw devices be set up to provide I/O to the database. The database resides on a raw disk partition, and the most efficient way to access the data is through the database utilities where the reads and writes to the file are controlled directly by the database environment, rather than UNIX. The database may run perfectly well using a standard disk device, but as the database grows, performance degrades because UNIX must track the disk space consumed by the data file. Setting up a raw disk device for a database capable of operating on a raw disk partition removes the redundancy of having UNIX track its data file space, thus improving performance.

For another example, if the application is to do disk striping (an implementation where data is spread across multiple disks), the raw disk device will support the hardware that accomplishes this task and once again avoid some of the overhead of the typical UNIX I/O process.

As an alternative to view a raw disk device, the **dd** command could be used. The **dd** command, with I/O directed toward the raw device, can look at the raw disk space. However, caution should be used here, because the **dd** command cannot replace the integrity checks used by a database application. Using it while the database is up could potentially corrupt raw disk space being read by the database.

Creating Special Files

For the most part, special files do not need to be created on a regular basis. Creating special files and installing new devices require the **mknod** command, which can only be executed by the superuser. You can execute **mknod** anywhere in a system, but to keep the system manageable, keep devices in the /dev directory. From the /dev directory, the proper syntax is

```
# mknod filename devicetype {c|b} major number, minor number
```

When this command is complete, the new device is created in the /dev directory. Give the new device a *filename* that is not already in use. Assign the *devicetype* c to a character device or b to a block device. Specify the *major number* depending on the type of device, and enter the *minor number* of the particular peripheral this new special file accesses, or in the case of a TTY device, the port of the device.

Some of this information can be gathered by a look at the last device of similar type. For example, back in the abbreviated /dev listing, the last TTY line printed was

```
crw-rw-rw-   1 root      other      19, 130 Apr 15  1994 tty010
```

To create another device file similar to this, enter

```
# mknod tty011 c 19 131
```

In this example, the previous filename was tty010 so the new filename tty011 is the next in the series. To assign the same devicetype add a c. The major number for a TTY remains 19, and the minor number is the next in the series, 131. When complete, use a list command (i.e., **ls -l**) to confirm that the file is created and that the proper permissions are set. (TTYs are discussed more fully in the next chapter.)

Some systems make creating a device file simpler by providing a **makedev** or **mkdev** utility. This utility looks for the appropriate numbers and type to assign to the named device. The execution of mkdev tape would create a special file for a tape drive called tape.

Hazards to Avoid

The /dev directory is very critical to the operation of a UNIX system. Any time a device is accessed, a file in this directory is used. Avoid the mistake of incorrectly directing output to a regular file in the /dev directory. For instance, to copy a file from your home directory to tape, the proper syntax using **cpio** is

```
# ls filename | cpio -ocvB > /dev/tape
```

But if, instead, you enter:

```
# ls filename | cpio -ocvB > /dev/tapw
```

you would be writing to the regular file tapw in the device directory rather than to the tape device tape. If this occurs for a large file, large number of files, or during a system backup, the regular file would grow, the root file system would fill up, and the system would degrade. In some cases, a system crash can occur where the errant file has filled the root file system, leaving no room for paging, temporary storage, or other I/O functions. As a result, system resources are consumed, new processes are unable to start, and the system become nonresponsive. Consequently, this process must be killed, the errant file removed, and the process that wrote to /dev corrected.

Such errant files in /dev are not always large. To avoid problems, check this directory on a regular basis and keep a backup of it in case of emergencies. To perform a check, for instance, you could create a file containing the contents of /dev every time you make a change and keep this file in a secure location. Running

```
# ls -l > /usr/admin/devchk/082796dev
```

from the /dev directory creates a dated file 082796dev in a directory called devchk, which was created to store these files. Routinely, you could execute the same process, either manually or automatically, creating a file with a different name, then run the **diff** utility with the dated file stored in devchk. Abnormalities could then be observed and compared against a master list, allowing you to remove unwanted files.

To find regular files in /dev enter

```
# cd /dev
# find . -print | grep "^_"
```

This finds all files in /dev and sends them to grep, which prints all lines that start with an underscore (_), indicating a regular file. Then you can go back and remove undesirables.

Also, if you experience an unrecoverable system crash and don't have the latest backup to recreate your /dev directory, it doesn't hurt to keep a hardcopy around in case you have to rebuild by hand. Because of the large size of some /dev directories, this may sound impractical, so be sure to keep a tape backup around, too. Then if your tape isn't the latest, the hardcopy can be used to make corrections in order to reset your system to mirror the last known good /dev configuration.

When looking through the /dev directory, be aware of the native syntax used by the operating system or the setup created by a previous system administrator. Not everything will follow convention, either by design or intervention. For example, it is possible to call all TTYs cons for console rather than TTYs. Likewise, file system naming conventions may not follow those established for the operating system. To avoid a lot of sleepless nights, do your best to keep your system within the naming conventions for files and devices used natively by the operating system (i.e., your defaults from the initial install) and by your organization. This will improve system maintenance and device troubleshooting.

Summary

Device special files are a core feature of the UNIX operating system. These files manage I/O in all of its forms. Even the pipe operation (|) is a special file controlled by the operating system. The administration and management of these files is crucial for maintaining the network, monitors, printers, floppy drives, hard drives, and any device attached to a system. This undoubtedly adds to the complexity of managing a UNIX system, but it also gives you the flexibility to assume control. Simply using the proper permissions on a device file can restrict usage for a specific device by owner, group, or the world. Improperly configured device files lead to low system reliability and increased risk to system security.

Hardware

## Chapter 5

Maintaining Hardware

Chapter 4 discussed configuring devices for I/O with the operating system. This chapter looks at how terminals and printers are maintained, to provide insight into the interaction of peripherals with UNIX, and offers tips for preventive maintenance on all hardware.

Terminals

Connecting a Terminal to a Port

When devices such as terminals are connected to a system, that connection must correspond with an actual port available on the system. The process of connecting to a port begins at bootup when the `init` daemon is started. `init` starts or "spawns" a process, primarily through the `getty` process. `getty` gets its information on a particular port through the `/etc/inittab` file (in some systems `inittab` is replaced by `/etc/ttys`), which allows the system to turn on the ports. The information provided determines the specific port to access, the speed of the connection, parity, and status of the process. Consequently, when booting to multi-user mode, all desired ports should be initialized. If coming up into maintenance mode, the configuration is limited because `/etc/inittab` determines what ports to turn on. In essence, `/etc/inittab` is a structured file containing data parameters for ports and device files specified in it. The system administrator can determine what ports to bring up at any particular run level.

The init daemon determines the run level of the system. When booting is complete, the init daemon becomes the first process to start and has a process ID of 1. Based on the run level specified, the /etc/inittab file gives init action information on which ports to open. The communications protocols used to interface with the terminals are obtained from the file /etc/gettydefs. While the system is up, the init must be running. During up time, init periodically wakes up and checks the /etc/inittab file. To force init to read /etc/inittab, enter **init** q (**telinit** -q on some systems) at the prompt. Sample output of an inittab file is shown below:

```
fs::sysinit:/sbin/rc ap S
is:3:initdefault:
p3:s1234:powerfail:/usr/sbin/shutdown -y -i5 -g0    >/dev/console 2>&1
s0:0:wait:/sbin/rc0                                 >/dev/console 2>&1 </dev/console
s1:1:wait:/usr/sbin/shutdown -y -iS -g0             >/dev/console 2>&1 </dev/console
fw:0:wait:/sbin/uadmin 2                            >/dev/console 2>&1 </dev/console
aA:234:respawn:/etc/getty tty010 9600 #Punch Block A24
```

The /etc/inittab file contains four fields separated by a colon (:). The first field provides an ID of one to four unique alphanumeric characters. The next field specifies the run states in which the process will run, so more than one run state can be entered. The next field specifies an operation to take (described in Table 5.1). The last field contains the program to be executed and any other argument that needs to be passed to the program. Many inittab files are also commented with the # character by the system administrator to make the them easier to read.

In the last line of the previous example, comment #Punch Block A24 tells the administrator to what wire this device is attached — an aid in troubleshooting in case of a failure. The 9600 before the comment refers to the baud rate being passed and points to the communications protocol in the /etc/getty file. Note in the first line that the sysinit operation does not have a specified run level. This is because this process is run before your console is online and the specified init level processes are run.

Not all UNIX systems follow the file layouts described above, but all UNIX systems follow the same type of process to communicate with various devices. Variations on the same theme include making the init.d file a subdirectory with /etc and including various system configuration files within this directory. Other systems keep the terminal information in /etc/ttytype and merge port and terminal type information into one /etc/ttytab file.

To pull all of this information together into a general cross-platform description, the most popular UNIX configurations have the ability to control port and device processes with the /etc/inittab, /etc/ttytab, or /etc/ttys files, depending on the flavor of UNIX. The setup arguments for getty in /etc/inittab are located in /etc/gettydefs. For /etc/ttytab or /etc/ttys, these parameters are found in /etc/gettytab. The terminal type for referenced terminals are either in the `/etc/ttytype` (and `/etc/inittab` files for systems that use `/etc/inittab`) or the `/etc/ttytab` and `/etc/ttys` files with their terminal types defined within themselves. Other systems such as Solaris have their own convention for these files administered through the `sacadm` process, which acts as a system configuration manager.

Table 5.1 `/etc/inittab` action operations.

`/etc/inittab` operation field type	Description
`boot`	Starts the process at boot time. When the process terminates, it does not restart, but the system continues to boot and does not wait for this process to terminate.
`bootwait`	Starts the process at boot time. When this process terminates, it is not restarted, but the system waits until the process terminates.
`initdefault`	The default run level. If no run level is specified, the administrator must supply the default level.
`off`	Checks to see if a process is running. If so, a warning is sent and the process terminates. A built-in delay is provided by the operating system prior to termination.
`once`	Starts a process once. Specifies that this process does not restart when it terminates, and the system continues to load processes, not waiting for this process to terminate.
`powerfail`	Starts the process only when a power fail signal is sent to `init`. This operation waits for the process to terminate before continuing.
`respawn`	Starts a process. Specifies that the system continue to load processes not waiting for this process to terminate. When this process terminates, the `respawn` operation restarts it.
`sysinit`	Loads a process before the `init` daemon initializes the console. This process must terminate before additional processing can continue.
`wait`	Starts a process and waits for it to terminate before going on to the next process.

Specifying Terminal Type

The terminal type allows users to access the system with terminal settings that match their workstation. If terminal types are incompatible, such as when the user uses an incorrect terminal type, the system administrator will get many calls. The main symptoms of an incompatible terminal type are keyboards or displays not working as expected. For instance, keys pressed may do unexpected things or nothing at all because the terminal type has incorrectly mapped the keyboard.

You can use the set TERM procedure described in Chapter 1 or the `tset` utility to change the terminal type. For instance, use `tset` in a `.profile` to query for a specific type of terminal. Or if your dialup usually expects a VT100 terminal, enter

tset -m dialup:?vt100

receiving a decision response from the system of

TERM = (vt100)?

To accept this terminal press Enter. For a different terminal type, enter a new one, such as wyse or whatever is supported by your local workstation. The information that defines the terminal types is found in the `termcap` or `terminfo` files. A common means for establishing the correct terminal type is to provide a command setup like the following when logging in:

set noglob
eval 'tset -s -Q -m dialup:?vt100 -m local:vt52'
unset noglob

Here, the `noglob` option is used to ignore unwanted characters that some terminals want to kick out to the terminal. The output of the **tset** command is suppressed with the -Q option and by requests through the -s option to use shell command input to set the environment. Next, `eval` checks for a connection through a dialup port. If true, the program prompts the user for the default terminal type vt100. If the login is not through a dialup, but rather through the local LAN or other defined access method, it assigns the local terminal type of vt52.

Diagnosing and Fixing Problems

To investigate terminals, the **stty** command is used. This command provides information on the terminal driver and changes terminal driver settings. **stty** displays a complete reading on a terminal by entering

stty -a

The output is system dependent but may look something like:

```
speed 38400 baud;
intr = ^c; quit = ^|; erase = ^h; kill = ^u;
eof = ^d; eol = <undef>; eol2 = <undef>; swtch = <undef>;
start = ^q; stop = ^s; susp = ^z; dsusp = ^y;
rprnt = ^r; flush = ^o; werase = ^w; lnext = ^v;
-parenb -parodd cs8 -cstopb -hupcl cread -clocal -loblk -parext
-ignbrk brkint ignpar -parmrk -inpck -istrip -inlcr -igncr
icrnl -iuclc
ixon -ixany -ixoff imaxbel
isig icanon -xcase echo echoe echok -echonl -noflsh
-tostop echoctl -echoprt echoke -defecho -flusho -pendin iexten
opost -olcuc onlcr -ocrnl -onocr -onlret -ofill -ofdel -tabs
```

The information displays the speed of the terminal device and how control characters and display requirements are interpreted.

stty defines parity, sets stop bits, baud rate, lines on the screen, and control characters. For instance, when logging in, the user is often unable to delete a character. All attempts to delete a character return the ^h (Cntl-h) symbol to the screen. Entering the command

stty erase ^h

fixes the problem by assigning ^h to the terminal as the character for erase.

If a terminal goes insane or acts strangely, the problem may be remedied with **stty sane** on System V UNIX or **reset** on BSD systems. The commands get the appropriate information from the terminfo or termcap files and return the terminal to a normal operating state.

If the problem cannot be fixed at the terminal, attempt to return terminal sanity from another terminal. Before starting, check the process that is running on the problem terminal. For instance, assuming terminal /dev/tty100 is acting strangely, enter

ps -t /dev/tty100

If there is a runaway process, **kill** it. Then use **stty** -a to check to see if the terminal parameters are correct. If you do not have a record of the terminal settings, go to another terminal and check it out. If the settings need to be reset, use the **stty sane** command.

If the problem terminal /dev/tty100 cannot be accessed directly, you need to correct the problem from another terminal, by entering

stty sane < /dev/tty100

Here, the problem device is being redirected toward the **sane** command so that it will not reset the terminal from which you are working.

If the terminal is locked or scrambled, you can also attempt to bring the terminal back to a normal operating mode with the following:

```
# ^j stty sane ^j
```

where ^j is Cntl-j. This command also resets the serial line to the terminal and restores echoing (the attribute of returning characters to your display from the keyboard).

Printers

Connecting a Printer

A printer in UNIX can be connected as either a serial or parallel device and as networked or remote. A serial printer interface transmits one character at a time, whereas a parallel printer interface transmits seven or eight bytes at a time and consequently is usually faster than a serial printer. The actual speed of the printer is measured by its output in characters per second (cps) or pages per minute (ppm).

The standard serial printer connection is an RS-232C cable. The initial communication between the printer and the computer through the interface is known as *handshaking*. Handshaking is used to establish communications and to control data flow.

Printer handshaking based on RS-232 was originally designed for modems. The printer documentation identifies the physical wire on which the UNIX serial port receives signals from the printer. However, the printer handshake requires all four wires used for the printer serial interface. The physical connection to the wires is made through the PINs in the cable. Table 5.2 explains the PINs used by the printer serial interface.

Because RS-232 was originally designed for modems, PINs 2, 3, and 7 are common between serial printers and modems. Nonetheless, PIN designations can vary between manufacturers. Some manufacturers reverse PINs 2 and 3 for transmit and

Table 5.2 RS-232 printer PIN connections.	
PIN number	***Description***
2	Transmit Data (TD)
3	Receive Data (RD)
7	Common Return
Manufacturer defined, PIN 20	DTR (Data Terminal Ready)

receive. The PINs used for handshaking vary even more by printer manufacturer and can be 5, 11, 19, 20, and in some models, a combination of PINs 5 and 6.

Table 5.3 defines the acronyms used to discuss printer handshaking and serial communication. Handshaking determines the DTE and DCE devices that will be communicating with each other. The computer or terminal connected to the printer (this could also be a modem) is the DTE. DTE devices can communicate with other DTE devices or DCE devices. The printer or modem is the DCE device. Because PINs 2 and 3 are the connections used to transmit and receive data, the other PINs are used to provide control of the data, such as, when to stop sending data, when to receive, when to stop receiving, etc. The handshaking takes place when the connected devices acknowledge the connection. First, the DTR on the DCE device sends a signal showing it is ready. The DCE then returns an acknowledgment that it also is ready. A DCE device does this through the DSR PIN. There are other scenarios as well. In some cases the computer sends a DTR and RTS and awaits a CTS and DSR signal from the printer. In any case, once the correct signals have been exchanged, handshaking is complete and the systems start to exchange data.

Data is sent to a printer and usually comes at a rate faster than the printer can process it, so the printer must signal the computer to stop and wait before sending additional data. Most printers have a buffer so that they can receive data at a faster rate than they can process it. The printer signals the computer to stop sending when the buffer is full, processes the buffer, then lets the computer know when to begin resending. The mechanism for doing this is software flow control called XON/XOFF. Faster hardware flow control also is usually available.

Table 5.3   Printer handshaking terminology.

PIN acronym	Description
TD	Transmit Data
RD	Receive Data
DTR	Data Terminal Ready
RTS	Request To Send
CTS	Clear To Send
DSR	Data Set Ready
DCD	Data Carrier Detect
GND	Signal Ground
RI	Ring Indicator
DCE	Data Communication Equipment
DTE	Data Terminal Equipment

Printing

Because the System V and BSD printing processes are significantly different, this section covers each separately.

System V Printing

Configuring the Printing Environment

In System V UNIX, **lpadmin** is used to configure the printing environment. It adds and deletes printers and printer classes and specifies names and paths for printers. The options available to **lpadmin** are shown in Table 5.4.

The minimum requirements for setting up a printer are the printer name (-p), an interface (-m), and the device file (-v). For example:

```
# /usr/lib/lpshut
# /usr/lib/lpadmin -plaser2 -mdumb -v/dev/tty10
# /usr/lib/accept laser2
# enable laser2
# /usr/lib/lpsched
```

In the above procedure, if the path is set to include the /usr/lib directories, you of course do not need to specify the full pathname. The procedure above first shuts

Table 5.4 Options to the `lpadmin` command.	
`lpadmin` option	**Description**
-c	Sets up a printer class (i.e., laser, jet, line, etc.).
-d	Specifies the system default destination through a printer or class name.
-h	Identifies a printer connected directly to the computer.
-l	Identifies a printer that is accessed with a log-in terminal.
-i	Specifies the absolute pathname of the interface program.
-m	Provides the name of the printer's interface program.
-e	Copies the name of an existing printer interface program for a specified printer.
-p	Specifies the name of the printer
-r	Removes a printer class
-v	Provides the pathname of the printer device
-x	Removes a specific printer by name.

down the scheduler using lpshut, then it defines a new printer called laser2 with -p and specifies an interface labeled dumb with the −m option, which allows it to operate as a standard printer. The −v option tells which device file is associated with this printer, in this case /dev/tty10. Note that this device file is also in the inittab file, through which the protocol to communicate with the printer is configured using gettydefs configurations. In /etc/inittab, the getty designation should be off to prevent a continuous print of log-in messages. You could also specify laser2 as a default by executing **lpadmin** -dlaser2 after the printer is established with the first **lpadmin** command.

Before you can use the printer, lpsched must be told to begin adding requests to the queue for this printer and to begin sending jobs to the printer. **accept** enables queuing to the specified printer, and **enable** starts printing to the specified printer. **accept** and **enable** only need to be used once when you add the printer, unless it is turned off for some reason using **reject** or **disable**.

You will probably want to use a printer's special features, so specify the appropriate interface file. Interface files allow your system to interact with the printer correctly; otherwise, you may get strange print results. Interface files are usually found in /usr/spool/lp/model.

To assign the printer to a class of printers, such as laser, enter **lpadmin** -plaser2 -claser. Printer classes are usually set up to aid the administrator to better manage printers. Establishing classes helps to standardize names of printers based on class type, giving the user a better understanding of how names are assigned to available printers. Classes also help the administrator distinguish between printer types, such as laser, dot matrix, inkjet, bubble jet, etc., using easily recognizable class names, such as las, dotm, inkj, and bubj, respectively.

To remove a printer from the system, stop the scheduler using **lpshut**, remove the printer with /usr/lib/**lpadmin** -xlaser2, then restart the scheduler using **lpsched**.

Shared printers on a network are very common, especially when an organization uses expensive color printers and plotters and wants to make them available to users on the network. **lpadmin** used with the −R option sets up remote machines to share print services. However, when purchasing a network printer, be sure to check that the manufacturer has the appropriate driver software for your type of UNIX so the printer can be set up and added to the network. Just knowing that a printer is a network printer is not enough to be a successful printer on a UNIX system.

Getting Printer Status

Before running lpadmin, lpsched must be stopped. After completing a task with lpadmin, the scheduler must be restarted, after which, you should verify that it is running, your print services are available, and the new printer is installed. Do this with the **lpstat** command. Various options listed in Table 5.5 allow you to see some or all of the status of the printing system.

Hardware

An example of the complete status of a print system using the −t option is

```
# lpstat -t

scheduler is running
system default destination: laser1
members of class jet:
jet1
members of class laser:
laser1
laser2
device for jet1: /dev/jet1
device for laser1: /dev/laser1
device for laser2: /dev/laser2
jet1 accepting requests since Aug 5 9:00
jet accepting requesting since Jul 1 6:00
laser1 accepting requests since Aug 5 9:05
laser accepting requests since Jul 1 6:02
laser2 accepting requests since Aug 7 13:43
printer jet1 is idle. enabled since Aug 5 9:01
printer laser1 is idle. enabled since Aug 5 14:12
Printer laser2 is idle. enabled since Aug 7 13:44
```

Table 5.5 **Options to the lpstat command.**

lpstat *option*	*Description*
−a	Shows the accept status of printers.
−c	Displays destinations of printer classes and printers within the class. Can request a specific class using −c[*classname*].
−o	Shows the status of output requests.
−p	Provides printer status.
−r	Returns the scheduler status.
−s	Returns a status summary.
−t	Returns a complete status of the print system.
−u	Returns the stats on request IDs. A specific request ID can be queried as −u[*request-id*[n]].
−v	Returns a list of printers and device names.

As Table 5.5 shows, you can also request information on specific printers using the -a, -p, and -v options. For example:

lpstat -plaser2

shows the status of printer laser2.

Starting and Stopping the Printing Process

The **lp** command starts a print job, and the System V print daemon, lpsched (short for line printer scheduler), spools the print request and tracks it from the time you enter the **lp** command. First, lp talks to the scheduler and creates a temporary file containing the request ID, which it places in the spooler subdirectory /usr/spool/lp/request. If the printer is currently busy, lpsched adds the print request to a First In First Out (FIFO) queue and waits until the printer is free before submitting the next request ID for printing. When the requested destination is available, lpsched transports the file to the requested device. (The acronym *spool* stands for *simultaneous peripheral operation off line.* Basically, a spooler takes data from computer memory and transports it to a peripheral device. The peripheral device runs slower than computer memory, so the data is placed in a file and added to a queue. When the requested destination is available, the spooler transports the file to the requested device.)

The **cancel** command removes a print request from the queue or cancels the currently printing job. When lpsched accepts the job, lp sends the user a response, like request-id is laser2-5677 (1 file), telling the user the destination of the print job and that the number 5677 is the request ID. To cancel the print job, the user simply enters **cancel** laser2-5677. If successful, lpsched responds with a message confirming that the print job has been cancelled. lpstat, described previously, can also provide the request ID and destination.

lpsched starts when the system is booted. To prevent having more than one copy of itself running at the same time, lpsched creates a lock file called SCHEDLOCK. If at startup lpsched finds a SCHEDLOCK file, the daemon terminates. Similarly, if the lock file does not exist at startup, lpsched creates this file to prevent other schedulers from running.

lpshut stops lpsched and removes the SCHEDLOCK file. After lpsched stops, lp can still send requests to the spooler subdirectory, but no jobs will be printed. lpsched can be restarted using the command /usr/lib/**lpsched**. If it was stopped by any process other than lpshut, SCHEDLOCK must be removed manually before lpsched can be restarted.

Hardware

Spooling and Printing Control

The key directories used by the lp spooler in System V are described in Table 5.6. Table 5.7 describes commands to control spooling and printing.

accept and reject tell lpsched whether or not to add a request to the print queue. enable and disable tell lpsched whether or not to send print jobs to a designated printer. When the **accept** command is executed, the system sends a response, such as destination laser2 now accept requests. Likewise, with the **enable** command, the system responds with printer laser2 enabled. The -r option can be used with **reject** to display a text message, such as why the printer is down. Similarly, a -r can be used with the **disable** command to display a text message. A -c flag used with **disable** cancels any print jobs pending for the printer that is to be disabled.

Table 5.6   Directories used by lp.

/usr/spool/lp	Main directory for the spooler.
/usr/spool/lp/model	Shell scripts that define variables and commands for specific types of printers.
/usr/spool/lp/request	Creates a filename with the request ID for a print job. When printed, the scheduler removes the file.
/usr/spool/lp/admins/lp/ classes	Contains files that classify printers by their defined classes.
/usr/spool/lp/admins/lp/ interfaces	Contains files of printer configurations.
/usr/spool/lp/admins/lp/ printers	Has files that contain printer-specific information set up with the **lpadmin** command, such as interface and port number parameters for the printer.

Table 5.7   System V commands to control spooling and printing.

Command	Description
accept	Accepts jobs for spooling to a device.
reject	Rejects jobs for spooling to a device.
enable	Enables printing to a device.
disable	Disables printing to a device.

Printing Options

`lp` can print either to the default printer or another printer on the system. To print to the default printer, the command line

```
# lp filename
```

is all that is needed. The –d option specifies a destination; otherwise, **lp** assumes the default destination. For example, the command line

```
# lp -dlaser2 filename
```

prints the specified file to the printer defined as `laser2`. The environment variable LPDEST tells `lpsched` what printer to use. Consequently, it is possible to configure different default printers for different classes or groups of users by setting up LPDEST for the group when the members log on, such as through `.profile`.

Other options available to the user of **lp** are listed in Table 5.8. In addition, the **lp** command can print multiple files by using wildcard characters. For example, to print all files that start with `sys` in a directory, enter **lp** `sys*`.

You can print to a desktop or other terminal with a printer attached locally, rather than through a network, using the **lpt** command. However, the local system (such as a PC) must have the proper printer protocols defined. The options to the **lpt** command differ from **lp**, although the syntax is the same. For example, to print three copies of a file, enter

```
# lpt -c3 filename
```

Table 5.8   Options to the `lp` command.

`lpstat` option	Description
–d	Sends the file to be printed to the supplied destination. Note: The LPDEST environment variable determines a user's default destination.
–m	Sends a mail message to the initiator of the print job when printing is complete.
–n	Prints more than one copy of the file. Example: **lp** –n2 *filename* prints two copies.
–s	Turns off message output from the spooler. If used, the user does not receive a request ID.
–t	Puts a title on the banner page.
–w	Notifies the user when a request is completed.

Hardware

Other print options to explore are remote print features as well as variations to **lp** that differ between UNIX versions.

BSD Printing

Starting the Printing Process

BSD systems use a different print method than System V. The **lpr** command queues data for printing and places the print data in the spooling directory. Then the BSD print daemon, lpd, checks the queue to find a print job and sends the job to the printer. lpd usually is located in /usr/lib. Other programs may be used for printing, such as pr, but these programs all call on lp for queuing and lpd for printing. Before lpr queues a print request, it must know how to handle the data; that is, it must know the destination, communications requirements, and details of the printing environment. lpr obtains this information from command line arguments for the **lpr** command, environment variables, and the global system configuration.

For example, to specify a printer with **lpr** use the -P option as follows:

```
# lpr -Plaser2 filename
```

Other command line flags are described in the UNIX documentation.

Configuring the Printing Environment

In the above example, the printer destination is specified. If a destination is not specified, lpr uses the default printer defined in the /etc/printcap file. The printcap file specifies printing environment variables in the same way that the termcap file specifies terminal information in System V. Some of the key variables in the printcap file are located in Table 5.9. Other variables are described in the UNIX documentation.

Print filters are also referenced in printcap. The filters are if, lpf, or of. The if and of filters are for input (i) and output (o) to the printer. lpf records the accounting data.

/etc/printcap also lets the print driver know where to spool the print jobs. As with the previous laser2 example, the typical location for spooling information is at /var/spool/laser2.

When job information is submitted, lpr creates two files. One file is the job number of the print request and the second file is the data file referenced by the job number. The job number allows you and the system to track and complete the print job and kill it if necessary. The name of the file that controls the print job, known as the control file, begins with the letters cf. Similarly, the name of the data file begins with the letters df. For information necessary for printing control on BSD systems, view print jobs by entering **lpq** at the system prompt. lpq provides status information for all requests on the queue, including rank on the queue, user making the request, job ID, where it came from (such as a file or a named pipe), and size of the job in bytes.

Hardware

Spooling and Printing Control

The **lpc** command controls spooling and printing. The interactive commands available to **lpc** are shown in Table 5.10. If you experience printer problems, lpc will not be the most reliable means of fixing your system. For the following lpc examples, use the actual name of the printer (e.g., laser2).

As the root user, you may want to remove all print jobs. To do this, enter

```
# lprm –
```

To remove all of the jobs from a specific printer enter

```
# lpc
# lpc>clean laser2
```

or just simply

```
# lpc clean laser2
```

where laser2 is the name of the printer.

Table 5.9   BSD /etc/printcap variables.

Variable name	Description
af	Accounting file variable for the printer. Provides information on printer usage.
br	Baud rate. Looks a lot like the termcap entry, such as br#14400
fc or fs	Variable to set flags. fs is also used to control parity, delays, data flow, echo, etc. for serial printers. Note: These are actually bit settings: fc clears the flag; fs sets a flag.
lf	Printer error log variable. Usually found at /var/adm/lpd-errs
lo	Variable providing the lock filename.
lp	Points to the actual device name of the printer. When this variable points to a nondescript printer file, it typically means that it should be pointing to a network printer.
rm or rp	Accesses remote printers.
sd	Spooler directory for each printer.

To specify a particular job, enter

lprm 235

where 235 references the ID of the job, which can be obtained with **lpq**. You can also remove the print jobs for a particular user by entering

lprm wetsch

where wetsch is the user ID of the user whose print jobs you want to remove.

Table 5.10 BSD **lpc** commands with syntax.

Command	Syntax	Description
abort	**abort** *printer*	Terminates current printing activity on *printer*. Restart print job using **start**. Considered more abrupt than **stop**. Print jobs remain in the queue.
clean	**clean** *printer*	Clears the print queue for the specified printer.
disable	**disable** *printer*	Prevents the printer from accepting new print jobs. To prevent an abrupt printer shutdown, use **stop** after a **disable** command.
down	**down** *printer* [*message*]	Disables the queue and stops printing. Add a message so that users are notified when they run lpq. The same as **disable** + **stop** commands.
enable	**enable** *printer*	To be run after **disable** to restore the print queue and printer for use.
help	**help** [*lpc command*]	Provides help on **lpc** commands.
start	**start** *printer*	Resumes printing jobs in the printer queue after an **abort** or **stop** command.
status	**status** *printer*	Provides status on the specified printer.
stop	**stop** *printer*	Stops the printer but still allows users to enter jobs in the print queue. Resume a **stop** with a **start** . A good command to use during routine printer maintenance.
up	**up** *printer*	Combines **enable** + **start** to enable the queue and resume printing.

Printer Troubleshooting

When your printer is not working, follow the systematic troubleshooting procedure that follows.

1. Check the printer and make sure it is on. If so, then check to make sure it is online.

2. Check the cable connections and make sure they are good.

3. Reinitialize the printer by turning it off and then back on again.

4. Check for any hardware errors, such as out of paper, no toner, printer jam, unable to talk to server, etc. Follow the vendor guidelines for correcting the problem.

5. Run lpstat to check the status of the printer. If disabled, try to enable the printer. If print jobs are rejected, use **accept** on the printer to get it to accept print requests.

6. Check your network connections to the printer if the printer is a network printer. If print jobs are going to the spooler but not printing or if printer status seems unpredictable after enabling the printer, a faulty network connection may be the culprit, even though cable connections to the printer look good.

7. Check the printer configuration and make sure that the system recognizes the printer port. Do this by sending some output to the printer device file. Send output directly to the device file using something like **cat** *testfile*> /dev/ *printer_device*, or use **stty** to direct output for serial printers. Also try redirecting output to a different port.

8. Run the **ps** command to look for print processes that may be in memory (use **ps** -ef | **grep** lp). Before killing these processes, first turn the problem printer(s) off and execute **lpshut**. After running lpshut, check the memory processes again. If lp processes are still trying to run in memory, then kill those processes. In a worst-case scenario, you may not be able to kill the processes even after trying to turn the printer on and off. You may have to reset your system so that all the processes in memory are reset. This would involve a shutdown to single-user mode and then a system restart to multi-user mode.

9. If you were successful in removing errant lp processes, but the printer still does not work, check in the spooler directory for the SCHEDLOCK file. If it exists (because lpshut did not remove it), remove it. Then restart lpsched.

10. Check that lpsched is included in your startup script with its full pathname, /usr/lib/lpsched. If it is missing or incorrect, add or correct it. If it is there and the scheduler is still not starting, check for the SCHEDLOCK file. On the line above /usr/lib/lpsched, enter

    rm -f /usr/spool/lp/SCHEDLOCK

Your shutdown script should also contain an absolute pathname call to `lpshut`. You do not have to add a `SCHEDLOCK` remove line here because `lpshut` is designed to remove the lock file when it executes properly.

Other options available include checking native printer troubleshooting techniques as recommended for your specific flavor of UNIX or contacting the appropriate customer support group. For instance, you may be experiencing problems such as bad characters, extra line feeds, and so forth. If the troubleshooting procedures do not help, dig deeper for causes, which could include an incorrect interface script, a faulty device file for the printer, or a defective printer.

Tips for Preventive Maintenance of Hardware

A large variety of hardware must be administered, monitored, and maintained in an enterprise-wide system that goes well beyond terminals and printers. Other common devices include hard disks, tape backup units, CD-ROMs, Jukeboxes, RAID (redundant array of inexpensive disks) arrays, cabling boxes, transceivers, routers, etc. The administrator must follow vendor instructions and obtain vendor support, if necessary, to properly integrate devices with a UNIX server or desktop.

The hardware administration layer covers all aspects of a UNIX system. Physical security is required to keep hardware intact. Software configuration is needed to allow the hardware to run properly. Device errors can cause problems ranging from small ones that may irritate a user to catastrophic failures that can bring an entire system down.

Incorporating preventative maintenance (PM) procedures on system hardware can save many headaches in the long run. Some PM procedures that should be seriously considered are:

- On a tape device, use a vendor-recommended cleaning/maintenance tape regularly to clean the drive. Dust and heavy use of a tape drive degrades the read/write capability of the tape. If you are doing daily backups, cleaning the drives at least once a week is recommended.

- Keep the physical environment of the servers clean, well ventilated, and as dust free as possible. This area should also be secure, so that unauthorized users are not messing with the machines. How secure depends on how critical the equipment is to the organization.

- Check cables on a regular basis. Moving hardware or just moving around in a computer room can lead to accidental pulls on cables or other incidents that loosen cabling. Periodic checks will minimize the incidence of loose connections.

- Check out all devices on a regular basis. Clean and do PM procedures on printers as recommended, reset modems, and check network connections. Note: The more reliable a device or connection, the less often you need to check it. For instance, a tape device may need weekly maintenance, but user network connections may only need annual checks.

- Set up regular maintenance periods to take down servers to single-user mode and perform disk maintenance. Planned maintenance also allows you to restart the system and reinitialize devices, computer memory, and software.

- Some administrators recommend completely powering off the server to clear out any unwanted variables when the system is brought down to init level 0. At times and on some systems, this may be necessary, depending on what the system is supporting, how long it would take to bring everything up from a cold start, and whether you need to transfer operations to a backup system before powering down.

- Some devices, such as large optical jukeboxes, may be beyond the realm of the local system administrator or PM technician to maintain. If this is the case, it is a good idea to budget vendor support contracts to keep some of the unwieldy devices in good shape.

- Have on hand the proper tools and some spare parts to support the environment. Tools may range from a simple set of screwdrivers to a good set of computer tools, cabling apparatus, and system diagnostic equipment. A good starter set of spare parts includes cables, connectors, cable converters, and network cards.

- If you have a lot of cabling for the network system, it is imperative that you properly label the cable connections from the computer room out to the communication devices and wherever else you have control of the cable. This will save countless hours of time in troubleshooting network problems, in case you need to actually trace the physical link between your server and a user connection. A good-quality cable tester is also essential to cable troubleshooting. In addition, if you have many peripherals, such as printers and modems, it is a good idea to label them as well.

- Keep your systems clean, but be careful in the use of cleaning agents. Many manufacturers sell cleaning supplies that will not harm the computer and some have antistatic capabilities. Regular detergents and cleaning solvents can damage or destroy some equipment, especially tape drives. As a minimum, lint-free wipes and isopropyl alcohol will serve you well. It may also be a good idea to have some canned air around to blow dust out of the computers.

Overall, hardware maintenance takes extra time, but it is an extremely important function. Putting time into supporting the hardware reduces user frustration; the time you must spend on troubleshooting problems (i.e., the frustration of the system administrator); and hardware repair or replacement costs. It also increases system reliability.

Hardware

Network Administration
Module

## Chapter 6

Introduction to Networking

In an enterprise, the network is the most complex part of the system. It must reliably transport data and operate continuously. Maintaining the network is a complex administrative task. The administrators on a network specialize in providing network services for a specific group of networks. For instance, providing network support to a Novell network is considerably different than providing a UNIX-based network with TCP/IP. Although the networking principles are the same, the actual technical details of maintaining and configuring the networks are different.

This chapter offers a foundation for understanding networks, but be prepared to dig much further into your own specific environment. Network implementations differ among UNIX variants. In complex enterprise-wide environments, good system administration requires technical specialties to cover the breadth and depth of the environment. To get a more practical understanding of a particular system, look for support from the vendor or a colleague who has worked on the system extensively.

Types of Networks

Small networks, usually contained within a geographically close environment, such as a single building, campus, or office park, are called Local Area Networks, or LANs. Larger networks that cover a wider geographic area, such as the network of an enterprise with offices in various cities or states, are called Wide Area Networks, or WANs. LANs are often the building blocks of WANs.

LANs can be grouped into two broad categories: peer-to-peer networks and server-based networks. In a peer-to-peer network, there is no subdivision of work. All computers on the network act as both client and server with the resources of any one computer supporting the local user; that is, the individual using the computer and any remote user on the network accessing the local computer. Security, maintenance, and resource sharing are at the discretion of the individual users on the network. Peer-to-peer networks operate best in small environments, such as an office with a limited number of computers and devices on the network, or in environments where security and maintenance needs are simple.

As a network grows, the performance of a peer-to-peer network may not be tolerable. In addition, the security and maintenance necessary on a larger network may make peer-to-peer services inadequate. In this case, a server-based or distributed system, the other major category of networks, is the alternative. In a distributed system, individual computers on the system perform work that contributes to a larger task; for example, providing network communications. Special computers called servers are dedicated to providing these services to the network, such as communication, print, database, mail, or fax services. Unlike a peer-to-peer network that can support few computers and must be geographically close, server-based or distributed networks can support thousands of nodes spaced as far away as another country.

Network Architectures

The architecture of a network describes not only the physical construction of the network (topology and transmission media) but also the way the software and hardware interact with each other (networking models and communications protocols). This book concentrates on the most popular implementation of networks for UNIX systems — an Ethernet network in a bus configuration — that follows the IEEE 802.3 standard for media access called Carrier-Sense Multiple Access with Collision Detection (CSMA/CD).

Physical Connections

Networking computers requires both physical connections and logical connections. The physical connections include the hardware, such as computers, cables, transceivers, and interface cards.

Cables and Connectors

Any computer or device, such as a printer, connected to a network is considered a node of the network. Nodes can be connected with wire or cable or can be connected using wireless technology, exchanging data using radio, microwave, or infrared transmissions.

The medium depends on your network needs. Bandwidth, the difference between the lowest and highest signal frequency a cable can carry, describes how much data a medium can transmit. For example, the theoretical Ethernet transport rate is 10 Mbps, whereas 100BaseX, or fast Ethernet, allows up to 100 Mbps. However, the actual throughput of a network is never 100 percent due to noise and other network overhead.

A network built using Ethernet cabling and connectors offers a selection of physical wire with differing characteristics. 10BaseT wiring, or twisted pair, has an effective range of 100 meters and a minimum of 0.5 meters between nodes. 10BaseT may have the lowest effective range, but it is one of the most common network connections because of its low maintenance and high flexibility.

10Base2, also known as thinnet, is a coaxial cable with a better range than 10BaseT. It has an effective length of less than 200 meters. About 185 meters is considered the maximum network segment length. Because it is less durable, 10Base2 cable is used in implementations where the wiring is less accessible to users, to protect it from being stepped on, pulled, bent, or otherwise mishandled. This reduces the maintenance task of replacing cable.

10Base5 cable, also known as thicknet, has an effective length of 500 meters and a minimum cable distance between the transceivers of 2.5 meters. It supports a maximum of 100 nodes. 10Base5 cable does not bend easily. This durability, in addition to its higher effective length, makes 10Base5 cable good for larger installations.

10BaseF, or fiber-optic, cable carries digital signals in the form of pulses of light. Fiber can carry the modulated light for miles without degradation. Fiber may be chosen over 10Base5 because it is more flexible, is not subject to electrical interference, and can be used for faster 100 Mbps networks like FDDI (Fiber Distribution Data Interface).

Different cable types use different methods of connection. 10BaseT requires an RJ-11 phone connector, whereas 10Base2 uses a BNC connector. Ethernet network interface cards (NICs) can range in their connection makeup from 10BaseT, 10Base2, and 10Base5 connections to only a single type of connection. NICs must support the same connection type as the medium in use.

Other Network Devices

In wired networks, such as an Ethernet network, a cable from a node is attached to an interface device called a transceiver. Transceivers ensure that there is a signal on the wire and manage the transmissions between the nodes. The NIC is the peripheral between the transceiver and the node. Usually, the transceiver is built into the NIC.

Another hardware device, a concentrator, allows several nodes to be plugged into one device connected to the network. In addition, a concentrator can also allow one network to feed into another, and through multiple concentrators, hundreds of network nodes can be accommodated. Concentrators are used in twisted pair networks.

As a network grows, the distance a signal must travel between nodes increases, sometimes exceeding the maximum of the medium used to transmit the signal. If the distance is too great, a repeater, which is a device used to boost a signal, can be connected between nodes. In addition to boosting a signal, repeaters connect wires. When using repeaters, only two can be placed between any two nodes. Repeaters are generally less expensive compared to other connection hardware. However, they require power and have electronic components that can fail. In addition, repeaters boost signals good or bad, so they can amplify noise as well as good signals, across the network.

Additional devices also connect networks to networks. For a complete enterprise-wide system, a router routes signals from one LAN to another and limits the connections of a LAN. For example, a network of many LANs can be broken into segments of three LANs per segment. A router can be installed between segments to prevent unwanted access between LANs. A special type of router, a bridge, connects similar networks. Another special router, a gateway, connects dissimilar networks.

Topologies and Access Methods

The topology of a network describes the physical arrangement of the nodes in the network. Commonly used topologies include bus, star, and ring configurations, as depicted in Figure 6.1. There are variation and hybrid schemes for network topologies, too. Each configuration has its advantages and disadvantages. The topology is an important component of the network infrastructure, so it must be selected to best fit the needs of the organization.

A bus topology connects many nodes with a single transmission line, called a backbone or trunk. Data is addressed to a particular computer on the network and sent to all devices on the trunk. Only the computer with the correct address can accept the data. Because it is sent to all nodes on the trunk, a signal will bounce from one unconnected end of the bus to another, preventing other nodes from transmitting until something stops it. A device called a terminator absorbs these free signals. All unconnected cables on an Ethernet bus require a 50-ohm terminator. An unconnected end can be a broken cable, a disconnected cable, or the ends of the backbone. When a node on the bus breaks or becomes disconnected, creating an unconnected end, the entire network goes down.

Traffic on the bus is controlled by CSMA/CD, defined in the IEEE standard 802.3. When a node wants to transmit, it tests the bus for a carrier, or signal. If it senses a carrier, it waits for a random amount of time before trying to retransmit. When two computers on the network send data at the same time, a collision occurs, causing both computers involved to stop for a random amount of time before trying to retransmit.

In a ring configuration, the nodes are linked to each other forming a circle of nodes. When one node on the network fails, the whole network goes down. Access on a ring network is often controlled by a method called token passing, in which an electronic signal called a token is passed continuously around the ring. When a computer on the ring wants to send a signal, it waits for the token. When it receives the token, it adds the destination address to the token, then sends the token and the data. The token and data move along the ring until they reach the computer matching the destination address. The destination computer copies the data then adds an acknowledgment to the token, which is passed through the ring until it reaches the computer that sent the data. After receiving the acknowledgment, the sending computer puts a new token on the ring.

A star configuration connects many nodes to a central node, or hub. The hub can be passive, simply retransmitting any received signal, or active, selectively switching received data to specified destinations and providing most of the processing for the network. When a node on a star topology fails or is disconnected, only the failed node is unable to send or receive on the network. The rest of the network is unaffected. If the central node fails, the whole network goes down.

In large systems, networks can be connected to networks in addition to computers and devices such as concentrators and repeaters. A possible setup is a bus topology with the nodes on the bus network occupied by star, ring, and other networks, as depicted in Figure 6.2.

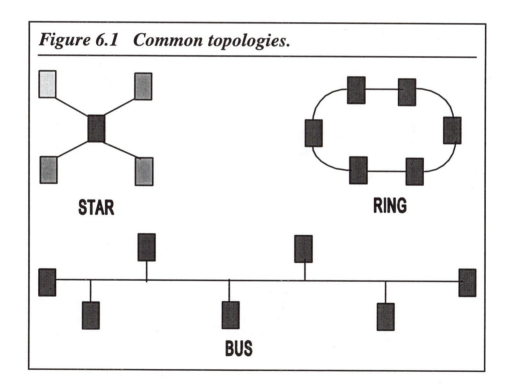

Figure 6.1   Common topologies.

STAR

RING

BUS

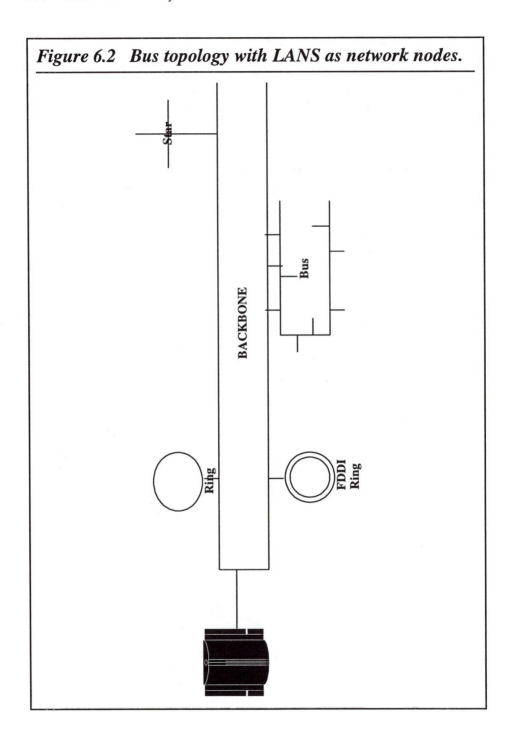

Figure 6.2   Bus topology with LANS as network nodes.

Logical Connections

The logical connections in a network follow rules and procedures called protocols for communications. Each protocol accomplishes a different communication task. A technique called layering allows the different protocols to work together by defining the sequence in which the protocols perform their tasks. The suite of protocols is called a protocol stack. Data transmitted on a network travels down the stack on the originating computer, through the transmission medium, then up the stack on the receiving computer.

Networking Models

Network protocol stacks follow models or standards created by computing communities. Two common reference models are the International Standards Organization and Open Systems Interconnect models (ISO/OSI). Table 6.1 shows the seven layers of the OSI model and gives an example of the function of each layer.

Network

Table 6.1   The OSI reference model (RM).

OSI layer	Layer name	Description	Example
7	Application	Services provided by an application.	Application program interface (API).
6	Presentation	Determines how the data is formatted.	Encryption and decryption routines. Data conversions.
5	Session	Provides for data flow. Assists the transport layer in maintaining data integrity.	Initial handshaking when a session is started.
4	Transport	Maintains integrity of network services between nodes.	Actual transport of the bit stream through the network medium.
3	Network	Allows bits to be routed and switched to network nodes.	Using a router.
2	Data link	Transfers bits to another physical link.	Data packets, or frames, sent across a network.
1	Physical	Physical hardware for data transmission.	NIC card. Cable.

The IEEE 802 standards enhance the OSI model by subdividing Layer 2 to further define data link communications, media access control, and the hardware used to build the network. Standards developed to enhance Layer 1 add more detailed specifications regarding the use of network interface cards and components used to build twisted pair and coax networks. Section 802.3 defines the access control method CSMA/CD. The network implementation that this book concentrates on, an Ethernet network in a bus configuration, follows the standards and specifications for cabling and media access as defined in the IEEE 802 enhancements.

More common than the OSI model is Transmission Control Protocol and Internet Protocol (TCP/IP), used by the Internet and numerous commercial enterprises. Simpler than OSI, TCP/IP uses a four-layer protocol stack as shown in Table 6.2

The TCP/IP model is missing some of the services provided by the OSI model and combines services from several layers. Though TCP/IP cannot be mapped to the OSI model exactly, the TCP protocol in the transport layer of the TCP/IP model provides services equivalent to the transport layer in the OSI model. Building the network using Ethernet bus topology and twisted pair cabling provides the connectivity specified in the data link and physical layers.

Network Protocols

A protocol stack is a suite of communications protocols, each providing a certain network communication service. Protocols can be added or removed much like drivers, although with a complete protocol stack, such as the OSI suite, that is not necessary. The number of available protocols adds to the complexity of successful network communications. Table 6.3 provides a selected list of protocols.

Addresses and Address Resolution Protocols

Networking models and communications protocols provide the vehicle for transmitting data but not its destination. Packet addressing schemes supply a logical destination for data in the form of an IP address.

Table 6.2   TCP/IP network model.

TCP/IP layer	Layer name	Description
4	Application	End-user applications
3	Transport	Communication among programs on a network
2	Network	Basic communication, addressing, and routing
1	Link	Network hardware and device drivers

IP Addresses

TCP/IP application layer protocols communicate with other nodes using an Internet address that specifies the network and the host (a node on the network) being accessed. The host can be a specific machine or another network, a subnet.

Table 6.3   Common network protocols.

Abbreviation	Full name
BGP	Border Gateway Protocol
CLNP	Connectionless Network Protocol
CMIP	Common Management Information Protocol
DAP	Data Access Protocol
DDCMP	Digital Data Communications Message Protocol
EGP	Exterior Gateway Protocol
FTP	File Transfer Protocol
ICMP	Internet Control Message Protocol
IDRP	Inter-Domain Routing Protocol
IGRP	Interior Gateway Routing Protocol
IP	Internet Protocol
IS-IS	Intermediate System — Intermediate System Protocol
LAP-B	Link Access Protocol — Balanced
LAT	Local Area Transport Protocol
MNP	Microcom Networking Protocol
NHRP	Next Hop Resolution Protocol
NSP	Network Services Protocol
RARP	Reverse Address Resolution Protocol
RIP	Routing Information Protocol
SMTP	Simple Mail Transfer Protocol
SNAP	SubNetwork Access Protocol
SNMP	Simple Network Management Protocol
SSCO	Service-Specific Connection-Oriented Protocol
TCP	Transmission Control Protocol
TCP/IP	Transmission Control Protocol/Internet Protocol
UDP	User Datagram Protocol
VMTP	Versatile Message Transaction Protocols

Network

IP addresses are four bytes long. The first two bytes identify a logical network. The third and fourth bytes identify a host. For example, in the address 250.100.99.35, the fields 250.100 specify the network and the fields 99.35 identify the host. Routers use the IP address to route the data to the correct destination (Figure 6.3).

A breakdown of the example address above into binary format is:

Network	First field	250	=	1111 1010
Network	Second field	100	=	0110 0100
Host	Third field	99	=	0110 0011
Host	Fourth field	35	=	0010 0011

IP addressing also follows a class structure that depends on the type of network. This structure provides a specific format for IP addresses. The following table shows the classes and their values in the first field of the IP address.

IP class	*First field range*
A	1–126
B	128–191
C	192–223
D	224–239
E	240–254

The classes allocate bytes to the network and host parts of an IP address differently. The format for a Class A address is net.host.host.host. Only very large networks receive this class of address. Class A addresses are virtually impossible to get. Class B addresses, format net.net.host.host, are assigned to large subnetted networks and are also very rare. The more commonly assigned Class C addresses, format net.net.net.host, are given to large or growing sites and can be obtained in blocks. Class D and E addresses are still in development or are experimental. These classes are needed to help fill the expanding world of TCP/IP and the Internet.

Note that the first field does not use the values 0, 127, or 255. These numbers are reserved for special purposes. The value 0 (in any of the four fields) stands for the local host or network. For example, an address of 0.0.45.50 refers to the host 45.50 on the local network. The value 127 identifies a loopback network, a virtual network that has no hardware interface and includes only the local host. The address 127.0.0.1 refers to the current host.

The value 255 identifies the network portion of an IP address that has been masked in a technique called subnetting. Subnetting extends the utility of the IP addressing scheme. Using subnetting, large networks limit the number of hosts recognizable to other hosts within the network by dividing the network into logical subnets. Assigning part of the host portion of the IP address to the network portion creates the logical subnets. For example, a Class B address can be changed from

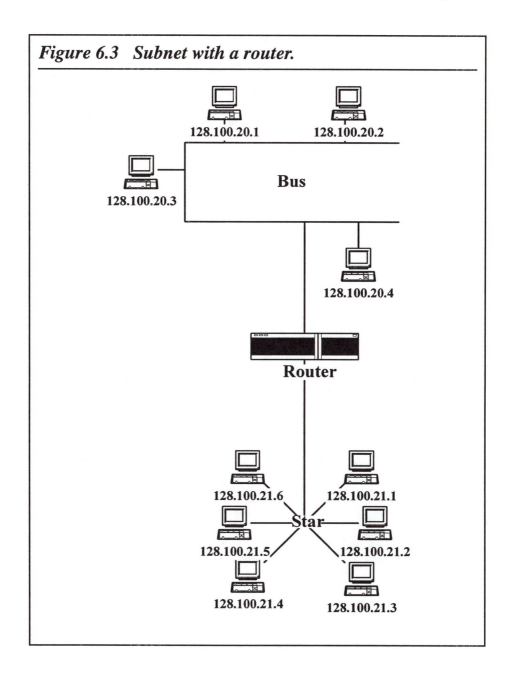

Figure 6.3   Subnet with a router.

net.net.host.host to net.net.net.host, reducing the potential hosts from more than 64,000 to a maximum of 254. Hosts outside the Class B network still see only one Class B address. Hosts within the Class B network see 254 Class C-like sub-nets, instead of the true number of hosts actually on the Class B network.

To implement subnetting, a subnet mask applied at startup overrides the kernel instructions to use the address class to determine the network portion of the address. The mask assigns the value of 255 (binary 1s) to the network bytes and 0 (binary 0) to the host bytes. The file used in UNIX systems to implement a subnet mask is /etc/ netmasks, shown in the following sample.

```
# The Netmasks File
# Use IP Address Type for Mask
#
# Format: Network-Address Mask-Address
#
# i.e. 128.35.0.0 255.255.255.0
#
132.55.0.0 255.255.255.0
```

As shown, the network address 132.55.0.0 is masked by hex ffffff00 to pro-duce the the subnet masked address 255.255.255.0 used by this host.

Port Addresses

IP addresses identify machines not processes. To specify certain processes, such as e-mail and ftp, a two-byte number called a port address supplements the IP address. Port addresses can have a value of 0 to 65535. When a machine connects to a system, it must be able to start up a process on the machine at the destination address. To do this, a port address is used that will be able to recognize the appropriate access method.

Certain port addresses are reserved for special uses. First, port 0 is reserved for use by the system. Ports 1 to 1023 are reserved for certain services and for assignment by the superuser. For instance, telnet services are assigned to port 23, ftp to port 21, SMTP (Simple Mail Transport Protocol) to port 25, and so on. Ports greater than 1023 can be used and assigned to any process. (For more information on network services see *Network Services* later in this chapter.)

Address Mapping

For convenience, the long number of an IP address is usually mapped to a text name. Complex networks and networks connected to the Internet use the Domain Name System (DNS), a distributed database that stores host name, IP address, and mail routing information. Simple networks use a UNIX file called /etc/hosts. In /etc/hosts, the IP addresses of the localhost and other hosts are mapped to their symbolic names. Whenever you add a server to your network, the /etc/hosts file must be updated to reflect the new server. A typical /etc/hosts file is shown below.

```
# host file
#
127.0.0.1 localhost
139.53.224.10 science.comp.com loghost
139.53.225.10 science.bio.com
139.53.224.13 science.eng.com
139.53.225.13 science.eng.com
139.53.224.14 science.admin.com
139.53.225.14 admin.serv.com
```

Another file, /etc/hosts.equiv, lists all hosts allowed to log in without a password, also known as trusted hosts. The /etc/hosts.equiv file is only updated when machines are added as trusted hosts. The machine names of the hosts added to this file include the name of the machine whose /etc/hosts.equiv file you are editing. When machines are made equivalent, the machine being accessed by the host checks to see if the user account exists. If so, the user is allowed to access the destination without reentering a password. Use caution when adding hosts to /etc/hosts.equiv. Diskless workstations should never be declared trusted and should always require a login to gain access.

In addition to mapping IP addresses to text names, hardware on a diskless workstation must be mapped to an IP address. The protocol called Reverse Address Resolution Protocol (RARP) provides this service. A newer, more frequently used protocol called BOOTP also provides this translation function. System hardware determines which protocol must be used.

On systems using the BOOTP protocol at startup, a diskless workstation broadcasts a request for boot information. When the bootpd daemon receives such a request, it reads the bootptab file looking for the Ethernet address of the requestor. If bootpd finds the appropriate information, it returns the requestor's IP address and the name of the file from which the requestor must boot. An entry in the bootptab file could be:

```
client:\
      :hd=/clientboot:\
      :ha=0600F56458FF:\
      :ip=185.124.110.220:\
      :bf=boot1:
```

In this example, the bootptab file gives a home directory (hd) of /clientboot, an Ethernet address (ha), an IP address (ip), and a boot file (bf) of boot1.

The bootptab file can include a group boot file from which individual clients can inherit boot parameters. This would be accomplished by setting up a bootptab directory that identifies boot parameters for a group of clients, such as, 486group. Then, any client could inherit the general bootup parameters by specifying the template host (tc) on the first line of the client parameters. In the following example, the group file 486group specifies parameters such as a subnet mask (sm) and home directory of the boot files (hd). The specified client, client25, inherits these and any others in the group file as directed by the variable tc in the first line of the client file.

```
486group:\
        :sm=255.255.255.0
        :hd=/clientboot:\
        :gw=185.102.5.2
        :ht=ether:
client25:\
        :tc=486group:\
        :ha=0600D564589F:\
        :ip=185.102.5.22:\
        :bf=boot1:
```

A legend of variables is located in the bootptab file.

On diskless workstations using the RARP protocol, the ethers file finds the correspondence between the hardware Ethernet addresses and the more symbolic IP addresses. The rarpd daemon reads the /etc/ethers and the /etc/hosts files to find the appropriate mapping.

Applying for Addresses

To ensure that all IP addresses are unique, they are controlled by the Internet Assigned Numbers Authority (IANA) and are administered by a group known as the InterNIC Registration Services, or InterNIC. An effort is currently underway to create a nonprofit, self-supporting, and independent organization to handle Internet protocol number assignments. The proposed organization is the American Registry for Internet Numbers (ARIN). You can check out the progress and developments of ARIN at http://www.arin.net.

InterNIC allows registry of a domain name and issues IP addresses. You can contact InterNIC by e-mail at hostmaster@internic.net. You can also ftp to Inter-NIC at internic.net. At the InterNIC site in the subdirectory templates is an Internet address application named Internet-number-template.txt. Also, you can get what you need at their Web site http://www.internic.net.

Routing Protocols

Routing protocols provide routing daemons with rules and procedures for choosing the path that data takes to a destination. Table 6.4 lists some common routing protocols. Whether or not routing services are necessary and, if so, which protocol to use is set by the network administrator. For information on configuring a UNIX system for routing, see *Network Services* below.

Network Services

Managing Services

An important daemon found on all UNIX systems, `inetd` manages the other daemons that provide TCP/IP network services. Known as the network superserver, `inetd` starts the appropriate daemon when it detects a service request. `inetd` can spawn more than one TCP/IP service, allowing more than one telnet, ftp, or other network process. To find `inetd`:

```
# ps -ef | grep inetd
```

This command provides the process ID (PID) for `inetd` in case the configuration file must be changed. Once you have the PID for the file (25 in this example), you can send the SIGHUP signal to `inetd` using the **kill** command

```
# kill -HUP 25
```

causing `inetd` to read the `inetd.conf` file and continue. Stopping `inetd` abruptly stops network services.

The `inetd.conf` file (Listing 6.1) provides the networking information for the `inetd` daemon. The # sign is used for comments and the fields are separated by white space. The first field names the service, the second field the socket type, followed by the protocol, wait status, user, server program, and server arguments. For example, in the line

```
telnet stream tcp nowait root /usr/sbin/in.telnetd in.telnetd
```

the service type is `telnet`, which is mapped to a port number. The socket type is `stream`. Other socket types available are: `dgram`, datagram sockets; `raw`, raw sockets; `seqpacket`, sequential packet socket; or `tli`, transport layer interface (TLI)

Table 6.4 Common routing protocols.	
Abbreviation	**Full name**
RIP	Routing Information Protocol
OSPF	Open Shortest Path First
IGRP	Interior Gateway Routing Protocol
EGP	Exterior Gateway Protocol
BGP	Border Gateway Protocol
DVMRP	Distance Vector Multicast Routing Protocol

Network

Listing 6.1 `inetd.conf` — *Networking information for the* `inetd` *daemon.*

```
#ident "@(#)inetd.conf 1.16 94/03/08 SMI" /* SVr4.0 1.5 */
#
# Configuration file for inetd(1M). See inetd.conf(4).
#
# To re-configure the running inetd process, edit this file, then
# send the inetd process a SIGHUP.
#
# Syntax for socket-based Internet services:
# <service_name> <socket_type> <proto> <flags> <user>
# <server_pathname> <args>
#
# Syntax for TLI-based Internet services:
#
# <service_name> tli <proto> <flags> <user> <server_pathname>
<args>
#
# Ftp and telnet are standard Internet services.
#
ftp     stream tcp nowait root /usr/sbin/in.ftpd in.ftpd
telnet  stream tcp nowait root /usr/sbin/in.telnetd in.telnetd
#
# Tnamed serves the obsolete IEN-116 name server protocol.
#
name    dgram  udp wait   root /usr/sbin/in.tnamed in.tnamed
#
# Shell, login, exec, comsat and talk are BSD protocols.
#
shell   stream tcp nowait root /usr/sbin/in.rshd in.rshd
login   stream tcp nowait root /usr/sbin/in.rlogind in.rlogind
exec    stream tcp nowait root /usr/sbin/in.rexecd in.rexecd
talk    dgram  udp wait   root /usr/sbin/in.talkd in.talkd
#
# Must run as root (to read /etc/shadow); "-n" turns off logging in
# utmp/wtmp.
#
uucp    stream tcp nowait root /usr/sbin/in.uucpd in.uucpd
#
# Time service is used for clock synchronization.
#
time    stream tcp nowait root internal
time    dgram  udp wait   root internal
```

endpoints. The protocol is TCP. This field must specify the correct protocol as listed in the /etc/protocols file. Wait status in the fourth field is nowait; the other option is wait. The user is root in the fifth field. This field specifies the user to whom the process should belong. Since no one other than root should be tinkering with telnet services, it is assigned to root. The sixth field is the absolute pathname to the daemon to be executed, /usr/sbin/in.telnetd. The last field contains specific arguments, in.telnetd in this case.

The service type designated in the first field of entries in Listing 6.1 is mapped to a port number using the /etc/protocols file, shown below. It has three fields and a comment. The first field is the name of the protocol, the second field is the protocol number, and the third field is the alias for the protocol. Notice that the alias field was added because UNIX is case sensitive. This allows variables to be referenced in upper- and lowercase.

```
#ident "@(#)protocols 1.2 90/02/03 SMI" /* SVr4.0 1.1 */
#
# Internet (IP) protocols
#
ip      0    IP       # Internet protocol, pseudo protocol number
icmp    1    ICMP     # Internet control message protocol
ggp     3    GGP      # gateway-gateway protocol
tcp     6    TCP      # transmission control protocol
egp     8    EGP      # exterior gateway protocol
pup     12   PUP      # PARC universal packet protocol
udp     17   UDP      # user datagram protocol
hmp     20   HMP      # host monitoring protocol
xns-idp 22   XNS-IDP  # Xerox NS IDP
rdp     27   RDP      # "reliable datagram" protocol
```

After adding a new service to inetd.conf, the /etc/services file, where port addresses are assigned, must be updated. This file indicates the network service being offered in the first field. The second field contains two pieces of information separated by a forward slash (/). The port number precedes the slash, and the available service — either TCP or UDP — follows the slash.

Below is a sample of the /etc/services file.

```
#
# Network services, Internet style
#tcpmux      1/tcp
echo         7/tcp
echo         7/udp
discard      9/tcp        sink null
```

```
discard     9/udp      sink null
systat      11/tcp     users
daytime     13/tcp
daytime     13/udp
netstat     15/tcp
chargen     19/tcp     ttytst source
chargen     19/udp     ttytst source
ftp-data    20/tcp
ftp         21/tcp
telnet      23/tcp
smtp        25/tcp     mail
time        37/tcp     timserver
time        37/udp     timserver
name        42/udp     nameserver
whois       43/tcp     nicname
domain      53/udp
domain      53/tcp
hostnames   101/tcp    hostname
```

Routing

A primary service UNIX systems provide is routing. Systems that need to contact a host on another network or implement a subnet must provide routing services.

Configuring the Network Interface

Connecting to another network with an interface card requires knowing that network's address. The command

ifconfig 1e0 128.110.52.32 up netmask 255.255.255.0

configures the network interface. Syntax for the command, which may vary across systems, says to assign the address 128.110.52.32 to interface 1e0 and set the netmask. The interface startup command is up. The command **ifconfig** 1e0 down shuts the interface down.

The interface configurations are normally entered in the bootup scripts. Although not advisable, interfaces can be added and shut down while the system is running. If not added to the startup script, the interface must be brought up manually when the system is restarted. (See Chapter 1 for more information on startup scripts.) Failing to keep track of an interface configuration can cause a lot of extra work restarting the interface each time the system comes up.

Interfaces are defined as a device, such as ie0 for an INTEL interface. To find out what interfaces you have available, run **netstat** -I. The **netstat** command is an extremely useful utility. It provides information on networking resources, open ports, and the overall status of the network. **netstat** -a | more supplies an overall look at the network configuration.

Configuring Static Routes

The **route** command at /etc/route defines static routes — routes that never change even when running a routing daemon. Usually executed at system startup, **route** syntax is

/etc/**route** *command destination gateway [metric]*

The commands available are add or delete. *destination* is the address of the next host associated with the route. *gateway* specifies where the data packets are to be addressed. *metric* is the number of hops to the destination; the default is 0, so unless the route is set up to loop back, the metric should be 1 or more.

Managing Dynamic Routing

Dynamic routing is used on larger systems and managed using internal route tables accessed by the standard routing daemon routed. In UNIX, routed controls routing using the RIP protocol. When routed receives an information packet, it checks its tables and determines the appropriate response. The daemon reads the etc/ gateways file to determine whether it is attaching to a network (net) or a host (host) and whether the connection is passive, active, or external. A passive gateway is always maintained in the routing tables, whereas active gateways can be deleted when no activity occurs over the specified address. An external gateway is stored the same way as a passive gateway, but it will not be included in any routing updates. This tells routed that this route will need to be installed by another process.

Basic Connection and File Transfer

Two of the most common network services are telnet and ftp. The terminal–remote host protocol, or telnet, is the TCP/IP standard connection package. Access a site by telnet using either the IP address or the symbolic name, as in

telnet 124.53.32.2

or

telnet access.asite.net

where access.asite.net is the symbolic name for a domain.

Network

The ftp command is a file transfer protocol. The syntax to reach a site is the same as telnet. A remote log-in command is very similar to telnet; it is called rlogin. In addition, there are remote commands such as rcp for remote file copy and rcmd for remote shell command execution.

File Sharing

Another UNIX service, called networked file systems or NFS, allows files to be shared among computers. NFS provides access to tools, services, and other information located on remote files. Also, NFS can allow client stations to access only selected file systems on a host. To the user, it seems that the file systems are available to the user's system just like any other file system. From an administrator perspective, these files are mounted and unmounted in a fashion similar to regular file systems.

NFS requires networking services and the nfsd, biod, exportfs, portmap, and rpc.mountd daemons. The nfsd daemon runs on the NFS server, accepting client file requests and passing them on to the kernel. The biod daemon provides read-ahead and write-behind block caching for a file system. exportfs handles the shared directories. portmap provides remote procedure call (RPC) mapping to port addresses, and rpc.mountd mounts the shared file system.

The rc startup scripts should start the nfsd daemon, which forks copies of itself to manage the traffic on the system. The number of copies of nfsd to specify depends on the number of connections nfsd needs to make at a given time. Too few copies cause netstat to report socket overflow errors. Too many and performance suffers. One way to determine the optimal number of copies is to add copies until socket overflow errors reported by **netstat** -s drop to zero. This indicates the maximum number of copies the system can support. To test system performance, add nfsd processes until performance suffers noticeably. This also gives an estimate of the largest number of nfsd processes allowed based on the processing load of the system.

The largest number of nfsd daemons to specify may not be the optimal number. The optimal number also depends on the number of biod processes specified. Just as with nfsd, biod takes as its argument the number of copies to fork. After determining the maximum number of nfsd copies, specify the same number of biod daemons, then check to see if system performance degrades. If performance is still unacceptable, continue reducing the number of copies of both daemons until performance meets requirements.

In the following example from a startup script, biod 12 and nfsd 12 tell the system to fork 12 copies of each process.

```
if [-f /usr/etc/biod] ;
then biod 12
if [-f /usr/etc/nfsd];
then nfsd 12
```

When establishing NFS on a server, the server must be told what file systems to share, and the workstations that access the server must know what file systems are available for sharing. To do this, the workstation reads a local /etc/fstab file and mounts the file system locally first. File systems found in fstab are considered permanent mounts. The **mount** command can be used for NFS, but these mounts are only temporary. When setting up an NFS system, using mount can be a good diagnostic tool to make sure desired services are available, especially when changes are made. Enter

mount -at nfs

to list the NFS file systems mounted on the system.

Once the local mount is done, the remote mount requests are managed by the rpc.mountd daemon. The actual file systems to be shared are stored on the server in /etc/exports, read by the /etc/exportfs daemon. The exports file can be edited freely to include the file systems needed for export by the server.

When you mount an NFS file system, you have the option of mounting the system with specified parameters to control its use. In System V, -f or -t is used to mount a system as an NFS file system, as follows:

mount -f nfs buddy:/usrec

This command mounts the file system /usrec from the node named buddy. In the file /etc/fstab, the following attributes may be entered to describe the file system as NFS mountable.

```
buddy:/usrdoc /usrec      nfs rw,hard,bg,intr,retrans=3 00
friend:/usres /personnel nfs ro,soft,bg 0 0
```

In the top line, buddy refers to the node name and mounts the file system /usrdoc on buddy as /usrec. On the first line, the fields after /usrec indicate an NFS (nfs) file system mounted as read–write (rw) with a hard mount (hard) and a background start (bg) if the mount should fail on the first try. intr allows users to interrupt hung processes, and retrans specifies the number of times a request to the file system is allowed — in this case 3. Finally, the numbers 0 0 set up the size, in bytes, of the read and write buffers, respectively.

In the second line, another node called friend has a file system /usres that is mounted as /personnel, using a different configuration. /personnel is a soft mount, mounted as read-only (ro) with no interrupts allowed (i.e., intr is missing). If an NFS file system is hard mounted, then NFS continues to try to process all requests even when the remote system in unavailable and all the retrans have been attempted. If the file system is soft mounted and is unavailable, NFS generates an error and cancels any additional requests. There are other NFS options available; check the local documentation to configure NFS properly.

Network Debugging

A simple utility (ping) is provided by every vendor of UNIX. It can be used to force a response from a particular machine. ping sends out a packet, verifies that it has been received, and in so doing, produces a report on how long it took to send the packet. If the packet was unable to get to its destination, ping reports a timeout. ping uses routing protocols, address resolution schemes, and gateways. When sent to a host known to be active, a successful ping indicates a functional network configuration. Local network services must be running to use ping.

The format for a ping is

```
# ping [-option] host [packetsize] [count]
```

An *option* field with -v provides a more detailed, or verbose, report. The *host* is a recognized symbolic name or a numeric IP address. *packetsize* is the desired size in bytes of the packet. (Defaults can vary and sizes are limited to a range of packet sizes.) *count* specifies the number of times the packet is sent. The following example pings a remote host at 128.32.10.2 and sends a packet size of 128 bytes 30 times to get the average transmission time to the remote server:

```
# ping 128.32.10.2 128 30
```

ping can connect and echo back to another server, verifying that servers are up on the network. The line

```
# ping 128.32.10.2
```

uses system defaults to verify a remote server.

When setting up a network, ping can stress the threshold of the network to see if network services are adequate. A script and test procedure could be written and subsequently kicked off by cron to determine the feedback from a node across a network. An example called forkit, described below, also tests the number of processes the system can handle to provide information for performance tuning.

Although time consuming, running such tests allows you to directly observe the degradation of the network. Increasing traffic reveals the impact of multiple packets from multiple processes being sent along the network to a specified host. A script such as forkit stresses the number of processes a system can handle until ping breaks down, leaving some ping statements unexecuted. forkit can be written to exceed the number of child processes a system can handle, resulting in fork errors that cannot build the requested process. Data from such tests can help build an assessment of network capabilities and processing. A look into system accounting to determine CPU usage and other factors of processing can add to the assessment established with the forkit procedure.

To establish forkit, determine at what level to test the system. Start the process by executing a single ping for several counts and recording the results to a file called level_1. Enter

```
# ping host 128 100 > /usr/data/level_1
```

If necessary, do this several times for increments of byte counts such as at 64-byte packets, 128-byte packets, and so on up to the limit available. Label the files level_1_64b, level_1_128b, and so on.

Next, create a file with an editor that executes consecutive pings through cron, as in the example below called npt (network performance test).

```
/etc/ping host 10 64 >  /usr/data/level_2_64b
/etc/ping host 10 64 >> /usr/data/level_2_64b
/etc/ping host 10 64 >> /usr/data/level_2_64b
/etc/ping host 10 64 >> /usr/data/level_2_64b
/etc/ping host 10 64 >> /usr/data/level_2_64b
```

If necessary, create several npt files to record a range of packet sizes.

For the second level, it is not imperative to execute from cron, but for the third level and beyond it is important to do so. For level three, kick off multiple npt files spaced in cron for execution at the smallest possible intervals of time. (The smallest interval used by cron is the minute.) The scripts should be such that all cron files are running at the same time. To do this, the first file to execute at Level 3 will have a large count, with counts scaling down from there, since the last file to execute won't necessarily need to run as long as the first. To increase time with count, packet size can be larger, but for each Level 3 test, the packet size should remain the same as that used for Level 1 and Level 2 tests.

Modem Communications

Early in its history, UNIX provided an implementation known as UUCP (Unix to Unix Communications Protocol) for file transfer and mail connectivity via modem connections. Because of the Internet and a demand for greater functionality, UUCP is being replaced by Serial Line Internet Protocol (SLIP) and Point-to-Point Protocol (PPP). Although outdated, UUCP is still a common protocol for communication between similar UNIX systems.

There are two commonly used flavors of UUCP, V7 and HoneyDanBer. The V7 flavor is similar to the original UUCP implementations. HoneyDanBer was written for AT&T flavors of UNIX by Peter Honeyman (Honey), David A. Nowitz (Dan), and Brian E. Redman (Ber). This discussion focuses on HoneyDanBer UUCP.

Essentially, UUCP is a collection of programs that provide networking over both serial and telephone lines. Programs that support UUCP services include cu, uucico, uucp, uuto, and uux. The **cu** command, a serial version of telnet, dials into another UUCP site. The **uucp** and **uuto** commands allow both binary and text files to be copied between machines. The **uux** command executes commands at remote sites. In addition, uname displays a list of systems that the local system can communicate with, providing these systems are precisely defined in the local system.

For UUCP to be successful, a machine must be able to call a remote site and write to a directory at the remote site. /usr/lib/uucp contains a permissions file also found on a remote site that specifies the directories to which a system can write. The general default directory is /usr/spool/uucppublic. To send a file to a remote machine that is configured for UUCP communication, enter

```
# uucp /usr/home/wetsch/sendfile blue1!~/sendfile
```

The sample is sending a file called sendfile to a machine called blue1. ~/sendfile is the pathname of the directory in which the sent file is placed, probably /usr/spool/uucppublic/sendfile. Omit the tilde (~) character when specifying the full pathname of where to send the file. The exclamation mark separates the sites where the file is being sent. To transfer the file to machines blue1, blue2, and blue3, enter

```
# uucp /usr/home/wetsch/sendfile blue1!blue2!blue3!~/sendfile
```

UUCP first transfers the files to the uucp spool directory and then attempts a transfer. The path also indicates the final destination as blue3 using blue2 and an intermediary hop. If the transfer is unsuccessful, the utility will notify the user and may also try to resend the file. To check on the status of UUCP jobs, use the **uustat** command.

To set up UUCP communications, the system must recognize the installed modem and be able to dialup. Once connected, the system must have a name that each machine recognizes and, as noted, can be found from the **uname** command. The name of your system is found with **uname** -n, whereas a complete list is gained using **uname** -a. The list is provided by the Systems file. Other files that must be set up include the Dialcodes file, which contains a dial-out sequence as well as a mnemonic to use that code. The devices used by UUCP are set up in the Devices file and must reference actual devices found in the /dev directory. Once these files are set up and a user account for uucp is ready, test the system with c to dial out to a remote site. You may have to do some debugging; use **uucico** with the −x option to specify the level of debugging appropriate for your system.

When deciding whether to implement a UUCP system, determine that you need it. If you already use SLIP and PPP, you may not have much need for UUCP unless you need to connect to a remote site that is not using SLIP or PPP. Also, as UNIX capabilities advance and because UNIX implementations vary, the implementation of UUCP may vary. Generally speaking, you must have a UUCP account, correct permission, the ability to dial out, and permission to access a remote site in order to use UUCP effectively.

Earlier, I mentioned that UUCP can send electronic mail. This service is provided through sendmail, which must also be configured for your system. Sendmail is configured in the `sendmail.cf` file and is also a networking daemon that allows mail to be sent over the Internet or locally. It has consequently evolved past its early UUCP implementations, which used SMTP (Simple Mail Transport Protocol) to send mail to users on a TCP/IP network.

The `sendmail` utility is another one of those UNIX pieces that really requires a thorough understanding. Due to the complexity and intricacies of the utility, the reader is referred to manufacturer and third-party documentation to research, study, and learn to successfully implement, maintain, and use `sendmail`.

Optimizing Networks

Networks must be able to provide solid performance. Problems such as traffic congestion or improper configuration can slow down a network, frustrating users. For example, a bottleneck significantly affects performance. Although easy to describe, finding a bottleneck can be more difficult. An overloaded transmission medium caused by too many connections is commonly blamed for the bottleneck. Although this can be a problem, other factors that add to network load must be investigated also, such as CPU utilization, available memory, or condition of the server.

Table 6.5 lists some of the factors that concern a system administrator. Dealing with these issues allows you to optimize your system, which in turn returns the best performance available based on hardware limitations and software constraints.

For an up and running UNIX network, optimization can be performed using a performance monitoring tool or even by making use of the system accounting utilities that are already available on your system. A very thorough optimization evaluation involves the use of statistical performance evaluation techniques using operational laws like Little's Law, the Utilization Law, the Forced Flow Law, and the General Response Time Law. In general, there is a considerable body of literature on performance analysis. The level of analysis required should correspond to the complexity of the system and the difficulty in determining the problem. Also, if you are prototyping a new system, a good knowledge of performance analysis is required so that you can provide benchmarks against which to measure your system development.

Table 6.5 *Definition of some network optimization terms.*

Optimization element	Description
Availability	Sometimes confused with reliability. However, it is really reliability over time. That is, you may have the system up and running and everything works but the access time is too long; therefore, availability is low.
Reliability	This is the actual dependability of the system. Can the system recover from errors without crashing?
Integrity	High integrity translates into a low number of errors. For instance, my system may be highly reliable in delivering an e-mail message but the integrity of the transfer may be low if the message arrives in a garbled state.
Overhead	The amount of processing that is taking place at a given time. Overhead is usually high when large numbers of users are on a system.
Reliability of delivery	An optimization measure that determines the percentage of network transmissions sent and received without error.
Throughput	The number of transmissions sent over time on a network.
Incidence speed	Also referred to as latency. Determines the minimum and maximum time of delivery. For instance, the fastest and slowest time to bring up an application would reference the incidence speed of the application.
Average speed	Refers to the average time of delivery of a specific application or a standardized data transfer.
Channel capacity	The limit of the ability to transfer data. For instance, the channel capacity or bandwidth of a 10Base2 Ethernet network is 10Mbps.
Reach	The capacity of the network in terms of the number of devices it can support. Reach can also refer to the limit of the length of the network medium.
Propagation delay	The delay caused as data is propagated through the medium, repeaters, gateways, routers, bridges, etc., of a network.

## Chapter 7

The Internet and Enterprise Systems

The Internet has become a global information tool, leading computing technology into the 21st century. The Internet provides information on many subjects and has the capability to download tools and utilities to simplify work. Business can also construct internal Internet connectivity and services, called intranets, not accessible to the outside world.

Almost a household word, Internet access is becoming more readily available through its use in businesses, libraries, and universities. Access providers offer free e-mail service. Network computers are being developed to connect directly to servers and the Internet. Also, a greater integration between telephone, television, and computer technology provides an increasing array of multimedia services that will eventually be incorporated into Internet sites.

Evolution of the Internet

Infrastructure

The Internet is not new. It started from a research program of the United States Defense Advanced Research Projects Agency (DARPA), which was an effort to determine methods for linking networks. By 1969, the Advanced Research Projects

Agency Network (ARPANET) began, and continuous growth through connected hosts continued through the 1970s. TCP/IP became the ARPANET standard protocol, and as growth increased, ARPANET was replaced by the Internet.

In the mid-1980s, the National Science Foundation installed a group of backbone sites, collectively known as NSFNET. NSFNET became the top layer of the hierarchical infrastructure of the Internet in the United States (Class A addresses accommodating 128 networks with 16,777,216 million hosts/network maximum). Since then, regional leased line networks have been attached to NFSNET by government agencies, research institutions, and businesses, including the National Center for Atmospheric Research (NCAR), WESTNET, the University of Colorado at Boulder (UCB), and the University of Utah. These backbones became the second layer of the Internet in the U.S. (Class B addresses supporting 16,284 networks with 65,536 hosts/network maximum). The third layer of networks (Class C addresses allowing for 2,000,000 networks with 256 hosts/network maximum) evolved from connections among government agencies, universities, and businesses on down to smaller networks and individual desktops, which must dial-in to a computer at a layer above it to access the Internet.

The Role of UNIX

UNIX led the way to the Internet and several character-based protocols were developed to allow improved computer interaction on the Internet. Services and methods were developed to provide increased usefulness of available tools. Sites were set up for anonymous ftp, which allows users on one host to connect to other hosts with a generic login called "anonymous" and without a password to download and upload files. Once anonymous ftp servers became abundant, servers were set up to archive

Table 7.1   Archie and anonymous ftp sites.

Site name	Site type
archie.ans.net	Archie
archie.internic.net	Archie
archie.rutgers.edu	Archie
archie.sura.net	Archie
archie.unl.edu	Archie
ftp.uu.net	Anonymous ftp
oak.oakland.edu	Anonymous ftp
rtfm.mit.edu	Anonymous ftp
sunsite.unc.edu	Anonymous ftp

files and McGill University developed Archie, which provides a database of accessible files on anonymous ftp servers. Table 7.1 provides a sampling of sites that are considered Archie or anonymous ftp sites.

Gopher, from the University of Minnesota, became a major character-based Internet service that provided a means to display files and menus as well as to select pages and services from a listed menu. With gopher, users saw an improved interface at the cost of more difficulty finding gopher resources on the Internet. Wide Area Information Servers (WAIS) became a means to access a large number of databases across networks. Both WAIS and Gopher systems require special software that runs at the client level.

Hytelnet was also introduced as a hypertext delivery service for telnet. Hytelnet is used to help users find library databases. The protocol for Hytelnet resides on the client.

World Wide Web

Eventually the Internet turned into a graphical interface known as the Web. The Web came out of the CERN research physics lab in Europe. With the Web (or World Wide Web or WWW), the use of the Internet mushroomed. The Web protocol developed was the hypertext transport protocol (http), which allowed links or addresses called URLs (Universal Resource Locators) to access files on Internet sites written in hypertext markup language (HTML). From HTML documents, one could attached links to other HTML pages, other sites, graphics, and e-mail services.

The browser became the tool of choice for people wanting to browse or "surf" through the Internet. Browsers are able to read multiple protocols on the Internet. The line

```
http://pages.prodigy.com/NC/drjohn/index.html
```

accesses a Web URL using a browser. The http at the start of the URL specifies the protocol. If it were a Gopher site, the http would be replaced with gopher. The symbolic name or the actual address of the site is given as pages.prodigy.com. This directly corresponds to an IP address for either a physical or virtual server. A virtual server is really a directory on a physical server that is accessible through the Web by an IP address.

Once the server has been reached, locating the file is a matter of moving through the directory structure. The characters after the address, /NC/drjohn/index.html, indicate the path to the actual file being accessed, index.html, which is read by the Web browser.

Advances to HTML are coming through products such as CGI (Common Gateway Interface) and Java, which provide for more interaction on the Web. CGI defines how http should communicate with gateway programs and allows requests to databases to be made by and returned to the client. Java is a tool like C++ that allows interfacing with databases, animation, and other programmer-defined interactions.

Not all Web services are available with all browsers, or some Web services may be turned off. For example, the USENET news service, which provides news groups on the Web, may be turned off. Many users may want to have the capability to telnet to sites, ftp to sites, use Archie, and other services. For some of these services, you may have to have access to a command prompt or to a similar interface.

Administration

As computer technology rapidly changes, so does the Internet. Faster networks are being researched and developed worldwide. Commerce on the Internet has increased to the point that users probably get unsolicited e-mail advertisements more often than they get unsolicited telephone calls from telemarketers. System protocols on the Internet that used to deal only in character-based information have expanded to graphics-based Web sites using http. Languages also have been developed to support Web servers, such as the HTML and Java.

Such rapid growth requires monitoring and coordination. Originally handled by government agencies such as DARPA, administration of the Internet is now moving away from government control and more toward the private sector. Now, administration of the Internet falls to organizations of commercial groups. Routine administration such as assigning IP addresses, managing the Domain Name System, and managing routing information for major backbones has been taken over by a group called the Network Information Center, or InterNIC. The members of InterNIC, Network Solutions, Inc., AT&T, and General Atomics, provide registration services, directory and database services, and information services. An agency called the Internet Architecture Board (IAB) provides long-term planning.

Internet Daemons and Commands

Table 7.2 provides a list and description of Internet-related daemons. Many of the daemons are also used on non-Internet sites for communications and file transfer.

httpd interprets Web requests on a UNIX machine, but another commercial or privately developed Web daemon could be used also. To see the number of httpd daemons running in memory, enter

```
# ps -ef | grep httpd
```

To see how many http ports httpd is using, execute

```
# ps -ef | grep httpd | wc
```

Table 7.2   Description of Internet daemons.

Internet daemon	Description
`fingerd`	Allows the `finger` program to provide information on users
`ftpd`	Handles ftp requests
`gated`	Interprets router protocols
`httpd`	Handles the http protocol and enables your site to participate on the Web
`innd`	Couples with the `nntpd` daemon to access news sites
`nntpd`	Handles the transfer of news through the Internet. Associated with the C-News package and uses the NNTP protocol
`popper`	Handles mail for non-UNIX users using POP (Post Office Protocol)
`rlogind`	Called by the daemon `inetd` that handles the login to a remote host
`routed`	Keeps track of the routing tables. Is being replaced by `gated` in some implementations
`rpc.rexd`	Handles the execution of remote procedure calls
`rshd`	Handles remote request from `rsh`, such as remote command execution and copy
`talkd`	Sets up the link between two machines so users can talk with each other with the **talk** command
`telnetd`	Handles remote logins. Similar to `rlogind`, only better
`timed`	Allows slave machines on the network to adjust their clocks according to a master clock
`xntpd`	Another clock daemon that uses NTP (Network Time Protocol)

Network

The word count command (**wc**) returns the number of instances of httpd that were retrieved by the **ps** command. The number of httpd daemons equals the number of http ports in use. wc counts the number of httpds piped to it. One of the processes counted will be the **grep** httpd command, so be sure to subtract one from the total.

Downloading Tools for UNIX

The Internet is an outstanding source of tools and learning material for the UNIX user and administrator. In news groups, you can share ideas, problems, questions, and complaints or just "lurk" about seeing what others are saying. In addition, through the various ftp sites, you can download a mountain of software that can be incorporated into your system — from editors and utilities to security programs and network daemons.

This book recommends software freely available at official and unofficial Web sites through The Free Software Foundation GNU project. In *GNU's Bulletin*, vol. 1 no. 5, the FSF describes its purpose (see http://www.cs.pdx.edu/~trent/ gnu/bull/05/bull5.html#SEC5).

> The Free Software Foundation is dedicated to eliminating restrictions on people's right to use, copy, modify, and redistribute computer programs. We do this by promoting the development and use of free software. Specifically, we are putting together a complete, integrated software system named "GNU" (pronounced "guh-new," "GNU's Not Unix") that will be upwardly compatible with UNIX. Some large parts of this system are already being used and distributed.

> The word "free" in our name refers to freedom, not price. You may or may not pay money to get GNU software, but either way you have two specific freedoms once you get it: first, the freedom to copy a program, and distribute it to your friends and coworkers; and second, the freedom to change a program as you wish, by having full access to source code. You can study the source and learn how such programs are written. You may then be able to port it, improve it, and share your changes with others. If you redistribute GNU software you may charge a distribution fee or give it away, so long as you include the source code and the GPL (i.e. General Public License).

> Other organizations distribute whatever free software happens to be available. By contrast, the Free Software Foundation concentrates on the development of new free software, working towards a GNU system complete enough to eliminate the need to use a proprietary system. Besides developing GNU, the FSF distributes GNU software and manuals for a distribution fee, and accepts gifts (tax deductible in the U.S.) to support GNU development. Most of the FSF's funds come from its distribution service.

The reader will want to explore the site at http://www.gnu.org for the latest information.

The Free Software Foundation can be contacted at

Free Software Foundation, Inc.
59 Temple Place - Suite 330
Boston, MA 02111-1307
Telephone: 617-542-5942
`gnu@prep.ai.mit.edu`

Using Internet search engines, such as Lycos, WebCrawler, Yahoo, NetSearch, and others, you can find many links to GNU sites and other UNIX information. Lycos can be found at `http://www.lycos.com` and Yahoo at `http://www.yahoo.com`. A good site with well laid out GNU information that includes the GNU Manifesto, Public License, and Coding Standards is at

`http://www.cs.utah.edu/csinfo/texinfo/texinfo.html`

Table 7.3 (pages 134 and 135) shows a sampling of files that can be found on the Web, through ftp sites, and through GNU.

When downloading files from the Internet, download only from reputable sites. For instance, if you were searching for the security analyzer SATAN and found a personal Web page offering a copy of the analyzer, or even advertising enhancements to the product, you would probably be doing yourself a favor by leaving it alone. Using a modified copy may allow unauthorized processes to run on your system and create security breaches that go undetected.

Internet and Enterprise

Challenges Facing Internet Development

A major challenge to development of the Internet is security. Misunderstood or poorly designed and implemented security measures create deficiencies, including insufficient access restrictions and out-of-date virus checking. The Morris Worm is an extreme example of the damage a hole in security can cause. Back in 1988, the Morris Worm exploited software security deficiencies and policy inadequacies. The worm relied on the fact that some administrators did not change administrator-level passwords from the vendor defaults. The `finger` daemon and `sendmail` also provided leaks into unauthorized areas. Overflowing the `finger` daemon's input buffer gave the worm access to the privileged shell under which the `finger` daemon ran. With sendmail, the worm gained access through the `DEBUG` feature, which was left turned on by an administrator.

In spite of the security risks, networks continue to be added, making uncontrolled growth arguably a bigger challenge than security. New addressing schemes are being

Network

Table 7.3 **UNIX and GNU software available on the Internet.**

Filename	GNU path	Description	Administration module
ange-ftp	http://www.ai.mit.edu/!info/dir/!!first	Remote file editing	Network
apache	http://www.apache.org	Sets your site up as a Web server	Network
autoconf	http://www.ai.mit.edu/!info/dir/!!first	GNU auto configuration file	Hardware
bash	http://www.cs.utah.edu/csinfo/texinfo/texinfo.html	The GNU Bourne Again shell	Software
cops	ftp://archive.cis.ohio-state.edu/pub/cops/1.04+	Checks for permission problems with directories, files, and devices	Security
crack	ftp://ftp.uu.net/usenet/comp.sources.misc/volume28	Checks for bad passwords	Security
diff	http://www.cs.utah.edu/csinfo/texinfo/texinfo.html	Checks differences between files	Software
emacs	http://www.cs.utah.edu/csinfo/texinfo/texinfo.html	A useful editor	Software
finger	http://www.cs.utah.edu/csinfo/texinfo/texinfo.html	Finds information on a user at a local site or on the Internet	Network
FreeBSD	http://www.freebsd.org/	UNIX OS	Software
Gzip	http://www.cs.utah.edu/csinfo/texinfo/texinfo.htmlgoodies/glimpse.tar	Compresses files (GNU)	Software

Table 7.3 (continued)

Filename	GNU path	Description	Administration module
g-whiz	http://www.ai.mit.edu/!info/dir/!!first	GNU C++ compiler	Software
perl	http://www.cs.utah.edu/csinfo/texinfo/texinfo.html	Scripting language	Software
satan	http://www.cs.ruu.nl/cert-uu/satan.html	Security analyzer to probe your site. Contains the latest updates and information on SATAN and its uses	Security
screen	http://www.cs.utah.edu/csinfo/texinfo/texinfo.html	Manages virtual terminals	Hardware
smalltalk	http://www.cs.utah.edu/csinfo/texinfo/texinfo.html	Object language	Software
tar	http://www.cis.ohio-state.edu/htbin/info/dir	GNU tape archive program	Software
termcap	http://www.ai.mit.edu/!info/dir/!!first	Terminal configuration	Hardware
vip	http://www.ai.mit.edu/!info/dir/!!first	A vi emulation program for emacs	Software
vm	http://www.cis.ohio-state.edu/htbin/info/dir	Mail interface compatible with mailx and elm folders. Used with emacs	Network
w3	http://www.ai.mit.edu/!info/dir/!!first	Web browser	Network
zsh	http://www.ai.mit.edu/!info/dir/!!first	The Z shell	Software

Network

studied to accommodate the growing number of networks being added. As users look for faster and more reliable access to improve the use of graphics, audio, and video on the Internet, the lack of bandwidth causes performance degradation. Users have responded by getting faster modems, and networks are requiring the same at their end. Nonetheless, user congestion is a problem, and the Internet infrastructure will undoubtedly grow as its user community grows.

Planning for Access

An enterprise system incorporates all the business needs of an organization on a scale that spans the entire organization. The need to communicate information and data, important assets to any organization, has made the Internet an essential tool in modern enterprise systems, standardizing the exchange of knowledge on a scale that also spans the entire organization.

Planning for secure and effective use of the Internet in an enterprise system requires evaluation of the processes and interactions in an enterprise, in all their complexity. The components of the system must be broken down and mapped out from end-to-end. Many questions must be answered down to the minutest detail, such as:

- At what point does a user gain entry to the system?
- What applications are available to the user?
- When the user executes a transaction what happens with the transaction?
- How is data moved among applications?
- What client/server methodologies are required to accomplish communication goals?
- Is software development needed to write applications from scratch or is off-the-shelf software available?
- What messaging strategy will be employed?

A study of the design of the enterprise can provide the answers to these questions. The design of an enterprise system has four steps. Failure to properly complete each step results in gaps in design and on-the-fly development. Enterprises based on an incomplete design can incur higher costs and longer development time caused by unanticipated requirements, features, and failures of various system components. Many informative books provide information on design, analysis, design notations, and data management of an enterprise, so this section offers a simple overview of the design process.

Step one toward designing an enterprise is to develop the Business Process Model (BPM). A BPM defines a system and the processes required for that system. Figure 7.1 shows a sample BPM for a fictional accounts receivable system called the ARS system, using a dynamic interaction graph (DIG). A complete BPM would be more comprehensive because ARS is a subsystem of a larger accounting business model.

Once the BPM is defined, establish the business rules in step two. Business enti- ties, such as objects and data elements, relate to each other through the processes used to transact business. Each relationship requires a rule. The business rules can be a part of the BPM and visualized using standard entity relationship diagrams. For example, the Inquiries process in the fictional ARS system allows customers to perform inquir- ies on their accounts and receive accounting information back. In one typical inquiry, account balance, the data elements `Account_Balance` and `Account_Number` inter- act. The business rule, the interaction between `Account_Balance` and `Account_Number`, can be described as: A valid account number will select the cur- rent account balance for the account.

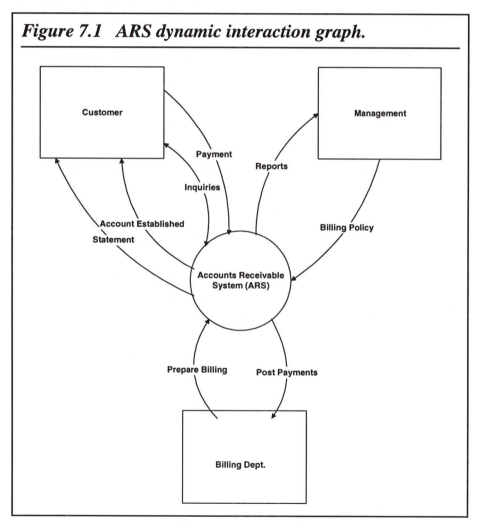

Figure 7.1   ARS dynamic interaction graph.

This business rule is depicted in Figure 7.2. The data element `Account_Number` has a relationship to the data element `Account_Balance` through a procedure called `Can_Select`.

When the business rules are established for a system, an Information Systems Model (ISM) can be developed in step three. The ISM puts the relationships gathered and built from the previous model into a form showing how information is delivered. Relationships and interactions are broken down through the subsequent diagrams. Figure 7.3 is the depiction of an ISM based on the business rule depicted in Figure 7.2.

When the ISM has been developed and the system is properly understood, the actual technical solution can be modeled in step four. A technical model of the system pins down the actual products that can be used to solve the problem and incorporate Information Technology (IT). The technical solution for the fictional ARS system could take on many forms, but one of them could be an Internet Web application that allows a customer to access the company's Web site and perform queries against an account database. Structured Query Language (SQL) could be used to establish the `Can_Select` procedure, and HTML and CGI could be used to build the customer interface.

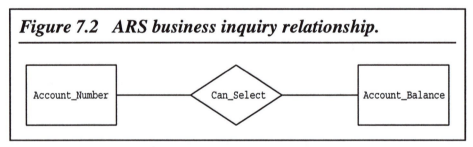

Figure 7.2   ARS business inquiry relationship.

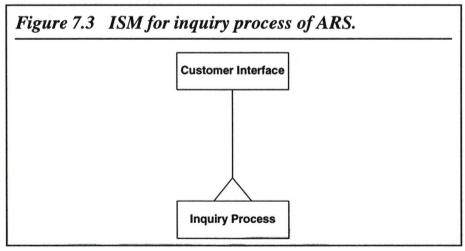

Figure 7.3   ISM for inquiry process of ARS.

Security Administration
Module

## Chapter 8

UNIX Security

Security administration is a primary concern of any computer system that holds business, industrial, government, or personal information. Information is an asset not necessarily meant to be freely distributed.

Security measures protect stand-alone and networked computers from deliberate and accidental harm. A deliberate attack on a computer system includes such events as someone breaking into a system and looking around and attacks that deny a service, destroy files, or cause a system to crash. Accidental harm occurs when files are unintentionally erased or during an unforeseen event, such as a major storm disrupting the system.

This chapter focuses on basic UNIX security provided by the kernel. The component of the kernel that provides this security is called the trusted computer base. Some security features available in the UNIX environment have already been discussed, such as permissions, the root user, and the directory structure.

Security Concerns

A system can be compromised at different levels, and an administrator must be aware of them all. Security measures must enhance rather than jeopardize these areas of concern, or they reduce the value and usefulness of a system.

First, data integrity must be kept intact by protecting data from alteration or removal by unauthorized persons or acts. Second, access to a system must be controlled, also referred to as isolation, so that existing files are not changed or unauthorized files added. Third, the level of service, or system availability, must be satisfactory for authorized users.

Related to access and availability are the additional security concerns of privacy and system behavior. Privacy controls access to information. For example in a business, access to personnel data should be limited to authorized management. Account numbers, social security numbers, and other identifying characteristics of customers and employees must be kept private, and a security scheme must be developed to protect this information.

System behavior is a variation of availability. Users expect a system to behave the same way each time they access it. Changing that behavior can create a problem. For instance, a database upgrade that loads new files without the correct permissions could exclude a qualified user from accessing necessary functions. A worse case would be if a utility started behaving with unpredictable results. For example, it is entirely possible for someone to replace a utility file such as `find` with a script file of the same name that contains a command to delete files owned by root.

An administrator must remember that no system is 100 percent secure. Protection from an outside attacker or a disaster does not protect against the actions of authorized users of a system. Authorized users may cause security problems intentionally or accidentally. The method used to track users on a system is referred to as auditing. Applications on a system may have their own audit trails built into them. At the system level, tracking who is using the system, and when, can be implemented. Although auditing may not prevent a security breach, it provides a way to trace the breach. Also, auditing may deter potential malicious users from attempting an attack.

When implementing security measures, a considerable number of system components must be monitored, as listed in Table 8.1.

User and Group IDs

Whenever a process is executed, it is given a process ID (PID). Additional IDs are also assigned to processes. These IDs are a user identification number (UID) and a group identification number (GID). It is through the UID and the GID that permissions can be assigned on a file at the user and group level. The identity of a user can be changed using the **su** command. To use su, a user, with the exception of root, must know the user's password.

The **newgrp** command changes a user to a different group. You can only change to a group to which you have been assigned. Assignments are kept in the /etc/ group file. The line

```
dbadm::0:root,admin,wetsch
```

Table 8.1 System components to monitor.

Security concern	Description
System files	The owner of key system files, usually `root`, is an authorized superuser with `rwx` privileges. World `w` privileges should never be granted. Group `w` privileges are not recommended unless the group is comprised of authorized users. Modification dates and times should also be consistent with these files.
Devices	Device files should be stored centrally in `/dev`. Permissions to these files should be monitored carefully. Setting a link to a storage device with world `rw` privileges should be provided to prevent direct `rw` access to the device. For TTY devices, world `w` permission should not be allowed. Modification dates and times should also be consistent with these files.
User files	A user's home directory should not have world or group `w` privileges. Check that hidden files (`.files`) cannot be written to or owned by someone other than the user. Also, if the administrator does not want the owner to modify startup dot files, the owner privileges should be set to `rx`.
Suspect files	Files on a system that resemble system executables, such as `cp`, `rm`, `ls`. that are not in the proper directory. These are suspect files that could cause damage or breach security when executed. Liken these files to suspicious packages.
Special files, devices, and daemons	There may be proprietary devices files, and daemons available and loaded on a system for special purposes. Check to make sure permissions are set correctly when installed and include checking permissions as part of a regular system level check. Generally, the owner has `rwx` privileges and the group and world may have `rx` authorization.
Network files	Network files can be invaded. Check `/etc/hosts` and `/etc/hosts.equiv` files for unauthorized IP addresses. An unauthorized address in `/etc/hosts.equiv` means an untrusted machine makes the local machine treat it as a trusted host to the local host.

Security

Table 8.1 (continued)

Security concern	Description
Log files	System log files should be checked on a regular basis (such as `lastlog`, `utmp`, and `wtmp`). If the system uses the **su** command, check the `sulog` file to monitor who uses it. Keep track of the contents in log files maintained for services used (i.e., ftp). Check services files. For greater protection, substitute `sudo` for `su`. Only authorized users are specified command privileges when using `sudo`.
Networking	1) When using `rlogin` to access a trusted host (i.e., hosts in the `/etc/hosts.equiv` file), a password is not required. 2) If using NFS, check and set the access privileges and authentication of files systems being exported, as required. Check `/etc/exports`. Security options can also be set for a mounted shared file system in the `/etc/fstab` file. The **exportfs** command lists what file systems are being exported. 3) If using `sendmail`, be sure the version does not predate 1989. Be sure that `debug` in `sendmail` is not active. Also, the `wizard` password should be disabled; otherwise, a user could execute a shell owned by `root`, which would exceed the privileges granted by a user. 4) Use a current version of `finger`. Older versions, up to November 1988, have the hole that was exploited by the Morris worm. 5) Be careful using `tftp`, also called trivial ftp. Usually user authentication is not part of `tftp`. If using it, try to access a file on the host without authentication. If access attempts fail, then the `tftp` version is probably OK, otherwise update it.
RPC	A remote procedure call that is used extensively in internetwork traffic. For secure network traffic, Secure RPC (from Sun) is a possible solution, or Kerberos authentication can be added to the system. Be sure you understand the features and limitations of implementing these methods before you choose one.

shows the fields in the file separated by colons (:). The first field is the group name field, dbadm in this example. The second field holds the encrypted group password, which is unused here. Some systems have an asterisk (*) in the password field. The third field is the group's GID, in this case 0. GID 0 is reserved for the group called root, or in some cases wheel, which has superuser privileges. The names of users, separated by commas, who belong to the group are in the fourth field, after the GID. This example creates a database administration group with superuser privileges for the groups root, admin, and wetsch.

The /etc/passwd file must be checked regularly for unauthorized superusers. Finding a questionable superuser may indicate that someone has cracked your system and is using it at the superuser level.

Encryption

In the mid-1970s, a Data Encryption Standard (DES) was proposed. DES has provided a means to secure unclassified files and messages, and it undergoes a periodic review. DES can operate in modes that determine the type of encryption being used.

Table 8.1 (continued)	
Security concern	*Description*
Modems	Modems are a means of access to a system. Be sure they hang up when a user leaves or is disconnected from a system. Give the phone numbers only to authorized users. Determine if the modems are to be one-way or two-way. This provides control over the number of lines for dial-out as well as separate lines for dial-in. Test modem connections on a periodic basis, or for more security, implement a callback feature to unsuccessful logins, have the phone company prevent third-party billing to the line, or get a leased line if dial-out is restricted to a single source.
Shell escapes	Many programs allow the user to escape to a shell by using ! or ~!. If shell access is to be denied, then access to a shell-escapable utility must be prevented or access to the service denied. For instance, a user denied shell access may be given the vi utility to create, write, or modify files. It would be entirely possible for the vi user to drop to the shell using !.

Security

These modes are Cipher Block Chaining (CBC), Cipher Feedback (CFB), Output Feedback (OFB), and Electronic Code Block (ECB). NIST provides publications on DES in the form of Federal Information Processing Standards Publications, more commonly referred to as FIPS PUBs. The DES is found in FIPS PUB 81. Due to restrictions on exports of encryption software, users outside of the United State may not have legal access to the DES utility.

Encryption utilities require a key to decrypt them and DES can be enhanced using multiple encryption iterations and multiple keys. A DES encryption tool is called des and sometimes uses a piece of hardware known as a DES chip. The syntax for the use of des can vary. One way to encrypt a file with a key is:

```
# des -e -k thekey -f inputfile outputfile
```

This line uses the -e option to encrypt using DES. The -k option specifies the user-defined key in the line as *thekey*. The -f option specifies the file to be encrypted (*inputfile*) and the name of the resulting encrypted file (*outputfile*). DES employs a technique called symmetric encryption, requiring the key be the same for both encryption and decryption.

To decrypt the file you must know the key. Enter

```
# des -d -s < encryptedfile > decryptedfile
```

Notice the input parameter is now the file that has been encrypted and the output file is the name of the file after it is decrypted. This line returns a prompt to enter the key. Just as when entering a password at login, the information entered for the key will not be displayed on the terminal.

A UNIX utility called crypt is part of the UNIX system and variations can usually be found on anonymous ftp servers and downloaded for use. Although there are various versions of crypt available, it is not considered the most secure encryption method. Using the UNIX compress utility and then crypt can improve security.

User Accounts and Passwords

Passwords protect data integrity and authenticity and enhance user privacy. Unfortunately, in the absence of an enforceable standard, many users take the easy way out, using easy-to-remember passwords such as first names, last names, names of relatives, or something trivial. In addition, when given a default password, users often retain it rather than change it. Passwords containing common names and system defaults are commonly referred to as "joe accounts." The ftp downloadable COPS program can be used to detect joe accounts on a system. To truly have a secure system, joe accounts must be eliminated. A system can enforce restrictions to a password in order to enforce a company standard. The ftp downloadable program called passwd+ allows a system to set and enforce security features on passwords.

A technique for creating a memorable password is to select two names that have no connected meaning, and either connect them or replace a letter or two with a special character or a number. For instance, the password *birdcage* may not be very secure, especially if the user is a bird enthusiast. A more secure password would be to use two disparate words like *birddirt,* which can be enhanced further using special characters and variations, such as *bird;dirt, b1rddir, bird7dir, 3irDi11.* Basically, the user comes up with an easy to remember but obscure mnemonic and then creates a variation of the mnemonic to make it more secure. Consequently, a good mnemonic allows the user to create many passwords with the same mnemonic, which comes in handy on systems that enforce password aging. When changing a password, keep the same mnemonic and just change the form or come up with a new mnemonic and start over.

Unlike passwords, naming accounts is much easier. Account names can include the person's last name with first initial or variations on this, in the case of multiple accounts with the same name. Account names are in the /etc/passwd file. Default permissions for this file usually allow read privileges by anyone.

When an account is first established, the initial password is set by the system administrator. New accounts should be monitored and deactivated after a certain period of time if they never get used. New users, when accessing a system for the first time should also be required to change their passwords. It is good policy to enforce password aging and make users change their passwords on a periodic basis. Once a month is considered a minimum time. If a user believes for any reason that his or her password has been compromised, that password should immediately be changed. The user should also contact the system administrator as well as any security groups within the organization. It is best to have a clear policy on what to do when a password is compromised. Change passwords with the **passwd** command.

The **passwd** command provides options to configure passwords according to accepted organizational policy. Some options to know are -f, which forces users to change passwords at the next log in; -n, which sets the minimum length of the password; -x, which sets the maximum length; and -w, which warns a user of the number of days left before a password must be changed. The options -n and -x should be used together. Be sure to check on the passwd parameters available for your UNIX release. In addition, adduser, the utility used to add new users to a system, can be configured to require a new user to enter a new password after logon.

Passwords are kept in the /etc/passwd file. The delimiter in the passwd file is the colon (:) just as it is in the /etc/group file. The layout of a couple of lines in the passwd file would look like

```
root:g74D34bf:0:1:Administrative User:/:/bin/ksh
wetsch:d8fej8sjG:100:10:John Wetsch:/usr/home/wetsch:/bin/ksh
```

The first field is the account name, followed by the encrypted password. The third field is the UID and the fourth field is the GID. The fifth field is populated by descriptive information about the user, usually the full name. The following fields are home directory and default shell, respectively. Once again, it is important to note that the UID for the superuser is 0. Any unauthorized users with a UID of 0 are suspect. Such a situation indicates that someone has penetrated the system and assigned superuser privileges to an account that should not have them.

The encryption of the password in the passwd file is kept more secure in all but the older releases of UNIX through the /etc/shadow file. A UNIX release rated below a C2 level of security is unlikely to include a shadow file. The shadow file provides a security mechanism to store encrypted passwords in a location separate from the passwd file.

The passwd and shadow files should always be backed up in the regular backup. To disable a user without deleting his or her file, add an * to the password field in the passwd file. Also, replacing the startup shell with /bin/false exits a user from the system when a log-on attempt is made. An empty password field allows a user to log in without a password. If something appears in this field that looks unusual, check it out, and, if necessary, deactivate the account. The user may be getting in on the account without authentication. Another area to watch in the passwd file is the startup directory or shell. An intruder may plant a program that runs at startup that gives unauthorized privileges.

Firewalls

A computer firewall prevents outside users from accessing a network. Systems can be open or closed. A closed system is an internal network or networks that must be kept secure. An open system allows anyone to have access, such as a world-accessible Internet Web site. Internal network users may have access to outside services or only access to other trusted hosts. Access to the open or closed system is determined by the originating IP address or other authorization. An effective firewall keeps intruders out of a system. If penetrated, a firewall can make it harder for an intruder to move beyond the firewall and attack other machines on the network. If the firewall is breached completely, an intruder will have access to the entire internal network.

A firewall is a node on the network set up explicitly to handle incoming connections. It can route authenticated users from the outside to the nodes they have authorized access to and keep outside users localized to a specific node. A firewall consists of two primary segments. The first segment contains control mechanisms that take actions allowing access to services based on the level of authorization of a user. Here, a user may be a customer who has access to a Web site and associated files and inquiry services available to that site. This could be expanded to allow customers who have accounts, such as a paid-for subscription to a service, additional privileges with the proper authorization. The control mechanisms will also be different for employees.

The next segment is a packet filter that filters out IP addresses and only allows authorized IP addresses; that is, those IP addresses to and from a trusted host. Anyone with an unauthorized IP address is filtered out and hence prevented access to the system. The control segment monitors and controls what actions a packet filter takes.

The features built into a firewall depend on the level of security and services required. First, the packet filter must be able to handle a wide variety of protocols that include services such as NFS, which is RPC based, other RPC-based services, UDP, ftp, http, etc. Second, a firewall should be able to audit the system, track access, and notify the administrator if abnormal actions against the filters are occurring. Third, the control modules must know the trusted computer resources and implement rules that support the level of access available to users. Fourth, the interaction of the firewall should appear seamless so that authorized users can move freely throughout their authorized domain and access applications. (Note: the exception to this is if you need to increase authorization and force users to log on and connect as they move between services.)

Firewalls are built commercially or can be downloaded and implemented. Free firewall software is available through anonymous ftp at `ftp.tis.com`.

Tools

Some tools, easily downloaded through ftp, provide a significant arsenal of security tools to the administrator, including `satan` for network security and `cops` and `crack` to test a UNIX server. An administrator can also build tools using common UNIX utilities.

To keep track of files in key directories, use **ls** -1 to build files that contain a listing of files with permissions. Create a master list, periodically run **ls** -1 against the system, and compare the results to the master list to see if any files are being changed. Also, expand the content of the master list to find just the files that can be seen with the -1 option, then use other options with -1, such as -a to find hidden files. SCO UNIX has a utility called `integrity` that reports changes in file permissions. Another important tool, the **umask** command, can explicitly specify the permissions allowed for all files generated by each type of user on a system. Enter a **umask** command in a user's /etc/profile startup file. For instance, **umask** 027 only allows access to a file by a user and his group.

The **find** command is also a very important tool for security. find can list files that can be written to by anyone, if the files are unowned. When a file is modified, be sure it has the proper SUID and SGID parameters. Table 8.2 shows some handy uses for find; there are considerable variations available to the usages shown.

A few notes on Table 8.2 concern implementation of these commands. First, executing several **find** commands in a script through cron can automate much of the file checking. When writing the files to a directory, put them in a secure place and give privileges to root only, so that others may not view or modify the files. Second, to save the information and have the results of these commands sent through mail. Substitute | **mail** root for > /*file_path*/*filename*.

To categorize files written out, specify a date by setting up the script variable:

```
LRGFILE = "/usr/adm/security/lrgf `date +%m%d%y`"
```

Table 8.2   Some incarnations of the **find** command.

find command	Description
find / -type f -size +1000 -print | xargs **ls** -1 > *lrgfiles*	Finds files that are greater than 1,000 blocks and writes them to a filename starting from the root directory (/). Modify the block size accordingly.
find / -name *file* -print -depth -exec **rm** {} \;	Finds a file with a specified name, or with use of wildcard characters, and deletes starting from root. Other commands with the -exec parameter increase the functionality of this statement. For some UNIX systems, -depth may be omitted. It is just a means to ensure that subdirectories will be searched. You may want to run this without -exec **rm** {} \; the first time to make sure you are not deleting needed files.
find / -type d -size 10 -print -exec **ls** -1d {} b \; > *lrgdirs*	Finds directories of more than 10 blocks and writes them to a filename (*lrgdirs*) starting from the root directory (/). Modify the block size accordingly; however, directory sizes in the double digit range can decrease performance.
find / -name core -exec **rm** {} \;	Removes those pesky core files left behind after abnormal terminations.

A simple script using the **find** command for large files would look like:

```
# An Example of writing out a file with a date stamp
#Administration File. Writing Out larger system files
#
#Set up your variable.
LRGFILE = "/usr/adm/security/lrgf `date +%m%d%y`"; export LRGFILE
#
#Executing your command
find / -type f -size +1000 -print | xargs ls -l > $LRGFILE
```

Table 8.2 *(continued)*

find command	*Description*
find / -type f -perm -777 -print > *permfile*	Checks the permissions of a file. The octal permission bit can be modified to check for whatever permissions you want and the results are written out to a file (*permfile*).The example checks for rwx permissions for the user, group, and others. If you want to check only for permissions to the world (other), substitute -007. Use -perm -4000 to check for unauthorized SUID, and -perm -2000 for unauthorized SGID files. -perm -1000 checks for the setting of the sticky bit on files.
find /*files_to_check* -mtime -7 -print > *modfile*	Finds specified files that have been modified over a specified period of time (in this case ≤7 days) and writes the output to a file. For key system files, you may want to make this a daily check (i.e., -mtime -1).
find . -exec **chmod** 744 {} \;	Changes the permissions for all files found in the current directory. (The dot specifies the current directory.)

This technique allows you to write files that do not overwrite files already existing. You can then set up your own checking and archiving methods to track and retain these files.

You could also set up variables for other file types in the same script as follows:

```
# An Example of writing out files with a date stamp
# Administration File. Permission and large file check.
#
# Setting up your variables
LRGFILE = "/usr/adm/security/lrgf `date +%m%d%y'"; export LRGFILE
SGIDFILE="/usr/adm/security/sgid `date +%m%d%y'"; export SGIDFILE
#
# Executing the find commands
find / -type f -size +1000 -print | xargs ls -l > $LRGFILE
find / -type f -perm -2000 -print > $SGIDFILE
```

If the file does not execute properly, check the pathnames. If pathnames are not properly set, change them or else explicitly set them in the script file.

Compare the following two statements:

```
find / -type f -size +1000 -print | xargs ls -l > lrgfiles
```

and

```
find / -type d -size 10 -print -exec ls -ld {} \; > lrgdirs
```

These statements accomplish the same task. The difference between the two is that one uses a pipe to xargs and the other uses the -exec argument. xargs is considered more efficient than -exec because it is designed for looping and reduces the number of times a command is executed. When working with a list of files, xargs is usually recommended, especially when writing a script file with a considerable amount of looping, because exec runs the associated files for each file matching the specified criteria.

When setting up script files for execution by cron, set up a strategy that staggers the execution time of security checks. If you set all of your security checks to look at your file systems at 1:00 AM how do you know there was unauthorized file access taking place between 8:00 AM and 5:00 PM. An intruder may change permissions to a file and then reset the permissions so that files look as if they have not been touched. Depending on the sensitivity of the system and the level of security, more frequent snapshots may be desirable. The information you generate here will be quite large so the more you do, the more work you are creating for yourself. The best rule of thumb is to use common sense and make this a workable routine and not a routine that will bog you down.

Backup Procedures

Backing up system files to tape is an important system management practice. It prevents loss to a system when files and directories are unexpectedly destroyed. The system administrator must restore them as soon as possible. A document that describes backup and restore procedures can communicate archive and storage methods to the organization. As systems are added or changed, backup and restore procedures will change, so any documentation of the backup process must be kept up to date as well.

In backup documentation, always specify the systems being archived and the equipment being used, and implement any additional specialty backup procedures, such as those required for a smooth database backup and restore. Keep a hardcopy log of tape backups. Label the tapes with the type of backup as well as the backup date, and indicate if the backup is an incremental backup (only files that have been changed or added since the last backup) or a full backup (a complete system backup). To help keep file systems straight, run backups on a file system basis. Backups could start with root and its associated file systems, followed by a tape for each subsequent file system. File systems that are fairly static can be backup less frequently than those that are used more frequently. A procedural outline may look something like:

1. In /etc/motd (the message of the day file) display the times when the system will be down for maintenance, including scheduled backup times.

2. A few minutes prior to bringing the system down, broadcast a message to all users that the system will be coming down for maintenance in a few minutes. Use the /etc/wall command and give users time to finish up what they are doing before they are logged off during shutdown.

3. When bringing the system down, use the **shutdown** command as follows: **shutdown** -i0 -g120 -y This gives users a two-minute grace period to log off. Backups should always be run in single-user mode to prevent users from accessing and using system files during the backup procedure.

4. After the system is down, enter system maintenance mode and run the **sync** command followed by the **fsck** command. If errors other than Possible File Size Error occur, rerun fsck until the system is error free.

5. Before starting the backup, mount the specified file systems.

6. For cpio transfer, the standard output parameters are -ocvB > /dev/ct (where /dev/ct specifies the cartridge tape device.). A cpio backup for root is **find** / -depth -print | **cpio** -ocvB > /dev/ct. (Note: cpio can also archive groups of files into another file for soft storage in an archive directory that can later be backed up and erased.)

7. During the backup procedure, the console printer, if you have one, should be turned on to record `fsck` activity, disk usage data, and commands executed during the backup. (This allows a hardcopy to be maintained.)

8. During the monthly full backup, the tape scan file created in the `tmp` directory using the **scan** command from the tape utility is printed and saved.

9. When executing all backup procedures, scripts, etc, be sure the console printer is turned on to record all input and output to the terminal.

10. An adequate supply of tapes to a tape pool should be made. At the beginning of each week the tape pool should be checked and additional tapes added if needed. Rotate tapes on a regular basis and do not use tapes beyond their normal life and wear expectancy.

11. The `cpio` utility should be used to restore tapes and files. Enter **cpio** `-icvB <` `/dev/ct` for the mounted tape.

12. Return to multi-user mode when backup is completed.

13. When dealing with tapes, consider storing them at an offsite location, a precaution the protects backups in case of catastrophic events like fires, hurricanes, tornadoes, and floods. If your organization does not have a secure offsite facility, commercial storage facilities in your area may take your backup tapes and even come and pick them up for you periodically.

Many administrators prefer the **tar** command or an off-the-shelf backup and restore product. Use whatever is preferable. Be sure when using off-the-shelf software that it can restore the system in case of a complete system crash. For instance, if the system fails, backup software on the system may have crashed too and must be reloaded. If the crash is destructive, the online system catalogs may be destroyed. Therefore, backup software should be able to do a no-catalog restore and be easily accessible after a crash; otherwise, the standby UNIX tape utilities `cpio` or `tar` may be a better backup option.

Security Standards

Certain government agencies and private organizations study computer security issues and attempt to standardize security policies and procedures. Within the federal government, agencies must follow the Computer Security Act of 1987. The Department of Defense has its Orange Book, which has become somewhat of a de facto standard. Agencies can also work with the National Institute of Standards and Technology (NIST), which has been given the task of developing security standards and evaluation methodologies. Private organizations such as the Association for Computing Machinery (ACM), the Computer Society of the Institute of Electrical and Electronics Engineers (IEEE), and the National Computer Security Association (NCSA) also deal with computer security issues, education, and research. The Computer Emergency Response Team (CERT) actively monitors computer security and sends out alert notices to help users prevent security problems. In addition, any group that deals either with computers or with security must also deal with computer security. There is really no way of avoiding the issue of computer security regardless of whether you are the sole user of a PC or a manager of the world's largest enterprise system.

One of the de facto standards mentioned earlier is known as The Orange Book (DOD 5200.28-STD). The Orange Book breaks the security of a system down into levels that have a specific security intent. Table 8.3 provides a brief description of the Orange Book security levels, listed from the lowest to the highest security level. Each successive level must incorporate the security standards of the previous level. The reader must be aware that the actual written standard breaks these levels down into specific criteria to define what constitutes a security level. The descriptions in Table 8.3 are generalities to give you an understanding of these levels. Note that there are also sublevels to the main levels.

Table 8.3 Description of Orange Book security levels.

Security level	Description
D	The lowest security level. Cannot be referenced by a higher class.
C1	Allows access to the system by allowing group or user passwords to be defined. Access mechanisms are at the discretion of the administrator.
C2	Allows controlled access to the system, incorporates auditing, and increases the ability of the system to isolate users and resources by authenticating a single user and by assigning permissions.
B1	Forces controls to access the system and provides auditing to data and devices.
B2	Modularizes the security functions further, such as separating the functions available to the administrator and to an operator. Provides security levels to devices and incorporates a formal security model.
B3	Consistently checks security mechanisms for flaws and provides increased auditing capabilities. Specific sections of the system can be broken down into specific security subsystems.
A1	The most stringent security level. Requires authentication for all levels of software deployment and access to software.

Security

The Orange Book provides a definition for secure environments. For instance, a home computer with no security but a virus checker is considered Class D. Off-the-shelf UNIX systems with security software purchased from vendors are usually C2 and sometimes B1 level.

The security level chosen must fit the system. Users do not want to be constantly frustrated by computer security, so a good balance must be struck between what is practical and what works for the users while still providing security to the system. Therefore, standards for computer security do not really exist. Industry may follow guidelines, but it implements security at whatever level deemed appropriate.

More Information

The Computer Emergency Response Team (CERT) is a major contributor to ongoing security issues and information on all aspects of computer security, including viruses, Trojan horses, firewalls, encryption, etc. CERT was started in 1988 and is a service mark of Carnegie Mellon University. CERT advisories and technical information can be found at the web site of `http://www.cert.org`. Files can be downloaded with ftp or you can go directly to `ftp://info.cert.org/pub`. E-mail can be sent to CERT at `cert@cert.org`. CERT is also known for its ability to assist during and after a break-in.

CERT is well known for its advisories. A CERT advisory provides information that will let the reader know how to obtain a solution to a security problem, and information on attacks is an ongoing effort. Advisories are found on the USENET newsgroup and advisories that have been archived can be found at `ftp://info.cert.org/pub/cert_advisories`.

Another excellent source of information is the National Institute of Standards and Technology (NIST). NIST houses a Computer Security Resource Clearinghouse on the Web, which offers NIST FIPS publications, including the Rainbow series. The Rainbow series of publications contains methods for handling security issues and includes the Orange Book. The home page for the NIST Computer Security Resource Clearinghouse is `http://csrc.ncal.nist.gov`. Information on establishing security criteria, incident response, security assessment, and security forums are accessible through this site.

The National Computer Security Association (NCSA), a membership-based private organization, is another significant source of security information and training. NCSA holds regular conferences and has established guidelines for certifying firewalls and securing a Web site. NCSA can be reached on the Web at `http://www.ncsa.com/ncsa.html`.

## Chapter 9

The Multilayered Security Model

To effectively implement and maintain a security system, all levels of the organization, from management to user, must support the effort. A security model including policies and procedures can help generate needed support.

Three documents describe a security system. First is a security plan that provides an overview of the security model, a description of the security methodology and physical environment, and an outline of policies and procedures found in the disaster recovery plan and the policies and procedures manual. The security plan should include where to find the disaster recovery document and the policies and procedures manual. The second document is the disaster recovery plan to take care of contingencies. The third document is the policies and procedures manual that describes in detail any procedures developed and used by the administrator. Because procedures change over time, the policy and procedures manual and the disaster recovery manual must be written and designed for easy revision as the system environment changes. Before a security plan can be implemented, a risk analysis must be completed.

The model presented here is called multilayered security. The multilayered security model offers a means to categorize security requirements. However, multilayered security does not provide a clear distinction between layers. This distinction can be made based on the level of granularity defined for a system. The better the system definitions, the easier it is to specify where to apply an administration policy or procedure.

Multilayered security ensures that the administrator has completely addressed system security issues. However, the extent of any assessment depends on the complexity of the system. No system is 100 percent secure.

Layer Overview

Multilayered security is an approach designed to ensure that the system administrator develops a security plan suitable for the environment. With or without knowledge of the DOD Orange Book security standard, the multilayered approach provides a means to address all levels of system security. The focus of any security implementation is to control access, protect data, and secure system resources. A security plan must be scalable from stand-alone systems to distributed client/server systems. In any environment, administrators must understand their environment and adopt appropriate security methodologies. To develop a comprehensive security plan, the administrator must consider security at network, system, application, data, and physical levels, also known as layers. Layers in this security model overlap, benefiting the administrator by connecting each layer and providing a comprehensive view of the system security.

Each layer provides a method of access to a system. Users access the system through the network layer, enter the system through the system layer, go through applications, find data, and may have access physically to system hardware. It is the responsibility of the administrator to configure the layers of a system in order to protect it.

Network Layer

The network layer is a complex system. It can range from a simple modem connection to a particular flavor of network implementation. With only modem connections, security may start with a fundamental log-in and password authentication at the server. A more advanced implementation might incorporate the security features found in some network operating systems (NOS).

Generally, the network layer is the weakest security layer. All types of users can be moving through a network to gain access to the system. If appropriate, a firewall can strengthen the network layer. Some systems further secure entry into the network by using encryption during the transport of information such as credit card transactions. A firewall is intended to stop and slow the progress of an intruder in a system similar to a physical firewall that is designed to slow the progress of a fire through a building.

A firewall segments access to the servers, admitting users only to needed servers or LAN systems. A simple firewall can be implemented on a networked system that will allow the administrator to control access to key areas. For instance, an Ethernet TCP/IP environment could consist of one LAN (machine name `alpha`) for development and another for production (machine name `beta`). In this type of environment, a firewall could keep the nonsystem users out of the development system but allow the development users access to both systems.

A front-end server (machine name `firewall`) where all users log in could be added to the network. In each user's `.profile`, adding the statement **rlogin** alpha for developers and **rlogin** beta for the production system users routes each to the appropriate LAN system. Additionally, users could be required to reenter another password to gain access. The user-defined authentication method for this firewall does not do IP filtering and is only recommended for small networks.

To ensure that users are logged off the system when they exit, add the statement **kill** -9 0 after the `rlogin` statement at the bottom of `.profile`, as in

```
rlogin machine-name #where machine-name is alpha or beta
kill -9 0            #Exits the user from the shell and
                    #removes user processes
```

giving the user only needed resources, but nothing more. Additional segmentation of resources could also be implemented by using the Network File System (NFS), if installed.

System Layer

Interaction with the system layer begins with log-in and password authentication. At the system layer, the system administrator can fully employ the tools available in the operating system to monitor and control user access.

Security at the system layer begins by knowing the key areas of the system and addressing each area as it pertains to the particular environment. Tasks to accomplish include:

- Know how the permission bits are set.
- Identify and monitor key file areas.
- Establish a password strategy.
- Set up the user environment.
- Establish system accounting.
- Establish system checking procedures.
- Monitor overhead.

Knowing how permission bits are set involves the proper settings of user and group IDs, sticky bits, and umask. umask is used to set the default permissions on files. It can also be used by shell users to set default permissions. A sticky bit is also employed by administrators to let only the superuser and the file owner modify the file.

Important file areas include the device directory, /dev; /bin for providing public access to UNIX commands and utilities; /etc for configuration files and other executables; /, the root directory; and others. When additional programs are installed, add /usr/local/bin as a public directory for these programs in order to avoid mixing them with the /bin utilities.

After learning the setup and location of key files, monitor both with a check utility activated using crontab. The following sample utility, called checksys, assumes the existence of a directory called /etc/checkfils, accessible only to the superuser. The script simply accesses key directories and writes an **ls** -l listing to a file. The script then runs a diff against a master file created prior to running the command and saves the contents of the diff command to a separate file. Processing the diff output through cat lists any changes to files made since the master was created. If the diff output looks good, update the master by running **rm** *master* and then **mv** *diffout master*. A regular run of checksys keeps the system administrator aware of what files change regularly and whether permissions and bit settings to key files have been changed.

```
# CHECKSYS SAMPLE SCRIPT
# This program will create a list to check your files and
# permissions against a master file. When running for the first
# time be sure to create a master. This can be done by
# commenting out the diff statement and then mv the checkfil
# file to master.
ls -l /etc/* > checkfil
ls -l /dev/* >> checkfil          #add other key files as required
ls -l /bin/* >> checkfil
ls -l /usr/adm/* >> checkfil
diff master checkfil > diffout
```

A password strategy includes addressing such areas as password restrictions, including length, password aging, the minimum time between password changes, whether or not to allow users to choose their own passwords, and whether or not the system should generate a password. A password strategy also includes establishing policies for setting up user accounts, removing inactive users, and removing user accounts.

Setting up the user environment involves defining paths users can access directly, the limits on failed log-in attempts, the maximum idleout time before automatic logoff, and whether or not to set a ulimit to prevent users from using too much disk space or an errant user process from writing a file that will fill up the disk.

Setting quotas can also restrict the amount of disk space available to users. To set quotas, create a quota file and configure it for quotas, then tell the file system to accept quotas.

To create a quotas file in a file system named /usrec, begin by entering

touch /usrec/quotas

then make sure that root is the only owner of the file and has the appropriate access by entering

chown root /usrec/quotas

then enter

chmod 600 /usrec/quotas

to set the proper permissions. The file system now has a quota file in it. Also, when the system reads the file system information at startup, it will enable the file system to accept quotas. A reboot is required for quota to work.

After setting it up, configure the quota and add users. Enter the **edquota** command as

edquota wetsch johnson edwards

where wetsch johnson edwards are three user names separated by spaces. The system then displays a vi interface to set quota limits. A soft quota establishes a level on disk space that generates a message warning users they are approaching their disk space limit. The hard limit is the real limit and cannot be exceeded. Specify both the hard and soft quota in bytes. To check on quota usage, enter the **quotacheck** or **repquota** commands. Other quota options are available also.

To tell a system that quotas are active, edit the file system file, such as /etc/fstab. A typical entry for the file system /usrec would be

/dev//1s1 /usrec rq 1 2

where rq specifies to read and write with quotas. An equivalent line is

/dev//1s1 /usrec rw,quota 1 2

To turn quota off, replace quota with noquota in the second line.

Finally, set up system accounting to track usage of the system. Establish procedures to maintain and track all security implementations. Without these procedures, files can become unmanageable. In essence, keep track of overhead. Any security implementation means additional work and system tracking. Security must be done on a regular basis — daily!

Security

Application Layer

Security in the application layer allows users access to the applications they need while protecting the shell. Not all users need access to the shell. In the previous network layer example, the development users probably need shell access but production system users only need access to their applications.

In a single application environment a startup to the application could be placed in the .profile between the rlogin statement and the kill statement. In this case, a user logging in will come directly up in the application. The kill statement forces a user off the system after exiting an application.

More likely, users need access to several applications. A user interface provides access to applications without letting users drop to a shell. If not using a graphical user interface (GUI), then implement a simple menuing script. Look back to the menux shell script provided in the Software Administration module in Listing 3.1.

A menu can improve the ease of using a system; however, access to some applications inadvertently allows access to the shell, leaving it unprotected. Allowing access to the vi editor through a menu is an example. Once the vi editor is invoked the user can enter shell commands using the ! operator. Effective application layer security depends on knowing the extent and limitations of system applications.

Finally, from the application layer, the system administrator can invoke particular security features of an application. For instance, when administering a database, consider database security features that include transaction logging; privileges on tables and fields such as add, modify, or delete, and access to specific data views.

Data Layer

Security at the data layer involves backup and restore strategies to protect data on a system as well as the system resources. The system administrator must establish policies and procedures for complete system backups and for daily, weekly, and monthly backup. Select the appropriate backup utilities such as tar, cpio, or an off-the-shelf package to standardize the backup environment. The backup methods must enable the administrator to restore any files lost, destroyed, or damaged on a system. Overall, the administrator must evaluate the environment to determine the best method to ensure data reliability.

Physical Layer

Physical layer security protects the hardware and licensed software. The administrator must address the security of the facilities that house the system. Can anyone approach the equipment, see a blinking light, and press a button? Does the organization have a contingency plan in case of fire, theft, or system failure? Is the backup media from the data layer stored in a secure location?

Implementing the various components of the network, system, and data layers is not enough if the physical layer is not addressed. In this layer, the administrator needs to set up a disaster recovery plan and address what needs to be done if any of the other layers should fail. If a plan is already in place, the administrator must make sure the plan is current and reflects the environment.

In conclusion, the layered approach to system security is designed to give the administrator a means to address user entry into the system. By addressing the system environment through each layer, the administrator has a means to collect all of the information required to write a security plan. It should also be emphasized that good system procedures are nothing if they are not enforced with good policy. Any security feature implemented must be maintained.

Implementing a Security System
Risk Analysis

Before an organization can implement a security system, or even write one of the basic documents, it must conduct a risk analysis. The complexity of a risk analysis depends on company size and its equipment and facilities.

A risk analysis inventories resources and identifies their importance to the enterprise. Each major resource represents one layer in the security model. Table 9.1 describes the levels of importance, or the criticality factors, that can be applied to a resource.

Table 9.1 Criticality factors.	
Criticality factor	**Description (based on availability)**
0	Loss of resource has no effect on the system or a specific layer.
1	Loss of resource has minimum effect on the system or a specific layer.
2	Loss of resource has some effect on at least one layer.
3	Loss of resource affects the integrity of a layer.
4	Loss of resource affects the integrity of the system.
5	Loss of resource decreases the availability of at least one layer.
6	Loss of resource makes at least one layer inaccessible.
7	Loss of resource decreases the availability of the system.
8	Loss of resource prevents access to the system for a short period of time.
9	Loss of resource prevents access to the system for a long period of time.

Security

The criticality factors are somewhat subjective because the local environment determines the impact of a lost resource to the rest of the system. Additional refinement can be added to the risk analysis by factoring in the frequency of an occurrence, such as losing a resource. For instance, loss of a network router may be rather frequent and could be assigned a criticality factor of 6 or 7. However, a fire that destroys a computer building is undoubtedly less frequent than a router going down but much more catastrophic with a criticality of a 9. The first draft of a risk analysis survey in Table 9.2 adds time weighted factors of 1 = low frequency, 2 = moderate frequency, and 3 = high frequency or likelihood of occurrence in column F.

Table 9.2 First draft of a survey for a risk analysis.

Survey question	L	Y/N	C	F	R	Comments
Is building access controlled?	P	Y	1	1	1	Building security
Is access to the computer facility controlled?	P	Y	3	1	3	Badge reader
Are ID badges required?	P	Y	0	0	0	
Are ID badges worn in the computing facility?	P	Y	0	0	0	
Are ID badges worn in the building?	P	Y	0	0	0	
Is the media storage facility separate from the computer room?	P	N	7	2	14	Separate facility required
Is the media storage facility locked?	P	Y	3	2	6	Same as computer room
Is a building emergency plan in place in case of disaster?	P	Y	9	1	9	Reference building security document
Is the building adequately maintained?	P	Y	8	1	8	Potential power losses due to old wiring
Is air conditioning provided?	P	Y	3	1	3	
Is a fire/smoke detection system available?	P	Y	9	1	9	
Is a raised floor available in the computer facility?	P	N	1	2	2	Potential for stepping on and pulling cables

Survey question	L	Y/N	C	F	R	Comments
Is there a UPS (power supply) provided for the equipment?	P	Y	8	1	8	
Is a disaster response team set up?	P	Y	9	1	9	
Is the computing facility free of combustible materials?	P	Y	9	1	9	Combustible cleaning supplies kept in separate storage closet
Is an offsite storage facility used for backup media?	P	Y	9	1	9	
Are procedures in place for setting up and removing user accounts?	S	Y	6	1	6	
Is system training provided to users?	S	Y	1	1	1	
Is security training provided to users?	S	Y	3	1	3	Security training provided to all new personnel with annual training to all employees
Are the following resources monitored regularly:						
Disk usage?	S	Y	0	1		
File system size?	S	Y	0	1		
File size?	S	Y	0	1		
CPU utilization?	S	Y	1	1	1	
Processor performance?	S	Y	2	1	2	
Network Performance?	N	Y	2	3	6	Monitored but not on a regular basis
Are levels of access privileges established and monitored?	S	Y	4	1	4	

Table 9.2 (continued)

Security

Table 9.2 (continued)

Survey question	L	Y/N	C	F	R	Comments
Are procedures in place to deal with unauthorized users?	S	N	4	3	12	Establish within 30 days
Is backup media used?	D	Y	5	1	5	Tape plus RAID
Are backups automatic and periodic?	D	Y	5	1	5	Nightly
Are manual backups done?	D	Y	5	1	5	User requested
Are redundant systems available for:						
CPU?	P	Y	7	1	7	
Network equipment?	P	N	7	3	21	Additional network equipment needed
Monitors?	P	Y	1	2	2	
Are superuser privileges restricted?	S	Y	9	1	9	Admin staff only. Passwords changed frequently
Are superuser and group access privileges established for the company database?	A	Y	6	1	6	Database administrator with accounts receivable and accounts payable groups
Are shell privileges restricted?	S	Y	4	1	4	
Are privacy controls in place?	A	Y	4	1	4	Public access to system is not allowed. Reporting is segregated into accounting, and decision support
Are key system files protected?	S	Y	7	1	7	
Is application data protected?	D	Y	8	1	8	

In Table 9.2 Risk (R) equals Criticality (C) times frequency (F) of an occurrence. The layers (L) in the table are Physical (P), Network (N), Application (A), System (S), and Data (D).

Table 9.2 covers just the basics of a risk analysis, but it demonstrates how detailed a risk analysis can be. However, the more detailed the analysis the better.

A risk analysis helps determined if the system is at high risk, moderate risk, or low risk. In an analysis such as that portrayed in Table 9.2, Criticality (C) times Frequency (F) equals Risk (R). Although no system is completely safe, if a 100-percent secure system could exist, the value for R would be 0, meaning no risk to the system. In a completely vulnerable system, everything would have a criticality of 9 and a frequency of 3, yielding an R per-line item of 27. In Table 9.2, 39 line items were assessed for a maximum risk factor of 1,053. The sum of the R column returns a value of 208.

To calculate the optimal risk factor (R_{optsys}) for a system, an organization must decide the criticality factor that allows enough security, backup, and procedures to get work done but minimize the impact on the system overall. In addition, the enterprise must decide on a tolerable frequency of failure. For a criticality goal of 2 with an optimal frequency of F = 1, $2 \times 1 = 2 = R_{optsys}$ as the optimal risk factor for the system. The actual R_{sys} for the risk analysis is the average of C times the average of F or $R_{sys} = C_{avg} \times F_{avg}$. In Table 9.2, this results in $170/39 = 4.4 = C_{avg}$, $45/39 = 1.2 = F_{avg}$, so $R_{sys} = 5.25$.

In plain English, these calculations show that one or more layers are at risk of being inaccessible. To predict which layer is most vulnerable, review the line items for questions answered with an N for No. The questions with No in the Y/N column are:

- Is the media storage facility separate from the computer room?

- Is a raised floor available in the computer facility?

- Are procedures in place to deal with unauthorized users?

- Are redundant systems available for: Network equipment?

Not having redundant systems for network equipment results in a risk factor of 21, suggesting that the layer at the greatest risk is the Network layer. No redundant network equipment for backup can greatly impede the network layer if a component should break down. Not having a raised floor provides for cabling nightmares around the walls and behind equipment, giving way to increased troubleshooting problems and pulled cables. In addition, when a required feature is needed and not available, the risk occurrence (i.e., frequency) increases.

In some organizations it is not practical to reduce certain risk factors. For instance, to reduce physical risk factors to below 9, an organization could implement a hot site where remote procedures are constantly updating another system. If the key system crashes, the hot site would take over operations in hours or even minutes. Thus, by having parallel layers, the nonavailability of one layer is replaced by a redundant layer. However, a fully redundant site may be impractical for some organizations.

Security

Some organizations have implemented their own risk assessment standards. These assessments are more detailed than the one presented here. Some will even compute the dollars lost when a system or component is unavailable. When risk is computed in dollars, the amount of risk is determined by the dollar value at stake. For example, if an organization relies on database data to conduct business and this data generates $10 million worth of revenue per year every year until it is obsolete, the unrecoverable loss of such data represents unconscionable risk.

Writing the Security Plan

Once the risk analysis is complete, the organization must implement a security plan. Recall that an effective security system requires a security plan that documents the security methodology and the physical environment. A security plan for a layered security system should cover, at a minimum:

- software auditing policies and installation guidelines to track the authorized use of software;
- access policies to include passwords, levels of access, workgroup assignments, and definitions of these levels;
- control of physical access to equipment;
- privacy of information, if applicable; and
- user accountability, to include usage and security training.

An outline of a security plan in the multilayered model can take on the following form.

XIV. Introduction: Describe what the system is used for, what its purpose is, and why a security plan is needed.

XV. Physical Security: Describe the following components:
  - System environment
  - Purpose
  - Location
  - Hardware
  - Software
  - Personnel controls
  - Internal controls

XVI. Access Security: Identify the security model. If it is a multilayered model, describe the layers as:
  - Network
  - System
  - Application
  - Data
  - Physical

XVII. Privacy: Describe the privacy concerns of the system and a plan to control them.

XVIII. Summary: Concluding remarks to the plan.

XIX. References: Attach any references used as the basis for your plan.

XX. Appendices: Include appendices that contain:

- Risk analysis
- Floor plan
- What to do for user security training

The following sample plan is based on this outline.

XYZ Company
COMPUTER SECURITY PLAN

TABLE OF CONTENTS {Enter Here}

INTRODUCTION:

The XYZ Company Computer Security Plan is developed in accordance with the published standards provided by [name references, industry, organizational, or government]. This document is prepared in accordance to these guidelines and references are located in the reference section and where appropriate. The scope of this plan is to provide policies and mechanisms to secure the information resources of the XYZ Company.

The XYZ Company is responsible for providing [name your business purpose]. The objective of this plan will be to provide security and protection to XYZ Company computer resources and services from natural and manmade hazards. This document is required by the XYZ Company for internal use. This document supports all automated data processing activities to protect from loss of data and involuntary disclosure of sensitive data. The basis for this plan is the XYZ Risk Assessment located in Appendix A.

PHYSICAL SECURITY:

A floor plan of the XYZ Company's computing facility is located in Appendix B. Building plans related to the location of and access to the computer facility are kept by building management [state place and location]. Internal security to the building is provided by building security, and alarm systems, fire equipment, emergency equipment, and inspection records are maintained by building security. Appendix C provides a description of such equipment available in the computer facility.

Security

System Environment:

Purpose:

The purpose of the computer equipment of the XYZ Company is to support the core business function of the business. [State business functions supported by the organization.]

Location:

The computer facility for the XYZ Company is located in room 328 of the XYZ Building, at 4423 Corporate St., Somewhere, State. Each computer system at this location is equipped with a Uninterruptible Power Supply (UPS). Air conditioning at this location is provided and each computer is housed in a secure cabinet. The cabinets can enclose the computers to protect them from potential water damage as well as make the enclosed equipment mobile. Fire detection equipment available in the facility includes a wet automatic sprinkler system, alarm, and emergency light. A raised floor is provided to allow for air circulation and cable housing. Physical access to the computer facility is controlled by badge access with access given to authorized employees.

Hardware:

[List the hardware and network configuration of the organization. Provide diagrams of what the basic setup looks like. Detailed information is required.]

Software:

[List the principle software components, including the operating system and major system applications.]

Personnel Controls:

Personnel controls to the XYZ Company computing resources are provided in the *Human Resources Manual* of the XYZ Company. Only qualified employees may have access to the XYZ computing resources. Appendix D provides the security training required by all system users.

Internal Controls:

Internal controls or procedures to the XYZ Company computing resources are available in the *XYZ Company Systems Policy and Procedures Manual.* Metacontrols are discussed further in this document.

ACCESS SECURITY:

The XYZ Company has established controls based on a multilayered security model with references to [list any available industry, organization, or government security references used to support controls].

[Provide a description of each layer and reference how users gain access to the layer. Do the layers from the top down as follows: network, system, application, data, and physical.

Network Layer:

Access to the XYZ Company WAN is through the AJAXNET X.25 system. Service password and mnemonics are released by the XYZ Company to authorized users. LAN connections are limited to XYZ staff and users who can gain access to a trusted host. Public access is limited to the XYZ Company web server. Direct modem access is limited to ten 14,400-baud asynchronous Z-Brand modems located in the computer facility. Two of the modem lines are limited to dial-in only with 3270 emulation.

System Layer:

All users who gain access to the XYZ Company system must provide a valid log-in ID and password. Once the log-in ID and password are authenticated, users are given access based on the following class structure:

Class 0 — superuser responsibilities. Assigned only to selected XYZ Company staff and managers responsible for system maintenance and management.

Class 1 — access to the shell. Assigned only to XYZ Company personnel requiring shell access but not superuser access.

Class 2 — application access. For XYZ Company staff and users who require access to application shells with file transfer capability in support of core business activities.

Class 3 — specialized application access. Limited application access for XYZ staff requiring only specialized system resources to do their job.

Class 4 — inquiry-only users. Users who are only allowed to view data and perform inquiries on specified databases. For outside business partners.

Class 5 — temporary users. Allows temporary accounts to be established for users. No shell access. Account valid for only 30 days.

Maintenance of these accounts is described in the *XYZ Company Systems Policy and Procedures Manual*. User classes are implemented by the XYZ Company to control shell access and provide greater accountability of user privileges.

Security

Application Layer:

With a proper user class, applications for the XYZ Company can be accessed. Class privileges are determined by a user's logon and password. For some class types, passwords may be grouped. Class 0 and 1 users may be assigned application superuser privileges. Class 2 and 3 users may have read, write, modify, update, or execute privileges based on their assigned application and job function. Class 4 and 5 users are given inquiry privileges only.

Data Layer:

The Data Layer is the actual files that reside on the hard disk. Class 0–2 users can have access to these files through the operating system or application shells. Class 3 users may modify this layer only through application shells. Because of the ability to manipulate files, users of Classes 0–3 are considered the most trusted users to the system.

Protection to this layer is provided by auditing and backup and restore procedures. These procedures are referenced in the *XYZ Company Systems Policy and Procedures Manual.* In the course of discovering fraudulent intent or a security leak at this layer (i.e., disruption or manipulation of files) procedures in the *XYZ Company Systems Policy and Procedures Manual* are to be followed.

Physical Layer:

System users, visitors, and technicians usually have access to the physical layer. Authorized technicians and Class 0 and 1 users may have unescorted entry to the computer facility. All other users must be escorted when in the computer facility by a Class 0 or 1 user. In case of a security breach, building security should be contacted immediately. In case of a system crash, natural disaster, or other unforeseen event, follow the procedures in the *XYZ Company Disaster Recovery Plan.*

PRIVACY:

[State whatever information the company has that is considered private and proprietary. Also cite any laws or company policies that address these issues.]

SUMMARY:

No computer, especially one on a network, is safe from intrusion. Intrusion into the system can be intentional or unintentional. This plan is designed to track intrusion through user access classifications and system accounting. In addition, it is designed to limit the number of users who must access critical system areas.

Maintaining and enforcing the system controls and office policies discussed in this plan and referenced in the *XYZ Company Systems Policy and Procedures Manual* will reduce the chance of unauthorized intrusion. By addressing each layer of the system, the chances of overlooking components that exist in each layer are reduced. This plan should be reviewed on an annual basis and updated accordingly.

REFERENCES:

[Cite whatever references used for the plan.]

APPENDICES:

[Attach your referenced appendices here.]

This sample provides an overview of a multilayered security plan. It references other documents as appropriate and incorporates detailed information as required. A general rule of thumb is that the more static the security information is, the better it is to include it in the security plan. Data that changes quickly, such as office policies or other procedures, should be included in supporting documents designed for change.

Before writing a security plan, the security requirements of the system should be addressed by management. The system administrator usually does not have the authority to implement security policy, and all policy must be supported by management. Without management consensus and support, users will run rampant on the system, including other managers who probably do not need the access level they insist on having.

User Security Training

The implementation of user security training and awareness is a key aspect to maintaining a secure computing environment. Security training does not have to be elaborate and should start with an authorized access form giving a user the right to access the computer system. These forms should be signed by an appropriate manager. To save paper, it is also good to put the company's security policy on the form that the manager signed and have the employee sign it to acknowledge having read the form. A copy of the form should be given to the authorized user. The content of the policy should be in a form that is easily readable and should include, at a minimum, such topics as:

- E-mail or messaging policy
- Equipment use policy
- Authorized access policy
- Disclosure of log-on IDs/passwords
- Who to contact

Security

- Information classification and disclosure standards
- Corporate ethics

These are all important considerations. Even for small organizations, they are important and they do not need to be elaborate. For instance, any business, large or small, considers its financial information confidential. Personnel working on the system must understand the need for security and the use of proper business ethics when dealing with any information system. A large part of policy is to prevent users from using company resources for personal business or even for a business on the side. Occasional personal e-mails are usually permissible, but much more is an improper use of computer resources. A company that monitors employee e-mail must make it known to them.

In case policy, and hence security, is breached, the consequences must also be spelled out. In addition, employees should know who to contact with questions on policy or to report a security breach. Security policy and consequences cannot violate employment law. Use common sense, be fair, but do not compromise the security of a system by being lax.

Annual training also should be done. This does not entail getting all of the employees together and spending a day going through security policies, issues, and concerns. Employees should already be aware of the requirements, but an annual reminder in the form of a memo on the established policy helps to reinforce system security. Similarly, if a policy changes, be sure employees are made aware as soon as possible; otherwise, unintentional security breaches may occur that will lead to aggravation and frustration.

Sample Security Policies

Based on the security plan and user class access, here is a sampling of some policies. The policy takes a standard form and is designed to meet rapid change. If a policy is added or modified, it easily can be inserted or replaced into the policy and procedures manual. In addition, the manual should contain preliminary information on the purpose and intent of the document in the form of an abstract, appropriate system definitions, and an outline of the various policies correlated to the multilayered model. A suggested layout for these policies follows.

Number: Approved By:
Title: Dept:
Effective Date:
User Level:
Init State:

Security Notes:

System Configuration

Misc. Notes:

References:

Notes and References are not mandatory, but all other areas should be included. You also may want to reference each policy with a number, such as SPP-01 for Systems Policy and Procedures.

Note that these policies are not referenced in any particular order. The User Level number refers to the class codes established in the Security Plan, and the Init State refers to the init level of the UNIX machine.

Number: SPP-01
Title: Annual and Miscellaneous Tasks
Effective Date: 10/1/1996
User Level: 0
Init State: 1–3

Security Notes: Annual tasks are annual reporting compilations of data and annual maintenance services.

System Configuration: To be used on all XYZ Company UNIX machines.

Implementation Procedures:

Calendar Year:
1. Update holidays file.

Fiscal Year:
1. Archive monthly fiscal reports and delete from system
2. Prepare annual report.

Misc. Notes:

Miscellaneous Tasks:
1. Update time zone changes as needed. Report change on the appropriate task checklist.
2. Perform biannual performance checks and diagnostics on the system. These are to be done during monthly downtime. Suggested times are January and July of each calendar year.

Number: SPP-02
Title: Automated Security Procedures
Effective Date: 10/01/1996
User Level: 0
Init State: 2, 3

Security Notes: Most XYZ Company automated security procedures are invoked from the `crontab` file. The file used by `crontab` is `/etc/admincron`. This file provides the automated security checks for XYZ Company computers. Modifications to this file can only be made by system superusers. The security files are contained in the `adm` directory with backups in the SA repository.

System Configuration: For use on all XYZ Company UNIX systems except for the training center computer. The machines involved are `xerxes`, `yarna`, and `zeus`.

Implementation Procedures: The security files used by `admincron` are:
• `joacctchk`
• `chklsfile`
• `autologout`
• `login`

`joacctchk` is a program run from `crontab` that tests the system for "joe" accounts. These are accounts whereby the user was able to establish a weak password that is the same as the log-in ID or an empty password account. The operating system protects against account passwords that are the same as account logins. The operating system requires users to use at least one nonalphabetic character in their passwords. Violations of system password integrity are therefore checked by `joacctchk`.

The `chklsfile` program, run from `crontab`, provides a list of files considered key system files. When this program is run, a copy of the files is checked against the master list. Because of the dynamic nature of some system files (i.e., password and shadow files) a new master list must be made on a periodic basis. When discrepancies are reported, they are checked to determine if the system has been checked or if an adverse condition exists.

The `autologout` program, run from `crontab`, is designed to check the system every 20 minutes for user inactivity. Users who have been inactive at their terminal for more than 20 minutes will receive a warning message and will then have 60 seconds to become active before being logged out. Warnings and logoffs are reported in the file `logoutlog`.

The log-in feature is inherent to the UNIX operating system and records unsuccessful log-in attempts. A user trying to access the system has five attempts. After the fifth unsuccessful log-in attempt, the system will record the login and TTY used in the file `loginlog`.

Misc. Notes:

1. Results of the `joacctchk` and `chklsfile` program are recorded daily on the daily checklist sheet and the printed console display.
2. The `loginlog` and `logoutlog` files are printed and reset every month.
3. On a weekly basis, the `checkfile` must be reset. The SA will move the old `checkfile` into an archival storage location and then **mv** the `checkfile.new` file to `checkfile`.

Number: SPP-03
Title: Automated System File Storage for Transfer
Effective Date: 10/1/1996
User Level: 0
Init State: 3

Security Notes: These automated procedures provide a monthly system backup of important system-related files. The files are moved to a central system storage area on a monthly basis and then are backed up to tape, after which they are removed from the system. The system requires the use of `crontab` on a monthly basis to do the required tasks.

System Configuration: `crontab` executes the file `/adm/store.month`. The files specified in `store.month` are transferred to `/translog/MONTHLY`.

Implementation Procedures: After execution of `store.maint` the files can be backed up to tape, verified, and removed from the system.

Misc. Notes: The command used in `store.month` is **mv**.

Security

Number: SPP-04
Title: Daily Incremental Backups
Effective Date: 10/1/1996
User Level: 0
Init State: 3

Security Notes: The file /adm/incback has only superuser -rwx privileges. This file is initiated by the cron daemon for off-hour automated incremental backups. A dated log file is placed in the directory /translog/back on machines xerxes and zeus. On yarna these files are placed in /usr/storage. These log files are archived to tape on a monthly basis to the monthly tape. The validation file is also stored in hard-copy format.

To prevent writing to backup tapes by all users other than superuser, the write privileges have been removed for normal user access on /dev/tape.

System Configuration: The daily incremental backup provides a backup of all modified and new files created during the date of the backup. This backup method serves to supplement the monthly backup system tapes. For tape verification, the incback file runs a cpio scan of the contents of the tape as well as a dd to verify the number of blocks written to the tapes against those scanned. Tape requirements for the backup are as follows:

1. yarna requires DC 6150 (150Mb) cartridge tapes for placement in the internal tape drive. Tape Device: dev/tape.
2. zeus and xerxes require a DC 6250 (250Mb) or DC 6150 (150Mb) cartridge tape for placement in the internal drive. Tape Device: /dev/tapeold (250Mb tapes are recommended).
3. zeus and xerxes require an 8mm tape (i.e., D8-112, 2.3Gb) for internal drive /dev/tape.
4. The default backup method for XYZ Company incremental backups is cpio using parameters -ocvB for file output to tape.

Implementation Procedures: To implement the daily incremental backup procedure it is first necessary to have the file incback placed in the /adm directory and to have the cron daemon running, allowing for the execution of incback. Once incback and cron are established, the daily procedures are as follows:

1. Enter the name of the tape placed in the drive in the backup log.
2. Correctly label the tape using XYZ Company tape labels.
3. Correctly place the tape in the drive bay using the appropriate tape for the appropriate machine. Make sure the tape is write enabled.
4. The tape must be placed in the drive bay prior to the established cron execution time.

5. Remove the tape the next business day. The following checks are also necessary:
   a. Cron output is sent to admin via mail. Print the mail received from the incremental backup. Record the blocksize of the backup in the backup log and on the tape label. For accuracy, check the blocksize of the files written to tape against the blocksize of the scanned (post-backup) tape.
   b. Scan the printout for anomalies. The following errors will result in having to do a manual backup:
      i. Tape write and scan file blocksize do not match.
      ii. Production area key files are missing. file.db, mxlogfile, and b-tree index files (*.ibx) are important files that may be backed up. However, these files may not change on a daily basis and the user should check them manually if a question arises.
6. Once incremental tapes have been verified and logged they will be placed in the onsite media storage facility. Be sure to engage the write-protect feature of each tape going to storage.
7. It is recommended to prepare the next day's incremental tape when verification of the current day's tape is completed.
8. The printout from the backup must be date stamped, initialed, and placed in the backup data file.

Misc. Notes:
1. An incremental tape may be removed temporarily from the drive bay to accommodate other tape backups, restores, loads, and unloads. The operator must remember to reinsert the incremental tape after the completion of any other tape procedures.
2. On the morning of the first business day of each week the previous week's incremental tapes will be shipped offsite. Check offsite tape storage procedures for further information.
3. To restore from backups see the restore procedures.
4. Verification of the incremental tapes is done automatically using **cpio** -icvBt and dd by the incback script. With the user write permission removed, tapes that are validated by the incback script do not necessarily need to be checked again. However, for system quality control it is recommended that at least on a weekly basis a tape set is pulled and verified manually using cpio or dd to ensure that the tape contents verify the incback verification procedures.

Number: SPP-05
Title: System Accounting
Effective Date: 10/1/1996
User Level: 0
Init State: 1, 2, 3

Security

Security Notes: System accounting is the monitoring of system resources. The scope of system monitoring also includes system maintenance chores not covered by other procedures. The system accounting reports can be used in conjunction with security checking to look for anomalous events.

System Configuration: These practices will be employed on all XYZ Company systems except the XYZ training computer. The dodisk, runacct, chkpacct, and monacct accounting files will be run from crontab.

Implementation Procedures: On a daily basis, the number of users that have used the system will be recorded on the daily checklist. **df** -v also will be run and printed with the data recorded on the daily checklist. The following classification for file systems is as follows:
- <80 percent full — OK
- 80–90 percent full — Warning
- 90 percent full — Critical

When a file system has reached 90 percent capacity or more, immediate action must be taken to reduce the file system to under 80 percent.

Weekly, du will be run against user directories. User directories that have exceeded their assigned limit will be sent a warning statement from the SA as follows:

> Your assigned directory has exceeded your usage limit by *xxxx* bytes. Please reduce your file system size. Failure to reduce your file system size within one week will result in one additional warning. After two warnings your account privileges will be suspended.

Users with no mail privileges will have reductions to their file system made at the discretion of the systems staff.

Assigned quotas for home directories:
- Class 0–1 : 5Mb (9,800 blocks)
- Class 2 :   2Mb (3,900 blocks)
- Class 3–5 : 5Kb (10 blocks)

The monthly system accounting record will be printed. Data from this report will be placed on the monthly checklist for use on the monthly SA report. The monthly reports are stored in the directory /usr/adm/acct/fiscal. These reports will be accumulated for each fiscal year then archived and removed from the system.

Each month, production areas will be monitored and checked. For production databases, this includes database statistics on the monthly SA report.

Number: SPP-006
Title: File System Cleanup
Effective Date: 10/1/1996
User Level: 0
Init State: 1, 2, 3

Security Notes: Cleanup affects system maintenance and file size. This procedure is designed to keep the system clean for file management and system performance purposes.

System Configuration: To be used on all XYZ Company systems.

Implementation Procedures:

Daily: On all systems, the script `rmtrash` is run by `crontab` to clean up `tmp` directories as well as `dead.letter` and core files.

Monthly: Monthly cleanup must be completed on the first business day of the month. Prior to the start of monthly cleanup, which will also include making the monthly backup, all tapes to the systems must be cleaned.

1. For the production areas, the files in the `../rpt/storage` directory must be backed up to tape.
2. Files in the `../rpt` directory are moved to the `../rpt/storage` directory.
3. Database load files for the previous month are moved to the `../rpt/storage` directory.
4. `yarna`: logs and data from the storage directories are moved to `/usr2/storage`, archived to tape, then removed.
5. `zeus/xerxes`: logs are moved to the `translog/rpt` directory, backed up, then removed from the system.

Misc. Notes:
1. When moving logs, be sure to print them first before removing them from the system. Using the line printer while in multi-user mode to print the logs is recommend.
2. When files from all areas are moved to the appropriate storage locations, they are then backed up prior to removal from the system.
3. Again, all logs must be zeroed after they have been backed up.
4. For correct logging, follow the recommended monthly procedures.

Number: SPP-007
Title: User Account Setup
Effective Date: 10/1/1996
User Level: 0
Init State: 3

Security Notes: User account setup is accomplished by systems personnel. These procedures are designed to eliminate unauthorized accounts on the system. Class levels for users are defined in the *XYZ Company Computer Security Plan*. Database groups are configured as follows:

ARECV	Access to Accounts Receivable
ACSPE	Account Specialists
APAYB	Accounts Payable
DISB	Disbursement Access
REPRT	Report Processing
SYSDM	System Administrators Menu

These groups are assigned to XYZ Company at the discretion of the XYZ Management Team. Class 3 users are primarily account specialist designations. Class 4–5 users are given inquiry-only status corresponding to their agency — such as REPRT. Superuser privileges to production databases are restricted to Class 0 users. Superuser privileges to test databases may be granted to Class 0–3 users. The above group designations decide what database views the user has access to and what the assigned user privileges are, such as add, modify, delete, and inquiry. A system group privilege report is printed monthly.

System Configuration: When a user account is approved, systems personnel will set up the account on XYZ Company resources that are relevant to the user's account and group privileges. Password aging is used when an account is established. Users not granted shell access privileges will be given a .profile file that allows access to the application only and that kills the user process when the application is exited.

Implementation Procedures: To activate a new account, the XYZ Company will establish the account on the appropriate machine. The account will also be set up with a designated default password and password aging. The password aging syntax used will be **passwd** -f -x 90 -n 7. This command will force the user to change passwords from the default setting when first logging in. It will also enable the user to maintain the password for 90 days before being required to change it again.

When the account is set up, the XYZ Company will notify the user that the accounts are established, what the default password is, and that the system guidelines are to be used.

Accounts will be deactivated by placing an * in the appropriate password field.

Once a sampling of policies and procedures have been reviewed, it is also possible to establish a daily checklist and a crash report to track your system and recommend crash recovery procedures.

Here is an example of a checklist for daily tasks.

DAILY SYSTEM CHECKLIST

Machine Name:
Date:
Checked By:

Systems:
[___] Verify, log, and store incremental backup tapes
[___] Load new incremental backup tapes
[___] Engage lockbox transfer
[___] Verify `rmtrash` routine
[___] Print, delete admin mail

Security:
[___] Verify `joacctchk`
[___] Verify `chklsfile`
[___] Verify superuser access
[___] Verify `crontab` activation with `autologoff`

Data Collection:
[___] Number of previous day users: _____
[___] Run **df** -v
[___] Place daily printout in datafile (backup files, **df** -v)

Comments:

Here is an example of a crash report form.

CRASH REPORT

This report is to be completed whenever system-wide downtime is noted. A complete system crash refers to a complete failure such as a CPU crash. A partial crash is the unavailability of a support system such as communications.

Machine Name:_____

Crash Date:_____
[____] Complete crash
[____] Partial crash
System Affected:_____
[____] Emergency system shutdown
Time of Downtime:_____
Time of Restore:_____
System Down For:_____ hours/minutes

Cause of Crash/Corrective Action Taken:

Signed _____Date_____

A crash report serves as a way to provide evidence of recurring crashes, detail what procedure was followed to remedy the system, and provide some guidance for the system administrator who may have forgotten what happened the last time the system crashed or who is new to the job and not familiar with the system.

Procedures and policy statements should be as explicit as possible, and every activity should have an assigned procedure. In a well-documented system, files won't get lost and the administrator can get a few nights sleep knowing that the system is running smoothly. In a disaster, documentation gives guidance and directions for recovery. A well-documented system also allows managers to know what the system administrators are doing and consequently allocate resources better and not burden the systems personnel.

Overall, policy and procedure tasks include routine system maintenance, system functionality, automated tasks, systems performance, reporting, and systems security. As a task requirements document, this manual provides proficient systems personnel with the necessary knowledge to complete key systems tasks.

Operations Administration
Module

## Chapter 10

Operations Administration

This chapter introduces the concept of operations administration, the module that assesses the system administration practices of the entire organization, not individual divisions and departments. An evaluation of system administration practices within an organization can determine the amount and location of risk caused by employing traditional data processing standards and methods of managing computing resources.

Overview

The task of operations administration begins with an assessment of system administration practices. Such an assessment starts by establishing a baseline that identifies the operational needs of the organization. This baseline, in turn, provides a benchmark for measuring the productivity of information resources.

Several important questions must be answered to understand the operational needs of an organization. These questions are:

- Does a standard administrative model for the organization already exist or does one need to be developed?

- Do the organization's system administration practices conform to acceptable data center operation practices?

- Can the organization's information resources be considered at risk?

- Are basic system administration functions accomplished?

- What is the effectiveness of automated systems in handling system workload?

Operations

When these questions are answered, a baseline can be established and standard practices and a model for system administration can be developed, unique to the particular enterprise. Using the model and standard practices, the job of operations administration can be completed; that is, the on-going and persistent effort of cataloging system tasks, ensuring that they are done, and coordinating system administration workload for a local system or an enterprise-wide system.

Developing Standards

System administration standards and practices are determined by an organization's system administrators. System administrators incorporate practices that work and discard those that don't, based on the technology in use. Over time, standard system administration practices have evolved from what government and industry expects of its information systems. From these practices, an administrative model can be developed that can be applied to a large range of organizations. Without a systems administration model, an organization's operational practices amount to letting the skilled administrators do their jobs and hoping that nothing catastrophic happens. In essence, a unique set of individuals, the sys admin gurus, controls the operations of a system. System management becomes reactive and chaotic.

Establishing a system administration model for an organization involves classifying the general aspects of distributed systems and working down to the level of the individual characteristics of the information system. This general overview must ignore specific environments in terms of location, the state of equipment, size, and individual organizational attitudes toward a systems environment. While gathering general characteristics, specific anomalies that are noted should be recorded so they can be addressed later in the definition of the systems administration model.

The same standards are not applicable to every situation; however, similar methodologies are needed to avoid undisciplined decentralization, especially when similar applications may be used in an organization whose users may not be physically near one another. Without clear internal policies, procedures, and controls, vulnerabilities creep into an organization's system as an enterprise responds to the increasing complexity of modern business.

The Role of the System Administrator

The standard model used in client/server and other distributed technologies is derived from methods of managing computing resources that have been available for decades; that is, the old administrative paradigm of efficiencies of operations, processing of basic business transactions, collecting and providing information relevant to managerial decisions, monitoring and recording employee performance, and maintaining records of status and change in business functions.

In the old paradigm, the system administrator acted as the information middleman between user and system. The decentralized nature of data processing today, however, has removed the middleman. Users are directly responsible for the transaction processing that allows an organization to maintain current business records and retrieve data. Users can build applications on a workstation or client system, connect to a data repository, and present nearly infinite views of data. In the old paradigm, users prepared data for processing (such as typing a series of punched cards) then submitted the data to the operator for input into the computer. Now, users submit data to a database directly or over a network. However, direct interaction between the system and the user has not eliminated the need for the system administrator; it has redefined the role. In the current model of system administration, the role of the administrator, crucial to the continuing operation of an enterprise, is to maintain the complex technical environment. The responsibility of insuring system availability and reliability falls to the system administrator. In addition, the systems administrator, or systems management, is responsible for deciding what rules are needed to govern the use of the computer system. The systems administrator implements those rules to provide the maximum amount of computing services within the limitations of the computing environment. Those rules correspond to regular policies, practices, and procedures that fit the data processing environment. In providing service functions for applications, the systems staff is supporting the man–machine interface.

In established, mature information processing environments, the roles of the systems staff are usually clearly defined in terms of policies and procedures because these are considered fundamental data center operations management methodologies. Job descriptions are poor measures of defining the needed system administration requirements of a technological infrastructure because in reality, there may be significant crossover in tasks. A system administrator may be doing database administration work, a network administrator may be doing system administration work, and so on.

Training for the System Administrator

The multidimensional aspects of operations management require training for systems staff to perform the functions of security administration, operations administration, and network administration. System administrator training begins with an introduction to UNIX and leads to an understanding of hardware, UNIX software and applications software and a means to keep basic administrative computer services available. However, formal training teaches only basic tasks, such as setting up and maintaining user accounts. Yet more advanced tasks, such as developing a security plan, are not taught in as much detail in system administration training, so over time, a system administrator must combine formal training, on the job experience, and personal studies and develop hybrid methodologies to administer his or her particular system. Within a distributed environment, it is rare to find homogeneous localized systems.

Experience allows the administrator to move between UNIX variations and other computer platforms to keep systems under control.

Conclusions

Although the modules provided in SAmatrix on the companion disk are not wholly automated, automated system tracking and risk analysis could be an end goal of a systems administration staff. An on-going and persistent effort would catalog system tasks, ensure that they are done, and cover all the management tasks for a local system or an enterprise-wide system. When new technologies are added to a system, the systems staff can incorporate the tasks required to implement and support a new piece of technology.

Seeing where new technology fits into the information system and the enterprise as a whole provides a means to assess the effect on security, networks, operations, hardware, and software. For instance, suppose a new piece of software is installed on the system. New security procedures as well as software maintenance procedures may have to be implemented. By defining these tasks, they are adequately addressed and added to the system administrators' standard operating procedures. These tasks can then be carried over to the next organizational group at another location that is responsible for the same tasks. Consequently, after the new software is installed, the software and security administration rating of a remote group may be lower than a group that merely installed the software without implementing the security and maintenance procedures.

There are many variations on this theme. An organization must develop an assessment for its particular environment, maintain the assessment matrix, and establish its own level of standards. These standards in turn become the benchmark by which the systems staff measures its productivity, effectiveness, and value to the enterprise. It also alleviates the concerns by other administrators and managers that certain tasks are not being done, since tasks can be tracked and compared across the matrix. If the task completion level is low, the performance level for a specific administration module and the system model will decrease and provide a quantifiable measure of completed system administration functions.

Chapter 11

Implementing a System Administration Matrix

An organization can develop a matrix to help automate periodic assessments of its system administration practices. The previous ten chapters introduced the primary administration variables — software, hardware, network, security, and operations administration — to acquaint you with the components of the ideal system administration model and to guide you in developing a model. This chapter describes how to create a survey or customize the one provided with SAmatrix and how to format the results into a matrix for use by SAmatrix. The results from analysis of the data gathered and processed with SAmatrix can help establish the baseline, or current state of system administration, against which further improvements can be measured.

The matrix provided on the companion disk is named SAmatrix. It can serve as a template for a matrix customized for a particular organization. SAmatrix comes from an assessment of an actual distributed UNIX environment. Forty-one specific sites were assessed. Many of the specific environmental task items have been rewritten to give the reader a better view of the tasks without involving technology used in a particular environment unfamiliar to the reader.

A matrix such as SAmatrix results in an Enterprise System Assessment (ESA). The ESA assesses the enterprise environment of an organization, determines if the resources of the organization are at risk, and provides information to steer a course of action to maintain or improve administration practices. The ESA supports the assertion that systems in an organization are at risk if any one of the key administration areas (primary variables) is neglected. The ESA identifies the areas in an enterprise system that require more system administration support and measures the risk of problems due to neglect in the identified areas. Problems caused by inadequate system administration services can range from the improper manipulation of data to unpredictable system crashes.

The initial ESA establishes the baseline that identifies the operational needs of the organization. This baseline, in turn, provides a benchmark for measuring the effectiveness of the chosen course of action.

Develop a Model

Over time, standard system administration practices have evolved from what government and industry expects of its information systems. From these acceptable practices, an administrative model can be developed that can be applied to a large range of organizations. System administration standards and practices are determined by an organization's system administrators. You already may have identified those used in your organization and created a model. If not, don't wait any longer. Before going on to develop a matrix for your organization, finalize your system administration model.

Here is the model used to develop SAmatrix:

Module 1: Software Administration

    1A: Procedures to maintain and tune the operating system.

    1B: Procedures to maintain and tune software applications

    1C: Procedures to measure software application performance.

    1D: Procedures to maintain operating system processes.

Module 2: Hardware Administration

    2A: Procedures to troubleshoot hardware faults.

    2B: Procedures to provide service and support.

    2C: Procedures to measure hardware performance.

    2D: Procedures to add and delete system peripherals.

    2E: Procedures to powerup and powerdown the system

Module 3: Network Administration

    3A: Procedures to provide network services to users.

    3B: Procedures to evaluate network performance.

Module 4: Security Administration

    4A: Procedures to ensure accuracy and integrity of the operating system and software applications.

    4B: Procedures to ensure data and system reliability.

    4C: Procedures to ensure access control.

    4D: Procedures to ensure information privacy.

    4E: Procedures to control the physical environment.

    4F: Procedures to implement and control automated tasks.

Module 5: Operations Administration
    5A: Procedures to handle user requests.
    5B: Procedures to monitor and maintain the system configuration.
    5C: Procedures to deliver information services to users.
    5D: Policies for data ownership.
    5E: Qualified systems personnel

The tasks prescribed by UNIX training and expected DP operations can be condensed and placed in a matrix, like that illustrated in Table 11.1, to see how the standard practices fit into your system administration model. In addition to the Task heading, the headings in this matrix are the five modules of the system administrative model: software administration (SA), hardware administration (HA), network administration (NA), security administration (CA), and operations administration (OA).

Table 11.1 System administration matrix.

Task	SA	HA	NA	SA	OA
System components		X	X	X	X
Powering down system		X		X	X
Powering up system		X		X	X
System backups	X			X	X
System restores	X			X	X
File system maintenance	X			X	X
File system structure	X			X	X
Database structure	X			X	X
Database maintenance	X			X	X
Disk structure	X	X		X	X
Disk maintenance	X	X		X	X
Physical connections	X	X	X	X	X
Peripheral services	X	X	X	X	X
Process maintenance	X			X	X
User access	X			X	X
Install new software	X			X	X
Personnel				X	X
DP management				X	X

Operations

The prominent feature of the matrix is that all aspects of required system administrative practices are included in modules 4 and 5, security administration and operations administration. Security relates to the reliability, integrity, and availability of the system and therefore pertains to the physical environment of the system, the type of system used, and access and controls to the hardware and software. The integration of these properties culminates in a computer security plan and a disaster recovery plan.

Software administration (Module 1) pertains to the maintenance of all software on the system. This includes the UNIX operating system and the BrandX database applications. System files and database backups are necessary to ensure the integrity and availability of the data. Restore procedures ensure that this data can be put back onto a system if the software is corrupted or deleted and must be tested. In the UNIX world, such utilities as cpio and tar are used to backup and restore files and directories. BrandX database administrators use the BrandX dbback utility for database backups and restdb for database restores. In addition, the operating system provides the necessary services to connect peripheral devices, run processes, create and delete file systems, and set tunable operating system parameters that allow the software to interact with the hardware and the user. The BrandX database utilities provide a means to check the status of the database, manipulate database environment variables, enable database security, and use features to rebuild damaged database entities such a b-tree indices and hash tables.

Hardware administration (Module 2) requires that the system administrator understand the hardware components of the system, how those components are interconnected, and how to diagnose hardware problems. The ability to troubleshoot a system enables the system administrator to quickly respond to crashes or the unavailability of a system component. In addition, the system administrator must also know who to contact for service and support when the resources at hand are inadequate to solve the hardware problem.

Network administration (Module 3) is closely connected to all other modules of the system. Networks can be viewed as peripheral to a system or as a system unto themselves. Nonetheless, networks are an area of major concern requiring their own particular brand of systems support. Networks deliver communications services that can range from a simple two-node LAN to a large-scale network environment. In the assessed environment, networking issues may range from the simple 9,600bps short-haul direct connections to LAN and WAN technologies.

Design a Survey

The actual implementation of procedures outlined in the model can vary with the physical locations of the organization. Therefore, the model must include specific tasks and practices dictated by the organization's particular information systems environment. You identify these variations with the survey instrument used to make the

ESA. The survey tests the availability of a service (a service being any service task provided by a systems administrator) and determines the status of the enterprise-wide information system as it relates to the established model.

Planning

Entire books are written about survey design and questionnaire construction, but some guidelines are common to all. An effective survey must have an objective and a goal; that is, you must know why you need it and what you need to learn from it. In the case of the initial survey, you need the survey of system administration practices to establish a baseline of activities that can act as a benchmark against which improvements can be measured. In addition, you need to identify the variations between the current system administration practices and the ideal model. Later surveys will be needed to learn whether a course of action resulted in improvement over the previous assessment and to identify variation from the ideal model.

In addition to the objective and goal, before designing the survey you must know:

- What will be done with the information after it is collected and analyzed?

    Although SAmatrix and other tools for automating the data gathering process can reduce the time and effort invested, the workload required to create and administer a survey and analyze the results can be great. Don't invest the time and effort if the findings will not elicit constructive action.

- What is the target group?

    Only the intended audience for the survey, experienced system administrators, can give valid responses to the questions. Experienced system administrators have the knowledge necessary to conduct a valid assessment with sufficient scope and representation of the content area.

- Will the entire group be surveyed or a sample of the group?

    Sample only when circumstances prevent a complete census. Circumstances preventing a complete census can include complexity of the assessment instrument, data collection method, geographical location of the system administrators, limited time frame, or limited budget. When sampling, use a methodology that produces a representative sample of the target group.

- How will the data be collected?

    A survey delivered and returned by way of e-mail, for example, has different design requirements than one administered over a browser-based form delivered on an intranet Web site. The answer to this question will affect the design of the physical product.

- How will the data be analyzed?

    Again, the answer will affect the design of the physical product.

Operations

Answering these questions before designing the survey can save time and effort and result in an assessment tool that provides a more accurate picture of the system administration needs of the enterprise.

Composing the Questionnaire

The questions needed to assess enterprise system administration support, although numerous, are not complicated. They require no opinions, only the special knowledge of the system administrators. They ask what technology is in use, what services are offered, and how often these services are rendered. The checklist-type questionnaire can be effective for gathering the information needed for the assessment. The challenge when composing the questions is ensuring their usefulness and completeness.

Each question must support the objective and goal of the survey; that is, it must provide information useful in establishing the baseline of system administration practices or help identify variations from the model. Each question must be worded to gather a specific piece of information or related pieces. For example, the question "How do you feel about the quality of the servers at company XYZ?" would elicit no quantifiable data useful for assessing the risk of network hardware failure, even if a checklist of possible answers were provided. Although the answer might contribute to a measure of system administrator satisfaction, it does not support the objective of establishing a baseline of practices or the goal of identifying variations from the ideal. Questions such as "How many hours of unscheduled downtime do you experience each month?" along with a checklist of ranges of time provides quantities that can reveal whether or not a vulnerability exists in that area. It supports the objective of establishing a baseline (company XYZ routinely experiences x hours of unscheduled downtime), and it identifies a variation from the model (the model experiences y hours of unscheduled downtime).

The questions on the survey must be complete; that is, they must solicit all the information needed to make an accurate assessment of the enterprise. Without a complete picture of the system administration function within the enterprise, the final assessment of risk can be dangerously wrong or, at best, misleading.

You may want to compose a document that gives background information on the assessment questions, such as the objective of the question, examples of compliance, or a sample response. The background document provides a system administrator or system manager with a common reference. It helps them to understand the meaning of a question and whether or not the system complies. It also helps to identify associated areas in which the system does or does not comply. This can vary between environments, so it is up to the organization to implement a standardized assessment. If assessment and risk analysis is already in place, you can break your assessment down into the appropriate data format for SAmatrix.

You can adapt the survey to a particular environment, such as non-UNIX, but it must be made relevant to the organization's needs and the technology it uses. It must be at least as detailed and in-depth as the one presented in this chapter to adequately provide meaningful results, useful for establishing a level of system administration performance and expected practice. The survey provided assumes that an organization may have rather homogeneous applications running in a distributed enterprise-wide environment.

System administrators are human beings. When formulating questions, consider the needs of the people you are asking to answer the questions. To motivate these human beings to willingly complete the survey, the questions must be interesting, convenient to answer, nonthreatening, and attractively formatted. Support by upper management and the organization as a whole is also important to obtaining good results.

The SAmatrix Survey

The major variables in this assessment are the five modules of the system administrative model: Software Administration (SA), Hardware Administration (HA), Network Administration (NA), Security Administration (CA), and Operations Administration (OA). The relationship of the survey to the variables is provided in Table 11.2. From the survey response, a correlation can be made between system administration activities and the administration model.

Table 11.2   Instrument questions and model module.

Instrument question number	*Relevant model module*
9	1, 3, 5
11a	5
11b	4, 5
11c	5
11d	1
11f	2
11g–i	1, 3, 5
11j–k	1, 3, 4, 5
11l–m	3, 5
11n–o	1, 3, 5
11p–q	3, 5
11r–s	1, 3, 5
11t	1, 2, 3, 4, 5
11u–w	1, 3, 5
11x–y	1, 2, 3, 4, 5

Operations

A customized survey must show consistency of results. The assessment instrument presented here was checked for reliability by evaluating how well the content and wording of the questions on the survey fit into the overall scope of the survey, their potential for eliciting the required information, and their acceptability to the target audience.

Table 11.2 lists the relevant modules that certain questions on the survey relate to, based on the matrix in Table 11.1. Questions 1, 2, 3, 4, 5, 6, 8, and 10 were used to establish the environment of the organization being surveyed. Question 1 relates directly to the UNIX environment. If a site does not have UNIX-based machines, the survey advances to question 31 to determine the extent of automation services within the organization. Questions 32–39 deal directly with operations administration to determine the technical expertise and background of the person completing the survey. This is important because technical expertise and knowledge of system administration will help to ensure that the system is adequately supported. Technical staff members or a team of system administrators and managers would be able to complete this self-assessment effectively. As noted earlier, 41 sites were assessed in the test case.

Table 11.2 (continued)

Instrument question number	Relevant model module
11z–aa	1, 3, 5
11ab	1, 2, 3, 4, 5
11ac	1, 2, 3, 5
11ad	1, 2, 3, 4, 5
12	3, 5
13	1, 3, 4, 5
14–15	3, 5
16	1, 3, 5
17	3, 5
18	1, 3, 5
20	2, 3, 5
21–22	1, 3, 5
23	1, 2, 3, 5
24	1, 3, 5
25	1, 3, 4, 5
32–34	5

System Administration Assessment Survey

1. Are your systems primarily UNIX?

[___] Yes
[___] No (Skip to Question 31.)

2. How many UNIX-based servers do you administer? (Check only one.)

[___] 1
[___] 2
[___] 3
[___] 4
[___] 5
[___] More than 5

3. Are your UNIX servers networked?

[___] Yes
[___] No

4. What hardware technology is your UNIX system(s) based on? (Check all that apply)

[___] a. Intel 386
[___] b. Intel 486
[___] c. Pentium
[___] d. RISC
[___] e. Other_____

5. How many users have access to your UNIX system(s)? (Check only one.)

[___] 1–20
[___] 20–40
[___] 40–60
[___] 60–80
[___] 80–100
[___] 100+

6. What company UNIX applications do you use at your site? (Check all that apply.)

[___] a. Financial Management System (FMS)
[___] b. Decision Support Reporting (DSR)
[___] c. Public User Access to Domain Services (PUADS)
[___] d. Other_____

7. What is your primary utility for doing system backups? (Check only one.)

[___] combkup
[___] cpio
[___] tar
[___] Other_____

Operations

8. What is your primary UNIX DBMS? (Check only one.)

[___] BrandX
[___] INFORMIX
[___] ORACLE
[___] Other_____

9. If you use a BrandX database application please check the following functions you perform at your location:

[___] a. Rebuild hash tables and b-tree indices.
[___] b. Set up database executables and register them with the database.
[___] c. Set up group user access to the database using grpmnt.
[___] d. Set up BrandX menus.
[___] e. Run appl programs.
[___] f. Perform dbback functions on a regular basis.
[___] g. Perform restdb functions as needed.
[___] h. Other_____

10. What network services do you provide to users? (Check all that apply.)

[___] a. LAN Ethernet connections
[___] b. UUCP
[___] c. Modem (dial-in, dial-out) other than UUCP
[___] d. Null modem/direct connect
[___] e. WAN
[___] f. Other_____

11. In providing system administration functions please check all areas below that pertain to services you or your systems staff provide: (Check all that apply.)

[___] a. Answer user questions regarding system functions.
[___] b. Evaluate user needs on a regular basis to better deliver company system services.
[___] c. Provide training support to users on an as-needed basis.
[___] d. Troubleshoot UNIX software problems.
[___] e. Interconnect your user office environments to your UNIX services.
[___] f. Troubleshoot UNIX hardware problems.
[___] g. Do file system backups on a regular basis.
[___] h. Do backups of database applications on a regular basis.
[___] i. Maintain backup media to completely restore the operating system.
[___] j. Set up user log-in accounts.
[___] k. Force users to change passwords on a regular basis.
[___] l. Have a written systems security plan.
[___] m. Have a written disaster recovery plan.
[___] n. Store backup media in an offsite location. (Offsite is to be interpreted as a separate building.)

[___] o. Store onsite backup media in a media storage room separate from computer facility.

[___] p. Maintain a system backup log.

[___] q. Maintain a system error reporting log.

[___] r. Monitor the permissions of systems files.

[___] s. Monitor the passwd file for unauthorized superuser access.

[___] t. Operate and maintain a crontab file to automate system tasks.

[___] u. Monitor the system date function for accuracy and time changes.

[___] v. Mount and unmount file systems.

[___] w. Set up new file systems.

[___] x. Maintain the inittab and gettydef files.

[___] y. Set up and troubleshoot printers.

[___] z. Do kernel reconfigurations, as necessary.

[___] aa. Install new software releases of database applications received from the HQ.

[___] ab. Set up terminal devices.

[___] ac. Set up data communications services.

[___] ad. Have completed a risk analysis of your facility.

[___] ae. Other_____

12. Have you ever had to restore your UNIX operating system?

[___] Yes

[___] No

13. Indicate which system resources you monitor. (Check all that apply.)

[___] a. Database size

[___] b. User usage

[___] c. File system size

[___] d. CPU utilization

[___] e. Other_____

14. How often do you monitor system resources? (Check only one.)

[___] Daily

[___] Weekly

[___] Monthly

[___] As needed

[___] Do not monitor system resources

[___] Other_____

15. What formal training do you supply to your users? (Check all that apply.)

[___] a. UNIX

[___] b. Security

[___] c. Database applications

[___] d. Other_____

Operations

16. How often do you provide UNIX training to your users? (Check only one.)

[___] Daily
[___] Weekly
[___] Monthly
[___] Annually
[___] As needed
[___] Do not provide UNIX training
[___] Other_____

17. How often do you provide security training to your users? (Check only one.)

[___] Monthly
[___] Biannually
[___] Annually
[___] As needed
[___] Do not supply security training
[___] Other_____

18. How often do you provide database application training to your users? (Check only one.)

[___] Daily
[___] Weekly
[___] Monthly
[___] Annually
[___] As needed
[___] Do not provide database application training
[___] Other_____

19. What is the primary source where systems personnel receive systems administration training? (Check only one.)

[___] Company training center
[___] Prior experience (job or academic)
[___] Local systems staff
[___] Training vendors
[___] Other_____

20. What procedures do you implement to maintain hardware? (Check all that apply.)

[___] a. Regular cleaning of tape drives
[___] b. Regular cleaning of disk drives.
[___] c. Check performance of UNIX server.
[___] d. Check network performance.
[___] e. Check for loose cable connections.
[___] f. Perform system shutdowns and reboots.
[___] g. Other_____

21. What procedures do you establish and implement to maintain software? (Check all that apply.)

[___] a. Check database statistics
[___] b. Full system backups
[___] c. Database backups
[___] d. Run `fsck` on all file systems
[___] e. Other_____

22. How often do you implement your backup procedures? (Check only one.)

[___] Daily
[___] Weekly
[___] Monthly
[___] As needed
[___] Do not implement
[___] Other_____

23. How often do you run `fsck` on your systems? (Check only one.)

[___] Daily
[___] Weekly
[___] Monthly
[___] As needed
[___] Do not run
[___] Other_____

24. How often do you check your database statistics? (Check only one.)

[___] Daily
[___] Weekly
[___] Monthly
[___] As needed
[___] Do not check
[___] Other_____

25. Have you established any automated procedures that include: (Check all that apply.)

[___] a. Automated backups
[___] b. Providing security checks (i.e., unauthorized logins, bad passwords, etc.)
[___] c. Logging off users after a specified time of inactivity
[___] d. Performing routine sys admin tasks
[___] e. Other_____

Operations

26. How many hours of scheduled downtime do you experience each month? (Check only one.)

[___] None
[___] 1–5 hours
[___] 6–10 hours
[___] 11–15 hours
[___] 16–20 hours
[___] More than 20 hours

27. How many hours of unscheduled downtime do you experience each month? (Check only one.)

[___] None
[___] 1–5 hours
[___] 6–10 hours
[___] 11–15 hours
[___] 16–20 hours
[___] More than 20 hours

28. What do you consider your average number of system crashes per year?

[___] 0
[___] 1
[___] 2
[___] 3
[___] 4
[___] 5
[___] 6–12
[___] More than 12

29. How many Personnel records do your automated systems support? _____

30. How many Customer records do your automated systems support? _____

31. Do you participate in establishing your information systems budget?

[___] Yes
[___] No

32. Do you procure automation equipment and supplies for your location?

[___] Yes
[___] No

33. In managing your computer resources please check all areas you are currently involved with:

[___] a. Facility design
[___] b. Equipment installation
[___] c. Determining use of automation resources
[___] d. Establishing automation operations procedures
[___] e. Other_____

34. From whom do you primarily receive automation support services? (Check only one.)

[___] Company support center
[___] Company headquarters
[___] Vendors
[___] Other_____

35. How many years of systems administration experience do you have? (Check only one.)

[___] None
[___] 0–1 years
[___] 2–4 years
[___] 5–7 years
[___] 7–9 years
[___] 10 or more years

36. How long have you been with the organization? (Check only one.)

[___] 0–1 years
[___] 2–4 years
[___] 5–7 years
[___] 7–9 years
[___] 10 or more years

37. What is your job title:_____

38. What is your educational background?

[___] a. High school graduate
[___] b. Some college
[___] c. Associate degree
[___] d. Bachelor's degree
[___] e. Graduate or professional degree
[___] f. Technical certification:_____
[___] g. Other_____

Operations

39. If you attended college, what was your major?

Undergraduate degree major:_____

Graduate degree major:_____

Thank you for completing this assessment. Please leave any additional comments you may have on the space provided below (additional space on the back of this page may also be used).

Administer the Survey

Theoretically, before beginning the hard work of creating the survey instrument, you must answer the question, "How will the survey be administered?" and "How will the data be analyzed?" The answers guide your choices for formatting the physical product. If you have done the legwork suggested before designing and composing the survey and the survey is a physical product, it can be distributed to the target audience, the system administrators.

System administrators are human beings. Therefore, you will need to solve the problem common to all surveys, achieving the highest possible response rate. This may not be a problem if the number of system administrators being surveyed is small enough to allow personal contact. However, if the target group is too large for personal contact, you can increase response rate by providing advance publicity for the survey, making the experience as rewarding as possible, and following up after a period of time with a reminder to respond.

Advanced publicity should describe:

- The benefits of taking the survey
- The purpose of the survey
- Methods to be used for data collection and sampling
- An overview of the contents
- Reassurance that the survey will not be difficult to take
- When it will be distributed
- When results will be reported

To make the survey experience as rewarding as possible, include a cover letter that repeats the messages in the advance publicity, emphasizing the importance of their participation, and thank the respondents in advance for their cooperation. In addition, follow the guidelines for composing the questions by making the instrument interesting, convenient to take, nonthreatening, and physically attractive.

Evaluate the Results

Before designing and writing a survey, you must answer the question, "How will the data be analyzed?" SAmatrix can save you some time and effort by analyzing the data gathered from the survey. The program is based on a more robust statistical application of system administration practices using a statistical analysis package to analyze data gathered from a manual survey. The simplification in SAmatrix reduces the statistical analysis to a set of rules that can be applied to the data provided. The analysis of data can then provide feedback to the user on whether or not the system is at risk. That is, as the risk to a system increases, the integrity and reliability of a system decreases. The methodology used in SAmatrix was successfully applied to a distributed system of national scope.

When the program is loaded with a properly formatted database file, you can immediately conduct an analysis of the data by clicking on the Analysis menu and selecting either a module to analyze or selecting System to analyze the entire system. The analysis depends totally on the quality of the input provided.

Module assessment will ONLY show compliance of the prime module assessments. Figure 11.1 shows an example of a module assessment from SAmatrix. A system assessment will show compliance of the entire system, including prime assessment areas and related compliance modules. Figure 11.2 shows an example of a system assessment from SAmatrix. Note, all fields contain 0 because the sample database contained no data.

Figure 11.1   A model assessment.

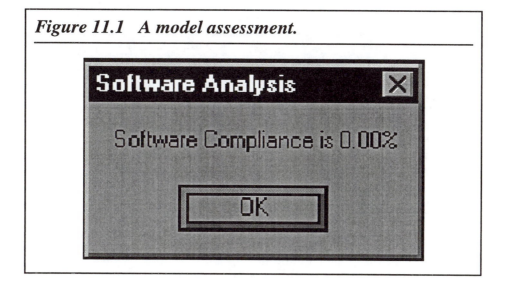

Operations

Figure 11.2   A system assessment.

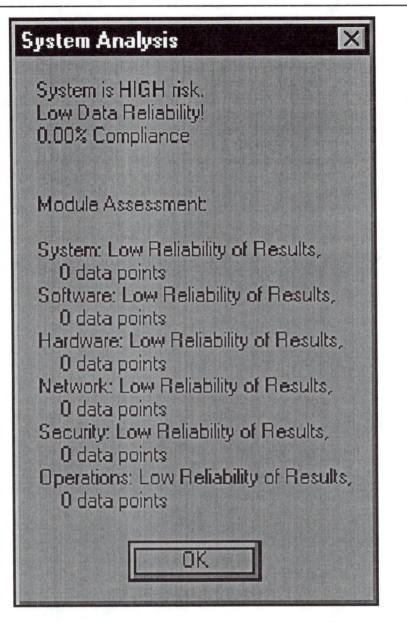

SAmatrix Data Format

An SAmatrix database file contains a matrix of information gathered with the survey in simple ASCII text. Each record contains seven data elements separated by a line break. The fields in each record must be in the following order:

- Assessment
- Module
- Software Compliance
- Hardware Compliance
- Network Compliance
- Security Compliance
- Operations Compliance

The values that can be assigned to these data elements are:

- Assessment = A text string of an assessment question.
- Module = a character value of S (Software), H (Hardware), N (Network), C (Security), and O (Operations).
- Compliance Data = either a 0 or a 1, where 1 = TRUE and 0 = FALSE

    For example, the last record in the sample is:

Do you provide security training to new users? (Assessment)
C (Module)
0 (Software compliance)
0 (Hardware Compliance)
0 (Network Compliance)
0 (Security Compliance)
0 (Operations Compliance)

Here is a three-question sample from samatrix.adm. In this example, all compliance values equal zero.

```
-------Sample records from samatrix.adm--------
Do you provide security training to new users?
C
0
0
0
0
0
```

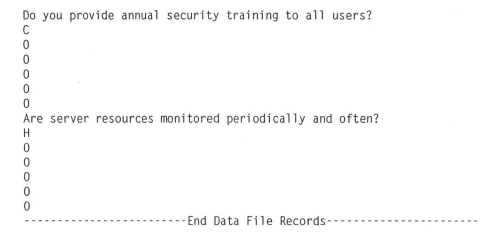

```
Do you provide annual security training to all users?
C
0
0
0
0
0
Are server resources monitored periodically and often?
H
0
0
0
0
0
-----------------------End Data File Records----------------------
```

Each assessment question must include a module. This makes the assessment question a PRIME question for the module. In the above example, the module assessment is for Hardware. The Hardware compliance value is 0 indicating that the administration of this resource is NOT in compliance. If this assessment were in compliance, the database record would read:

```
------------Hardware Assessment Record in Compliance----------
Are server resources monitored periodically and often?
H
0
1
0
0
0
-------------------------------------------------------------------
```

The above record now indicates that the system complies with the assessment question.

An assessment may affect other areas than its primary module. When the assessment affects more than one module, the person doing the assessment may want to assign a value to the record to indicate that a procedure for the additional module(s) is in place and enforced. In the above example, the question "Are server resources monitored periodically and often?" is also an operations issue. To show compliance in both the hardware and operations modules the record would now look like:

```
-------Data Record Showing Hardware and Operations Compliance--------
Are server resources monitored periodically and often?
H
0
1
0
0
1
-----------------------------------------------------------------
```

Statistical Tests

It may help if you understand how SAmatrix results were analyzed during the development stage. To gain some meaningful results from the survey, correlation methods were employed to relate the results of the survey to the administrative model using Pearson r correlation statistics. The correlation results were used to test the research hypotheses using t-test statistics. The hypothesis was tested by correlating and checking the results of the instrument to the major variables. Computer-based research methodologies were employed using the SPSS (Statistical Package for the Social Sciences) statistical software package. (However, any decent statistical package can be used to provide the needed results.) The results of the tests provide a quantitative picture of how the information systems of the organization as a whole perform in relation to the administrative model.

The significance of the correlation coefficient r was tested using t-test statistics. Two-tailed significance was used for the assessment assuming the null hypothesis is rejected with a 95 percent level of confidence ($\alpha = 0.05$). The null hypothesis in this case is that the organization's information systems are not at risk.

What to Expect

An ideal operation would be 100 percent compliant in all model modules. Greater than 90 percent compliance indicates that some minor services are missing but puts a system at low risk. Less than 90 percent but more than 80 percent indicates that attention to the overall aspects of the model are provided but that gaps in major areas undoubtedly exist and can place a system at risk. Any evaluative score less than 80 percent indicates that the lack of proper administration for a module exists throughout the organization or area assessed.

Operations

Current research does not provide an accepted degree of compliance to any administrative model; therefore, the assessments made during development of SAmatrix attempt to quantify practice to modeled operations. It was expected that the organization's information systems would not be compliant with the system administrative model. It was also expected that the reliability of the organization's systems were directly dependent on the degree of compliance to the administrative model. To have a reliable system, each location needs to show that it provides system administration services for each module. Because the model supports all aspects of system administration, it is reasonable to expect that overall, the organization should rate 90 percent or better with all of the major variables. This would indicate that attention to all areas of system administration have been addressed to a significant degree.

Chapter 12

The SAmatrix Case Study

This chapter presents a description and interpretation of the results of the case study done during development of SAmatrix.

In the actual case study, 50 assessment instruments were sent to 50 locations out of a total population of 94 sites within the organization. Forty-one responses to the instrument were received representing a return of 82 percent of the sample population. Four responses were rejected in whole or in part for invalid data or refusal by the respondent to participate in the study. The valid returns evaluated for the study consisted of 37 cases or 74 percent of the sample population. This compares to a return rate of 70 percent, which was conducted in a pilot study.

The results to each survey question appear in Appendix A. Question numbers and variables reported in Appendix A are matched to the instrument questions in Chapter 11. An SPSS data file and the associated variables applied to each question was constructed and the appropriate t-tests and Pearson r statistics were run against this data to determine linear relationships of the variables and reliability of the instrument. The data file appears in Appendix B and illustrates the SPSS script used. The t-test results are in Appendix C.

Matrix Results

The matrix of Table 11.1 was applied to the assessment results. The questions were inserted into the relationship model of Table 11.2. Questions were considered affirmative (Yes) when a task or response on the survey was checked. When tasks or

Operations

responses were blank, the answer was considered negative (No). A few questions were graded as affirmative if the response was in a specified range.

Questions where responses were dependent on a range of responses were:

14. How often to you monitor system resources? Acceptable responses were Daily, Weekly, or Monthly.

16. How often do you provide UNIX training to your users? Acceptable responses were Daily, Weekly, Monthly, Annually, or As needed.

Table 12.1 Software administration module.

Value	Freq	Percent	Valid percent	Cum percent
0.500	1	2.4	2.7	2.7
0.686	2	4.9	5.4	8.1
0.714	1	2.4	2.7	10.8
0.742	1	2.4	2.7	13.5
0.743	2	4.9	5.4	18.9
0.771	1	2.4	2.7	21.6
0.800	6	14.6	16.2	37.8
0.828	2	4.9	5.4	43.2
0.829	3	7.3	8.1	51.4
0.857	2	4.9	5.4	56.8
0.886	4	9.8	10.8	67.6
0.912	2	4.9	5.4	73.0
0.914	3	7.3	8.1	81.1
0.943	6	14.6	16.2	97.3
1.000	1	2.4	2.7	100.0
9999	4	9.8	MISSING	
TOTAL	41	100.0	100.0	

Table 12.2 SA statistics.

Mean	0.838	Median	0.829		
Mode	0.800	Std Dev	0.098	Variance	0.010
Valid Cases	37	Missing Cases	4		

17. How often do you provide security training to your users? The acceptable responses to this question included Monthly, Biannually, and Annually.

18. How often do you provide database application training to your users? The acceptable responses were Daily, Weekly, Monthly, Annually, or As needed.

22. How often do you implement your backup procedures? The acceptable responses were Daily or Weekly.

23. How often do you run `fsck` on your systems? The acceptable responses were Daily or Weekly.

24. How often do you check your database statistics? Acceptable responses were Daily, Weekly, or Monthly.

For the organization to qualify for analysis of its matrix modules, except for network administration, it had to answer yes to question 1 (Are your systems primarily UNIX?). To qualify for analysis of the network administration module, a site had to answer yes to either question 3 (Are your UNIX servers networked?), 10a–10f (What network services do you provide to users?), or 11e ([Do you] interconnect your user office environments to your UNIX services?). These questions help determine the environment at the specified location because not all sites were considered mature in their implementation of the organization's technological infrastructure.

The matrix results are derived from Tables 11.1 and 11.2. This derivation starts with the module categories from Table 11.1 providing the basis for the instrument questions. Each instrument question was assigned to one or more modules and reported in Table 11.2. Variable names were assigned to each question. Definitions of each variable name are provided in Appendix B. The matrix of Table 11.2 provided an efficient means to cross question assignments with their applicability to the modules of Table 11.1.

The number of variables assigned to Software Administration (SA), Hardware Administration (HA), Security Administration (CA), Network Administration (NA), and Operations Administration (OA) were 35, 14, 60, 16, and 70, respectively. These variable assignments accounted for the maximum number of affirmative answers for each assessed site per module (MAX). Negative responses from each site (NEG) were subtracted from MAX and this result was divided by MAX. In cases where responses to the instrument questions were deemed invalid, the variable MAX had to be adjusted accordingly. The result of equation 1 provided the matrix result value (MATX) for each site per module.

$$(MAX - NEG)/MAX = MATX_{Mocule} \qquad \text{(equation 1)}$$

The matrix results for SA, HA, CA, NA, and OA are located in Tables 12.1, 12.3, 12.5, 12.7 and 12.9. (Tables appear at the end of this chapter.) The statistics on each matrix module are located in Tables 12.2, 12.4, 12.6, 12.8, and 12.10, respectively. The descriptive statistics reported in these tables are mean, median, mode, standard deviation, and variance.

Tables 12.11 and 12.12 include the composite averages of the matrix modules and the statistics on the composite values. The composite values are the overall matrix scores computed as the average of the major variables of SA, HA, CA, NA, and OA. The composite average variable is designated COMP.

Pearson r statistics are used to compare the major variables software administration (SA), hardware administration (HA), security administration (CA), network administration (NA), and operations administration (OA). Table 12.13 illustrates the correlation of the variables to each other and to the composite value. The composite value (COMP) is the score that each case in the sample received based upon its response to the survey instrument.

There are three lines of data for each variable in Table 12.13. The first line is the r correlation coefficient value, the second line indicates the number of valid cases used to calculate r, and the third line is the two-tailed significance value (P) computed at a 95 percent confidence interval. For values of $P = 0.000$, the significance value is less than 0.0005.

Table 12.3   Hardware administration module.

Value	Freq	Percent	Valid percent	Cum percent
0.500	2	4.9	5.4	5.4
0.571	3	7.3	8.1	13.5
0.643	6	14.6	16.2	29.7
0.714	7	14.6	16.2	45.9
0.786	8	19.5	21.6	67.6
0.846	1	2.4	2.7	70.3
0.857	5	12.2	13.5	83.8
0.928	5	12.2	13.5	97.3
1.000	1	2.4	2.7	100.0
9999	4	9.8	MISSING	
TOTAL	41	100.0	100.0	

Table 12.4   HA statistics.

Mean	0.754	Median	0.786		
Mode	0.786	Std Dev	0.129	Variance	0.017
Valid Cases	37	Missing Cases	4		

Table 12.5 Security administration model.

Value	Freq	Percent	Valid percent	Cum percent
0.508	1	2.4	2.7	2.7
0.633	1	2.4	2.7	5.4
0.650	3	7.3	8.1	13.5
0.667	3	7.3	8.1	21.6
0.700	1	2.4	2.7	24.3
0.717	2	4.9	5.4	29.7
0.733	4	9.8	10.8	40.5
0.750	1	2.4	2.7	43.2
0.767	3	7.3	8.1	51.4
0.783	1	2.4	2.7	54.1
0.800	1	2.4	2.7	56.8
0.814	1	2.4	2.7	59.5
0.817	4	9.8	10.8	70.3
0.833	1	2.4	2.7	73.0
0.850	1	2.4	2.7	75.7
0.862	1	2.4	2.7	78.4
0.867	2	4.9	5.4	83.8
0.883	2	4.9	5.4	89.2
0.900	2	4.9	5.4	94.6
0.933	1	2.4	2.7	97.3
0.950	1	2.4	2.7	100.0
9999	4	9.8	MISSING	
TOTAL	41	100.0	100.0	

Table 12.6 CA statistics.

Mean	0.773	Median	0.767		
Mode	0.733	Std Dev	0.098	Variance	0.010
Valid Cases	37	Missing Cases	4		

Operations

The r value of COMP to each of the major variables has a range of 0.7721 to 0.9729, indicating a strong linear relationship.

To test the relationship of COMP to actual system administration practices, the number of responses from the assessment that were regarded as incorrect as determined by the model are indicated in Table 12.14. The statistics of these results are reported in Table 12.15.

A t-test was done to test the null hypothesis by testing the matrix model COMP value to the number of incorrect procedures reported by each site. This test centered around the mean COMP value of 0.781. Of the 37 valid cases, 19 (Group 1) were selected as having a COMP value greater than or equal to the mean, and 18 cases (Group 2) were used having values less than the mean. For Group 1, the mean number of incorrect procedures was 27.21 with a standard deviation of 8.40 and a standard error of 1.93. For Group 2, the mean number of incorrect procedures was 55.83 with a standard deviation of 10.18 and a standard error of 2.40. The pooled variance estimate for 35 degrees of freedom yielded a t-value of –9.35 and a two-tailed significance

Table 12.7   Network administration module.

Value	Freq	Percent	Valid percent	Cum percent
0.500	1	2.4	2.7	2.7
0.563	3	7.3	8.1	10.8
0.625	8	19.5	21.6	32.4
0.688	6	14.6	16.2	48.6
0.750	4	9.8	10.8	59.5
0.813	5	12.2	13.5	73.0
0.875	5	12.2	13.5	86.5
0.938	3	7.3	8.1	94.6
1.000	2	4.9	5.4	100.0
9999	4	9.8	MISSING	
TOTAL	41	100.0	100.0	

Table 12.8   NA statistics.

Mean	0.745	Median	0.750		
Mode	0.625	Std Dev	0.134	Variance	0.018
Valid Cases	37	Missing Cases	4		

value of less than 0.0005 for a 95 percent confidence interval. The F-value for this test was 1.47 with a probability of 0.427. The separate variance estimate of the t-value was also computed for 33.03 degrees of freedom yielding –9.30.

Value	*Freq*	*Percent*	*Valid percent*	*Cum percent*
0.536	1	2.4	2.7	2.7
0.657	1	2.4	2.7	5.4
0.686	2	4.9	5.4	10.8
0.700	1	2.4	2.7	13.5
0.710	1	2.4	2.7	16.2
0.714	1	2.4	2.7	18.9
0.729	1	2.4	2.7	21.6
0.743	2	4.9	5.4	27.0
0.757	2	4.9	5.4	32.4
0.770	1	2.4	2.7	35.1
0.771	2	4.9	5.4	40.5
0.779	1	2.4	2.7	43.2
0.786	2	4.9	5.4	48.6
0.800	2	4.9	5.4	54.1
0.814	3	7.3	8.1	62.2
0.826	2	4.9	5.4	67.6
0.829	1	2.4	2.7	70.3
0.843	1	2.4	2.7	73.0
0.857	2	4.9	5.4	78.4
0.871	1	2.4	2.7	81.1
0.886	1	2.4	2.7	83.8
0.897	1	2.4	2.7	86.5
0.900	2	4.9	5.4	91.9
0.914	2	4.9	5.4	97.3
0.957	1	2.4	2.7	100.0
9999	4	9.8	MISSING	
TOTAL	41	100.0	100.0	

Table 12.9   Operations administration model.

Operations

Table 12.10 OA statistics.

Mean	0.795	Median	0.800		
Mode	0.814	Std Dev	0.085	Variance	0.007
Valid Cases	37	Missing Cases	4		

Table 12.11 Composite matrix module.

Value	Freq	Percent	Valid percent	Cum percent
0.521	1	2.4	2.7	2.7
0.644	1	2.4	2.7	5.4
0.665	1	2.4	2.7	8.1
0.669	1	2.4	2.7	10.8
0.675	2	4.9	5.4	16.2
0.684	1	2.4	2.7	18.9
0.702	1	2.4	2.7	21.6
0.711	2	4.9	5.4	27.0
0.719	1	2.4	2.7	29.7
0.734	1	2.4	2.7	32.4
0.738	1	2.4	2.7	35.1
0.746	1	2.4	2.7	37.8
0.753	1	2.4	2.7	40.5
0.758	1	2.4	2.7	43.2
0.764	1	2.4	2.7	45.9
0.781	1	2.4	2.7	48.6
0.789	1	2.4	2.7	51.4
0.790	1	2.4	2.7	54.1
0.793	1	4.9	5.4	56.8
0.795	1	2.4	2.7	59.5
0.816	1	2.4	2.7	62.2
0.834	2	4.9	5.4	67.6
0.839	1	2.4	2.7	70.3

From the survey results, an overview of system administration can be ascertained when looking at each major administration module. Overall, nearly 44 percent of the sites administer more than three servers per site supporting an average of 1,688 personnel records and a customer base of 11,684 records.

In the area of software administration in such areas such as running `fsck`, checking `dbstats`, doing backups, monitoring file system size, performing shutdowns and reboots, and automating tasks, nearly all of the locations responded to doing these routines. It is noted that nearly one-fourth of the respondents had never done a kernel reconfiguration or set up new file systems on their systems. Nonetheless, 63.4 percent of the respondents indicated that the company support centers are their primary automation support service. The majority of sites also follow company recommendations

Table 12.11 (continued)

Value	Freq	Percent	Valid percent	Cum percent
0.521	1	2.4	2.7	2.7
0.841	1	2.4	2.7	73.0
0.842	1	2.4	2.7	75.7
0.844	1	2.4	2.7	78.4
0.870	1	2.4	2.7	81.1
0.881	1	2.4	2.7	83.8
0.885	1	2.4	2.7	86.5
0.906	1	2.4	2.7	89.2
0.908	1	2.4	2.7	91.9
0.927	1	2.4	2.7	91.6
0.928	1	2.4	2.7	97.3
0.929	1	2.4	2.7	100.0
9999	4	9.8	MISSING	
TOTAL	41	100.0	100.0	

Table 12.12 COMP statistics.

Mean	0.781	Median	0.789		
Mode	0.711	Std Dev	0.094	Variance	0.009
Valid cases	37	Missing cases	4		

Operations

Table 12.13 Pearson r correlation coefficients of major variables.

X	SA	HA	CA	NA	OA	COMP
SA	1.0000	.5331	.8563	.6723	.8188	.8734
	(0)	(37)	(37)	(37)	(37)	(37)
		P = .001	P = .000	P = .000	P = .000	P = .000
HA	.5331	1.0000	.7103	.3952	.6968	.7721
	(37)	(0)	(37)	(37)	(37)	(37)
	P = .001		P = .000	P = .015	P = .000	P = .000
CA	.8563	.7103	1.0000	.7549	.9703	.9729
	(37)	(37)	(0)	(37)	(37)	(37)
	P = .000	P = .000		P = .000	P = .000	P = .000
NA	.6723	.3952	.7549	1.0000	.6908	.8161
	(37)	(37)	(37)	(0)	(37)	(37)
	P = .000	P = .015	P = .000		P = .000	P = .000
OA	.8188	.6968	.9703	.6908	1.0000	.9423
	(37)	(37)	(37)	(37)	(0)	(37)
	P = .000	P = .000	P = .000	P = .000		P = .000
COMP	.8734	.7721	.9729	.8161	.9423	1.0000
	(37)	(37)	(37)	(37)	(37)	(0)
	P = .000	P = .000	P = .000	P = .000	P = .000	

Table 12.14 Number of incorrect procedures reported.

Value	Freq	Percent	Valid percent	Cum percent
11.00	1	2.4	2.7	2.7
12.00	1	2.4	2.7	5.4
17.00	1	2.4	2.7	8.1
19.00	1	2.4	2.7	10.8
22.00	1	2.4	2.7	13.5
25.00	2	4.9	5.4	18.9
26.00	1	2.4	2.7	21.6

to support their BrandX (i.e., ORACLE, Informix, etc.) database applications, which are considered the primary UNIX database for the organization's systems. In addition, only 12.2 percent of the sites use the company-supplied backup software combkup, whereas 78.1 percent of the organizational sites opted to use the standard UNIX cpio utility or some other option. Respondents using the BrandX vendor-supplied dbback/

Value	*Freq*	*Percent*	*Valid percent*	*Cum percent*
27.00	1	2.4	2.7	24.3
28.00	1	2.4	2.7	27.0
29.00	1	2.4	2.7	29.7
31.00	2	4.9	5.4	35.1
32.00	2	4.9	5.4	40.5
33.00	1	2.4	2.7	43.2
34.00	1	2.4	2.7	45.9
40.00	1	2.4	2.7	48.6
41.00	1	2.4	2.7	51.4
42.00	2	4.9	5.4	56.8
44.00	1	2.4	2.7	59.5
48.00	2	4.9	5.4	64.9
50.00	1	2.4	2.7	67.6
52.00	1	2.4	2.7	70.3
54.00	1	2.4	2.7	73.0
57.00	2	4.9	5.4	78.4
58.00	1	2.4	2.7	81.1
59.00	2	4.9	5.4	86.5
62.00	1	2.4	2.7	89.2
63.00	1	2.4	2.7	91.9
64.00	1	2.4	2.7	94.6
65.00	1	2.4	2.7	97.3
83.00	1	2.4	2.7	100.0
9999	4	9.8	MISSING	
TOTAL	41	100.0	100.0	

Table 12.14 (continued)

Operations

restdb database functions to backup and restore their BrandX (RDBMS) applications stood at 80 percent. Overall, 78 percent of the organization received a software module matrix value of 80 percent (0.800) or greater. One location received a perfect 100 percent (1.000).

In hardware administration, all sites reported that they troubleshoot hardware problems and set up terminal devices. In maintaining hardware, a significant majority of the sites regularly clean their tape drives; however, 41.5 percent do not check the performance of their servers, 73.2 percent do not clean disk drives, 85.7 percent of the sites use an Intel 486 platform that uses a disk recovery procedure, 46.3 percent do not check for loose cable connections, and 61 percent do not check on their network performance. Only 32 percent of the sites received a hardware module matrix value of 80 percent or better. One site received a 100 percent score.

Security administration results report that 22 percent of the sites do not force users to change passwords on a regular basis, 31.7 percent do not monitor system file permissions, and 26.8 percent do not check for unauthorized superuser access.

In the area of disaster recovery all respondents reported that they maintain backup media to restore their operating system and have backups to restore their database; 85.4 percent also reported that they store backup media offsite, 29.3 percent do not have a written disaster recovery plan, and 41.5 percent store their onsite backup media in the same room as the computer facility.

The security administration module results indicate that the majority of valid respondents (46.3 percent) do not have a written security plan, and 80.5 percent have not completed a risk analysis of their facility. In addition, only 4.9 percent of the sites provide annual security training, 36.6 percent do not provide any security training, and 48.8 percent provide this training only as needed. Only 46 percent of the sites responding received a security module matrix value of 80 percent or more.

Network administration in assessed sites is varied. LANs, UUCP modem connections, and other modem connections comprise a significant part of the site environment. A significant number of the locations set up their own data communications services. In network administration, 26.9 percent of the sites report four or more system crashes per year. Only 41 percent of the sites received a network module matrix value of 80 percent or better. Two sites scored a perfect 100 percent.

Table 12.15   Incorrect procedures table.

Mean	41.135	Median	41.000		
Mode	25.000	Std Dev	17.165	Variance	294.620
Valid Cases	37	Missing Cases	4		

The majority of the respondents were responsible for budgeting for equipment, procuring equipment, facility design, establishing procedures, and determining how automation resources were to be used. Within operations administration, 51 percent of the sites scored 80 percent or higher on their operations matrix module. Overall, 41 percent of the assessed locations received a composite matrix value of 80 percent or greater. Of those, 14 percent received a value of 90 percent or above. On the other end of the organization's system administration spectrum, 16 percent of the sites received a composite matrix value under 70 percent. The under 70 percent value for software administration was for 8 percent of the sites: 30 percent for hardware administration, 22 percent for security administration, 49 percent in network administration, and 11 percent in operations administration.

Implications

The results of this ESA assessment indicate that from a systems-level perspective, the organization's resources are at risk because the proper system administration practices are not followed in all locations of the enterprise. Managing the organization's information systems has become the responsibility of the local system administrator with support provided by the company support centers. The model employed in this study was designed to show that systems personnel provide support to computer hardware, software, networks, security, and operations. The support of these systems provides services to the organization's users (i.e., clerks, management, support staff, etc.) and protects a significant corporate resource. The significance of that resource is that millions of dollars of information technology is used to control millions of dollars worth of information through the customer information base.

The null hypothesis (H0) of this study stated that the organization's systems are not at risk by providing adequate system administration practices to key administration areas. In contrast, it was asserted that the assessed systems are at risk if key administration procedures are neglected. To accept or reject the null hypothesis, the correlation of the major variables to the model matrix were examined.

From the t-test, you can conclude that there is a difference between the matrix COMP value and the number of incorrect responses reported. The result indicates that the number of incorrect procedures followed increases as COMP values decrease; thus, the null hypothesis is rejected and our assessment accepts the statement that the organization's systems are at risk.

You can also conclude through the assessment that known data processing standards are not followed by the organization. In particular, procedures recommended by the company during system administration training are primarily software practices to maintain the operating system and database. Low matrix scores in software administration are due to sites that are neglecting procedures to maintain their operating system, database, and other software applications. The significance of incorrect

Operations

responses for each major variable, with the exception of HA, for each matrix module indicates increasing matrix module scores with a decreasing number of incorrect responses. The t-test values that support the results are located in Appendix C and are centered around the mean value for each major variable.

This assessment indicates that there are some severe gaps in system administration practices within the assessed organization. In the area of software administration, the organization did very well overall. Of concern is that nearly one-fourth of the respondents had never done a kernel reconfiguration or set up new file systems on their systems. UNIX kernel rebuilds are a necessity when it comes to performance tuning or installing new device drivers. It is possible that those who have not done these tasks rely on the company support centers for these services. The majority of sites also follow company recommendations to support their BrandX database applications that are considered the primary UNIX database on the organization's systems. As previously noted, the results indicated that most of the sites have opted not to use the company-supplied backup software for system backups, relying mostly on standard UNIX archiving utilities. More than 80 percent of the respondents used the vendor-supplied BrandX dbback/restdb database functions to backup and restore their BrandX applications.

Hardware administration practices indicated some inconsistencies. Although all sites reported that they troubleshoot hardware problems and set up terminal devices, maintenance practices varied. For instance, a large majority reported that they clean their tape drives, but only a small percentage reported cleaning disk drives. Cleaning disk drives is irrelevant for some of the hardware platforms, but because a significant number of sites use Intel 486 platforms, the reliability of system recovery using boot disks comes into question. Additional hardware reliability questions are raised because there is a significant number of sites that do not regularly check for loose cable connections or, to a greater degree, hardware performance. This may imply that greater troubleshooting efforts are required to maintain hardware.

Significant gaps in security administration are noted. On average, one-fourth of the sites do not regularly monitor passwords, file permissions, and superuser access. This significant minority can allow for unauthorized intrusion into systems without detection, with possible disastrous effects on the rest of the system. This is particularly significant when 56.2 percent of the sites responded as having more than 60 users (24.4 percent had over 100 users).

There are good indicators that disaster recovery practices are implemented by a majority of sites. However, a significant minority do not properly implement disaster recovery. A weighty indicator is evidenced by those sites that have not adopted a disaster recovery plan. To a lesser degree, sites that store their onsite backup media in the same room as the computer facility may loose valuable backup media in the event of a disaster to their physical environment.

Of primary concern is the security administration of the organization's systems. The majority of respondents do not have a written security plan and have not completed a risk analysis. Without a security plan, the organization may not be able to recognize all of the risks they are exposed to and how to minimize their impact. Without a risk analysis sites cannot assess the impact of a break-in or disaster to automated systems.

Sites with a security plan but no risk analysis may also have questionable security plans in place. For instance, a working security plan prescribes regular computer security training. Only a handful of sites indicated that they do annual computer security training. Irregular training or no training decreases security awareness and can cause security breaches. In addition, the lack of a security plan and not providing security training indicates noncompliance with company policy.

The varied network environment will become one of increasing complexity as network technology expands and becomes more pervasive in the organization. Like hardware administration, networks must be monitored for performance, cable connections checked, and network services provided. This study only touched the surface of network administration, which by itself encompasses most aspects of system administration because it is a major subsystem that provides information to users. Nonetheless, most sites employed some type of network system (i.e., LANS, modems, etc.) and are responsible for maintaining this interface. Overall, increased network administration will be required based on assessment results.

Overall, the assessed locations scored well in operations administration because systems personnel have input or control of system procedures, budgeting, procurement, facility design, and allocation of resources. However, site operations administration was negatively affected because this area was a primary indicator in the establishment of appropriate system policies and procedures. Significant procedures, such as a security plan, disaster recovery plan, and a risk analysis, have not been completed for a majority of the sites.

The overall composite matrix values indicate the level of system administration procedures that are followed by the organization as a whole. It was expected that a composite mean of less than 80 percent (0.80) would indicated significant gaps in system administration practices. The composite mean of 0.781 received by the organization would then indicate that a major gap or lapse in administration practices does exist. The previous notes on the analysis of each module support this conclusion.

Individual sites that received low scores may already be experiencing significant system troubles ranging from frustration in maintaining systems to significant reliability problems that did not appear on the assessment instrument. It is possible that other sites are proceeding smoothly but are unprepared for any significant disruption to a regular routine.

Reasons for the system administration deficiencies noted are beyond the scope of this assessment. It is necessary to determine first what the problems are before trying to eliminate them. From this assessment, it may be conjectured that lack of support, over-tasked personnel, apathy, lack of knowledge, frustration, or other factors may contribute to these findings. It is up to management to get down to core issues and solve existing problems.

Operations

Insight into this speculation comes from comments given by the respondents. One respondent, when referring to the types of information resource tasks they are involved with stated, "many many other areas." In automation support, another response was, "we mostly rely on ourselves." A security-related comment received stated, "They are tired of hearing me talk about passwords, logging out, etc."

The above comments come from an educated and experienced systems staff. Of the respondents, 78.1 percent had a bachelor degree or better with only 51.2 percent having a degree in computer science, management information systems, or a technical discipline. The experience level of the respondents indicate that 80.5 percent had five or more years of system administration experience and 56.1 percent had five or more years of experience with the organization. From the comments and respondent data, it appears that additional questions need to be raised and postulates asserted to answer the "why" question.

A further analysis of the data acquired in this assessment did not show a direct correlation between system reliability and the staff not following procedures. The literature cannot be rejected in indicating that improper procedures lead to decreased system reliability. The inability of the results to affirm this hypothesis may be the result of factors not addressed by the assessment. These factors may include but are not limited to (a) how often sites receive support from their support centers, (b) how much time is spent on each support call, (c) what the cause of a reliability problem is, (d) problem repetition, and (e) actual documentation and reporting of system problems. Consequently, more questions can be added to the survey, and the scope of the assessment can be increased. This can be done incrementally. After an initial assessment is made, the door is open for additional comments and suggestions. Input can then refine the model so that the assessment instrument is kept current and up to date with technology.

Recommendations

The analysis of this general assessment of the system administration practices of an organization yields an urgent need for the organization to complete a risk analysis of their automated facilities. This analysis should be used to develop and implement a security plan for each site and establish proper system policies and procedures. A complete risk analysis will give the organization a more accurate estimate of the effect that system downtime and equipment loss will have on operations. A risk analysis will also validate security plans. Security plans need to address the physical security as well as the operational procedures that are in place to protect the organization's systems. Such issues as information privacy and regular security training also need to be included in a site security plan.

Other areas of system administration could be easily addressed by the sites by adopting a control systems matrix. This matrix could be adaptable to the environment of each system of the enterprise and assessed by each site on an annual basis to pinpoint deficiencies in administration practices. In essence, the sites should adopt a comprehensive methodology that will develop a system administrative model that is adaptable to the needs of each site. Such a model should allow each site to implement system administrative practices that pertain to their present environment and are adaptable to expanding information technology needs. Within the context of this assessment the sites should strive for a comprehensive matrix score of 0.90 or better.

As reliance on automation continues and increases, the need to assess the value of these systems in terms of the information they hold becomes increasingly important. The organization needs to take an approach to address its deficiencies in order to minimize the effect of factors that do not support system integrity and reliability. Based on the results of this assessment, it is also possible that the same deficiencies carry over into other systems that the organization may support, use, or maintain that were not addressed by the assessment. These systems should also be assessed and analyzed to determine the type of control systems that need to be put in place. The job of the system administrator is far-reaching and varied, and good system administration practices smooth the relationship between the system user and the systems they come to rely on to perform their job.

Summary

From the beginning of this book we have taken a look at system administration practices. It was noted that actual practice can vary because of the wide variety of UNIX system environments. Studying UNIX system administration gives the administrator a means to discover what others are doing in the administrator world as well to incorporate acceptable administration practices. The difficulty in system administration comes down to actually quantifying what is expected in a systems environment. Even when policies and procedures are established it is not possible to know if they are being followed, if they have been bypassed, or if they are comprehensive enough to address the enterprise system as a whole. Taking a look at the detailed aspects of system administration and stepping back to view the job as an integral part of the "big picture" of systems support reveal that a more scientific approach to quantifying these tasks is needed.

A statistical analysis of detailed and broad functions as they relate to the administration modules shows an overlapping of tasks between modules. For instance, all modules have tasks related to security. The assessment incorporates relevant tasks as they relate to one module such as networks and then reassesses the task as part of the overall security module. Therefore, security within the network module may be sufficient but if neglected everywhere else would probably give a security module score of 0.20 (20 percent), indicating major security weaknesses. The analysis of the system would then show that the security tasks are there for the network module but are lacking elsewhere.

Operations

From a management perspective, the assessment instrument gives a manager an overall view of the computing environment. Assessments can be made locally or globally for the enterprise. In either case, a detailed assessment of system administration functions will help support the information infrastructure of the organization. It can also provide a means for the systems staff to report on the reliability of a system in a objective quantitative manner instead of subjectively, using casual and anecdotal communications as evidence for a position. It can also help eliminate subjective and reactive system administration practices that are primarily "find it and fix it." Systems staff can be proactive and, through their assessment, more effective to ensure that the proper system administration tasks are in place and adaptable to changing environments.

Appendices

Results of System Administration Assessment Survey

1.(UX) Do you have applications running in a UNIX environment?

Value label	Value	Frequency	Percent	Valid percent	Cum percent
Yes	1	38	92.7	92.7	92.7
No	2	2	4.9	4.9	97.6
No data	9	1	2.4	2.4	100.0

2.(UXSER) How many UNIX-based servers do you administer?

Value label	Value	Frequency	Percent	Valid percent	Cum percent
1	1	8	19.5	19.5	19.5
2	2	12	29.3	29.3	48.8
3	3	17	41.5	41.5	90.2
4	4	1	2.4	2.4	92.7
No data	9	3	7.3	7.3	100.0

Appendices

3.(UXNET) Are your UNIX servers networked?

Value label	Value	Frequency	Percent	Valid percent	Cum percent
Yes	1	20	48.8	48.8	48.8
No	2	17	41.5	41.5	90.2
No data	9	4	9.8	9.8	100.0

4.What hardware technology is your UNIX system(s) based on?

a. (UXHDA) Intel 386

Value label	Value	Frequency	Percent	Valid percent	Cum percent
Yes	1	13	31.7	31.7	31.7
No	2	25	61.0	61.0	92.7
No data	9	3	7.3	7.3	100.0

b. (UXHDB) Intel 486

Value label	Value	Frequency	Percent	Valid percent	Cum percent
Yes	1	35	85.4	85.4	85.4
No	2	3	7.3	7.3	92.7
No data	9	3	7.3	7.3	100.0

c. (UXHDC) Unisys 5000

Value label	Value	Frequency	Percent	Valid percent	Cum percent
Yes	1	17	41.5	41.5	41.5
No	2	21	51.2	51.2	92.7
No data	9	3	7.3	7.3	100.0

d. (UXHDD) Motorola 4 Phase

Value label	Value	Frequency	Percent	Valid percent	Cum percent
Yes	1	4	9.8	9.8	9.8
No	2	34	82.9	82.9	92.7
No data	9	3	7.3	7.3	100.0

e. (UXHDE) Other hardware platform

Value label	Value	Frequency	Percent	Valid percent	Cum percent
Yes	1	2	4.9	4.9	4.9
No	2	36	87.8	87.8	92.7
No data	9	3	7.3	7.3	100.0

5.(UXUS) How many users have access to your UNIX system(s)?

Value label	Value	Frequency	Percent	Valid percent	Cum percent
1–20 users	1	1	2.4	2.4	2.4
20–40 users	2	5	12.2	12.2	14.6
40–60 users	3	9	22.0	22.0	36.6
60–80 users	4	9	22.0	22.0	58.5
80–100 users	5	4	9.8	9.8	68.3
100+ users	6	10	24.4	24.4	92.7
No data	9	3	7.3	7.3	100.0

6.What UNIX applications do you use at your site?

a. (UXAPA) FMS

Value label	Value	Frequency	Percent	Valid percent	Cum percent
Yes	1	37	90.2	90.2	90.2
No	2	1	2.4	2.4	92.7
No data	9	3	7.3	7.3	100.0

b. (UXAPB) DSR

Value label	Value	Frequency	Percent	Valid percent	Cum percent
Yes	1	21	51.2	51.2	51.2
No	2	17	41.5	41.5	92.7
No data	9	3	7.3	7.3	100.0

Appendices

c. (UXAPC) PUADS

Value label	Value	Frequency	Percent	Valid percent	Cum percent
Yes	1	19	46.3	46.3	46.3
No	2	19	46.3	46.3	92.7
No data	9	3	7.3	7.3	100.0

d. (UXAPD) Other UNIX applications

Value label	Value	Frequency	Percent	Valid percent	Cum percent
Yes	1	18	43.9	43.9	43.9
No	2	20	48.8	48.8	92.7
No data	9	3	7.3	7.3	100.0

7.(UXUT) What is your primary utility for doing system backups?

Value label	Value	Frequency	Percent	Valid percent	Cum percent
combkup	1	5	12.2	12.2	12.2
cpio	2	27	65.9	65.9	78.0
Other	4	5	12.2	12.2	90.2
No data	9	4	9.8	9.8	100.0

Other system backup utilities reported were: dobkup, bru, and sbmbackup.

8.(UXDB) What is your primary UNIX DBMS?

Value label	Value	Frequency	Percent	Valid percent	Cum percent
UNIFY	1	38	92.7	92.7	92.7
No data	9	3	7.3	7.3	100.0

9. If you use a UNIFY database please check the following functions you do at your location:

a. (UFYFNA) Rebuild hash tables and b-tree indices.

Value label	Value	Frequency	Percent	Valid percent	Cum percent
Yes	1	36	87.8	87.8	87.8
No	2	2	4.9	4.9	92.7
No data	9	3	7.3	7.3	100.0

b. (UFYFNB) Set up database executables and register them with the database.

Value label	Value	Frequency	Percent	Valid percent	Cum percent
Yes	1	36	87.8	87.8	87.8
No	2	2	4.9	4.9	92.7

c. (UFYFNC) Set up group user access to the database using grpmnt.

Value label	Value	Frequency	Percent	Valid percent	Cum percent
Yes	1	38	92.7	92.7	92.7
No data	9	3	7.3	7.3	100.0

d. (UFYFND) Set up BrandX menus.

Value label	Value	Frequency	Percent	Valid percent	Cum percent
Yes	1	35	85.4	85.4	85.4
No	2	3	7.3	7.3	92.7
No data	9	3	7.3	7.3	100.0

e. (UFYFNE) Run appl programs.

Value label	Value	Frequency	Percent	Valid percent	Cum percent
Yes	1	34	82.9	82.9	82.9
No	2	4	9.8	9.8	92.7
No data	9	3	7.3	7.3	100.0

Appendices

f. (UFYFNF) Perform `dbback` functions on a regular basis.

Value label	Value	Frequency	Percent	Valid percent	Cum percent
Yes	1	35	85.4	85.4	85.4
No	2	3	7.3	7.3	92.7
No data	9	3	7.3	7.3	100.0

g. (UFYFNG) Perform `restdb` functions as needed.

Value label	Value	Frequency	Percent	Valid percent	Cum percent
Yes	1	34	82.9	82.9	82.9
No	2	4	9.8	9.8	92.7
No data	9	3	7.3	7.3	100.0

h. (UFYFNH) Other BrandX DBMS applications.

Value label	Value	Frequency	Percent	Valid percent	Cum percent
Yes	1	5	12.2	12.2	12.2
No	2	33	80.5	80.5	92.7
No data	9	3	7.3	7.3	100.0

Other BrandX database applications reported were: Run SQLs and RPTs as needed; rbuild <*rebuild database*>, screens, create and modify screens, fa <*field attribute assignments*>; Shell programs, SQLs, etc.; dbstats, reconfigure; SQL/RPT; Too numerous too mention; maint, redokey, redopoint, and redoconfigure.

10.What network services do you provide to users?

a. (USNETA) LAN Ethernet

Value label	Value	Frequency	Percent	Valid percent	Cum percent
Yes	1	22	53.7	53.7	53.7
No	2	16	39.0	39.0	92.7
No data	9	3	7.3	7.3	100.0

b. (USNETB) UUCP

Value label	Value	Frequency	Percent	Valid percent	Cum percent
Yes	1	32	78.0	78.0	78.0
No	2	6	14.6	14.6	92.7
No data	9	3	7.3	7.3	100.0

c. (USNETC) Modem (dial-in, dial-out) other than UUCP

Value label	Value	Frequency	Percent	Valid percent	Cum percent
Yes	1	36	87.8	87.8	87.8
No	2	2	4.9	4.9	92.7
No data	9	3	7.3	7.3	100.0

d. (USNETD) Null modem/direct connect

Value label	Value	Frequency	Percent	Valid percent	Cum percent
Yes	1	32	78.0	78.0	78.0
No	2	6	14.6	14.6	92.7
No data	9	3	7.3	7.3	100.0

e. (USNETE) WAN

Value label	Value	Frequency	Percent	Valid percent	Cum percent
Yes	1	6	14.6	14.6	14.6
No	2	32	78.0	78.0	92.7
No data	9	3	7.3	7.3	100.0

f. (USNETF) Other network services

Value label	Value	Frequency	Percent	Valid percent	Cum percent
Yes	1	2	4.9	4.9	4.9
No	2	36	87.8	87.8	92.7
No data	9	3	7.3	7.3	100.0

Other network services reported were: LAN ARCNET; Wide area e-mail.

Appendices

11. In providing system administration functions please check all areas below
that pertain to services you or your systems staff provide:

a. (SAFNA) Answer user questions regarding system functions.

Value label	Value	Frequency	Percent	Valid percent	Cum percent
Yes	1	37	90.2	90.2	90.2
No data	9	4	9.8	9.8	100.0

b. (SAFNB) Evaluate user needs on a regular basis to better deliver system services.

Value label	Value	Frequency	Percent	Valid percent	Cum percent
Yes	1	35	85.4	85.4	85.4
No	2	2	4.9	4.9	90.2
No data	9	4	9.8	9.8	100.0

c. (SAFNC) Provide training support to users on an as-needed basis.

Value label	Value	Frequency	Percent	Valid percent	Cum percent
Yes	1	36	87.8	87.8	87.8
No	2	1	2.4	2.4	90.2
No data	9	4	9.8	9.8	100.0

d. (SAFND) Troubleshoot UNIX software problems.

Value label	Value	Frequency	Percent	Valid percent	Cum percent
Yes	1	37	90.2	90.2	90.2
No data	9	4	9.8	9.8	100.0

e. (SAFNE) Interconnect user office environments to UNIX services.

Value label	Value	Frequency	Percent	Valid percent	Cum percent
Yes	1	28	68.3	68.3	68.3
No	2	9	22.0	22.0	90.2
No data	9	4	9.8	9.8	100.0

f. (SAFNF) Troubleshoot UNIX hardware problems.

Value label	Value	Frequency	Percent	Valid percent	Cum percent
Yes	1	37	90.2	90.2	90.2
No data	9	4	9.8	9.8	100.0

g. (SAFNG) Do file system backups on a regular basis.

Value label	Value	Frequency	Percent	Valid percent	Cum percent
Yes	1	37	90.2	90.2	90.2
No data	9	4	9.8	9.8	100.0

h. (SAFNH) Do backups of database applications on a regular basis.

Value label	Value	Frequency	Percent	Valid percent	Cum percent
Yes	1	37	90.2	90.2	90.2
No data	9	4	9.8	9.8	100.0

i. (SAFNI) Maintain backup media to completely restore operating system.

Value label	Value	Frequency	Percent	Valid percent	Cum percent
Yes	1	37	90.2	90.2	90.2
No data	9	4	9.8	9.8	100.0

j. (SAFNJ) Set up user log-in accounts.

Value label	Value	Frequency	Percent	Valid percent	Cum percent
Yes	1	37	90.2	90.2	90.2
No data	9	4	9.8	9.8	100.0

k. (SAFNK) Force user to change passwords on a regular basis.

Value label	Value	Frequency	Percent	Valid percent	Cum percent
Yes	1	28	68.3	68.3	68.3
No	2	9	22.0	22.0	90.2
No data	9	4	9.8	9.8	100.0

Appendices

l. (SAFNL) Have a written systems security plan.

Value label	Value	Frequency	Percent	Valid percent	Cum percent
Yes	1	18	43.9	43.9	43.9
No	2	19	46.3	46.3	90.2
No data	9	4	9.8	9.8	100.0

m. (SAFNM) Have a written disaster recovery plan.

Value label	Value	Frequency	Percent	Valid percent	Cum percent
Yes	1	25	61.0	61.0	61.0
No	2	12	29.3	29.3	90.2
No data	9	4	9.8	9.8	100.0

n. (SAFNN) Store backup media in an offsite location. (Offsite is to be interpreted as a separate building.)

Value label	Value	Frequency	Percent	Valid percent	Cum percent
Yes	1	35	85.4	85.4	85.4
No	2	2	4.9	4.9	90.2
No data	9	4	9.8	9.8	100.0

o. (SAFNO) Store onsite backup media in a media storage room separate from computer facility.

Value label	Value	Frequency	Percent	Valid percent	Cum percent
Yes	1	20	48.8	48.8	48.8
No	2	17	41.5	41.5	90.2
No data	9	4	9.8	9.8	100.0

p. (SAFNP) Maintain a system backup log.

Value label	Value	Frequency	Percent	Valid percent	Cum percent
Yes	1	32	78.0	78.0	78.0
No	2	5	12.2	12.2	90.2
No data	9	4	9.8	9.8	100.0

q. (SAFNQ) Maintain a system error reporting log.

Value label	Value	Frequency	Percent	Valid percent	Cum percent
Yes	1	33	80.5	80.5	80.5
No	2	4	9.8	9.8	90.2
No data	9	4	9.8	9.8	100.0

r. (SAFNR) Monitor the permissions of systems files.

Value label	Value	Frequency	Percent	Valid percent	Cum percent
Yes	1	24	58.5	58.5	58.5
No	2	13	31.7	31.7	90.2
No data	9	4	9.8	9.8	100.0

s. (SAFNS) Monitor the passwd file for unauthorized superuser access.

Value label	Value	Frequency	Percent	Valid percent	Cum percent
Yes	1	26	63.4	63.4	63.4
No	2	11	26.8	26.8	90.2
No data	9	4	9.8	9.8	100.0

t. (SAFNT) Operate and maintain a crontab file to automate system tasks.

Value label	Value	Frequency	Percent	Valid percent	Cum percent
Yes	1	35	85.4	85.4	85.4
No	2	2	4.9	4.9	90.2
No data	9	4	9.8	9.8	100.0

u. (SAFNU) Monitor the system date function for accuracy and time changes.

Value label	Value	Frequency	Percent	Valid percent	Cum percent
Yes	1	33	80.5	80.5	80.5
No	2	4	9.8	9.8	90.2
No data	9	4	9.8	9.8	100.0

Appendices

v. (SAFNV) Mount and Unmount file systems.

Value label	Value	Frequency	Percent	Valid percent	Cum percent
Yes	1	35	85.4	85.4	85.4
No	2	2	4.9	4.9	90.2
No data	9	4	9.8	9.8	100.0

w. (SAFNW) Set up new file systems.

Value label	Value	Frequency	Percent	Valid percent	Cum percent
Yes	1	28	68.3	68.3	68.3
No	2	9	22.0	22.0	90.2
No data	9	4	9.8	9.8	100.0

x. (SAFNX) Maintain the `inittab` and `gettydef` files.

Value label	Value	Frequency	Percent	Valid percent	Cum percent
Yes	1	37	90.2	90.2	90.2
No data	9	4	9.8	9.8	100.0

y. (SAFNY) Set up and troubleshoot printers.

Value label	Value	Frequency	Percent	Valid percent	Cum percent
Yes	1	37	90.2	90.2	90.2
No data	9	4	9.8	9.8	100.0

z. (SAFNZ) Do kernel reconfigurations, as necessary.

Value label	Value	Frequency	Percent	Valid percent	Cum percent
Yes	1	27	65.9	65.9	65.9
No	2	10	24.4	24.4	90.2
No data	9	4	9.8	9.8	100.0

aa. (SAFNAA) Install new software releases of database applications received from the HQ.

Value label	Value	Frequency	Percent	Valid percent	Cum percent
Yes	1	37	90.2	90.2	90.2
No data	9	4	9.8	9.8	100.0

ab. (SAFNAB) Set up terminal devices.

Value label	Value	Frequency	Percent	Valid percent	Cum percent
Yes	1	37	90.2	90.2	90.2
No data	9	4	9.8	9.8	100.0

ac. (SAFNAC) Set up data communications services.

Value label	Value	Frequency	Percent	Valid percent	Cum percent
Yes	1	35	85.4	85.4	85.4
No	2	2	4.9	4.9	90.2
No data	9	4	9.8	9.8	100.0

ad. (SAFNAD) Have completed a risk analysis of your facility.

Value label	Value	Frequency	Percent	Valid percent	Cum percent
Yes	1	4	9.8	9.8	9.8
No	2	33	80.5	80.5	90.2
No data	9	4	9.8	9.8	100.0

ae. (SAFNAE) Other

Value label	Value	Frequency	Percent	Valid percent	Cum percent
Yes	1	3	7.3	7.3	7.3
No	2	34	82.9	82.9	90.2
No data	9	4	9.8	9.8	100.0

Other system administration functions reported were: Trouble-shoot problems with our RACER system <Remote Access to Company Electronic Records> and provide support to outside users of the system. (i.e., configuring their communications package,

Appendices

etc.). Support company PC Based applications, maintain and order computer supplies as well as new equipment. In-house repair of PC equipment or contact outside source; Whatever needs to be done; Monitor dial-in activity for unauthorized use.

12.(UXRS) Have you ever had to restore your UNIX operating system?

Value label	Value	Frequency	Percent	Valid percent	Cum percent
Yes	1	28	68.3	68.3	68.3
No	2	9	22.0	22.0	90.2
No data	9	4	9.8	9.8	100.0

13.Indicate which system resources you monitor

a. (UXMNA) Database size

Value label	Value	Frequency	Percent	Valid percent	Cum percent
Yes	1	37	90.2	90.2	90.2
No data	9	4	9.8	9.8	100.0

b. (UXMNB) User usage

Value label	Value	Frequency	Percent	Valid percent	Cum percent
Yes	1	24	58.5	58.5	58.5
No	2	13	31.7	31.7	90.2
No data	9	4	9.8	9.8	100.0

c. (UXMNC) File system size

Value label	Value	Frequency	Percent	Valid percent	Cum percent
Yes	1	35	85.4	85.4	85.4
No	2	2	4.9	4.9	90.2
No data	9	4	9.8	9.8	100.0

d. (UXMND) CPU utilization

Value label	Value	Frequency	Percent	Valid percent	Cum percent
Yes	1	20	48.8	48.8	48.8
No	2	17	41.5	41.5	90.2
No data	9	4	9.8	9.8	100.0

e. (UXMNE) Other

Value label	Value	Frequency	Percent	Valid percent	Cum percent
Yes	1	1	2.4	2.4	2.4
No	2	36	87.8	87.8	90.2
No data	9	4	9.8	9.8	100.0

Another response was: `sar` (system activity reports).

14.(TMMN) How often do you monitor system resources.

Value label	Value	Frequency	Percent	Valid percent	Cum percent
Daily	1	12	29.3	29.3	29.3
Weekly	2	9	22.0	22.0	51.2
Monthly	3	1	2.4	2.4	53.7
As needed	4	13	31.7	31.7	85.4
Other	6	1	2.4	2.4	87.8
No data	9	5	12.2	12.2	100.0

Another responses was: Every few days.

15.What formal training do you supply to your users?

a. (USTRA) UNIX

Value label	Value	Frequency	Percent	Valid percent	Cum percent
Yes	1	9	22.0	22.0	22.0
No	2	28	68.3	68.3	90.2
No data	9	4	9.8	9.8	100.0

Appendices

b. (USTRB) Security

Value label	Value	Frequency	Percent	Valid percent	Cum percent
Yes	1	7	17.1	17.1	17.1
No	2	30	73.2	73.2	90.2
No data	9	4	9.8	9.8	100.0

c. (USTRC) Database applications

Value label	Value	Frequency	Percent	Valid percent	Cum percent
Yes	1	35	85.4	85.4	85.4
No	2	2	4.9	4.9	90.2
No data	9	4	9.8	9.8	100.0

d. (USTRD) Other

Value label	Value	Frequency	Percent	Valid percent	Cum percent
Yes	1	9	22.0	22.0	22.0
No	2	28	68.3	68.3	90.2
No data	9	4	9.8	9.8	100.0

Other responses included: Word processing; DOS-based applications; DOS, Windows, Wordperfect, Excel, etc.; UNIX e-mail (elm); wp; Mail; PC Applications; Office Automation Applications; Wordperfect, Windows, Excel.

16.(UXTR) How often do you provide UNIX training to your users?

Value label	Value	Frequency	Percent	Valid percent	Cum percent
As needed	5	25	61.0	61.0	61.0
Do not	6	11	26.8	26.8	87.8
No data	9	5	12.2	12.2	100.0

17.(SCTR) How Often do you provide security training to your users?

Value label	Value	Frequency	Percent	Valid percent	Cum percent
Annually	4	2	4.9	4.9	4.9
As needed	5	20	48.8	48.8	53.7
Do not	6	15	36.6	36.6	90.2
Other	7	1	2.4	2.4	92.7
No data	9	3	7.3	7.3	100.0

The comments received for this question were: Whenever I get a chance; They are tired of hearing me talk about passwords; Logging out.

18.(TRDB) How Often do you provide database training to your users?

Value label	Value	Frequency	Percent	Valid percent	Cum percent
Daily	1	1	2.4	2.4	2.4
Monthly	3	1	2.4	2.4	4.9
As needed	5	34	82.9	82.9	87.8
Do not	6	2	4.9	4.9	92.7
No data	9	3	7.3	7.3	100.0

19.(TRSA) What is the primary source where systems personnel receive systems administration training?

Value label	Value	Frequency	Percent	Valid percent	Cum percent
Training center	1	21	51.2	51.2	51.2
Prior experience	2	6	14.6	14.6	65.9
Local staff	3	8	19.5	19.5	85.4
No data	9	6	14.6	14.6	100.0

20. What procedures do you implement to maintain hardware?

a. (SAHDA) Regular cleaning of tape drives.

Value label	Value	Frequency	Percent	Valid percent	Cum percent
Yes	1	32	78.0	78.0	78.0
No	2	6	14.6	14.6	92.7
No data	9	3	7.3	7.3	100.0

b. (SAHDB) Regular cleaning of disk drives.

Value label	Value	Frequency	Percent	Valid percent	Cum percent
Yes	1	8	19.5	19.5	19.5
No	2	30	73.2	73.2	92.7
No data	9	3	7.3	7.3	100.0

c. (SAHDC) Check performance of UNIX server.

Value label	Value	Frequency	Percent	Valid percent	Cum percent
Yes	1	21	51.2	51.2	51.2
No	2	17	41.5	41.5	92.7
No data	9	3	7.3	7.3	100.0

d. (SAHDD) Check network performance.

Value label	Value	Frequency	Percent	Valid percent	Cum percent
Yes	1	13	31.7	31.7	31.7
No	2	25	61.0	61.0	92.7
No data	9	3	7.3	7.3	100.0

e. (SAHDE) Check for loose cable connections.

Value label	Value	Frequency	Percent	Valid percent	Cum percent
Yes	1	19	46.3	46.3	46.3
No	2	19	46.3	46.3	92.7
No data	9	3	7.3	7.3	100.0

f. (SAHDF) Perform system shutdowns and reboots.

Value label	Value	Frequency	Percent	Valid percent	Cum percent
Yes	1	38	92.7	92.7	92.7
No data	9	3	7.3	7.3	100.0

g. (SAHDG) Other

Value label	Value	Frequency	Percent	Valid percent	Cum percent
Yes	1	3	7.3	7.3	7.3
No	2	35	85.4	85.4	92.7
No data	9	3	7.3	7.3	100.0

Other comments consisted of: `fsck`; Regular hardware preventative maintenance; A huge variety of things.

21. What procedures do you establish and implement to maintain software?

a. (SASWA) Check database statistics

Value label	Value	Frequency	Percent	Valid percent	Cum percent
Yes	1	38	92.7	92.7	92.7
No data	9	3	7.3	7.3	100.0

b. (SASWB) Full system backups

Value label	Value	Frequency	Percent	Valid percent	Cum percent
Yes	1	37	90.2	90.2	90.2
No	2	1	2.4	2.4	92.7
No data	9	3	7.3	7.3	100.0

c. (SASWC) Database backups

Value label	Value	Frequency	Percent	Valid percent	Cum percent
Yes	1	37	90.2	90.2	90.2
No	2	1	2.4	2.4	92.7
No data	9	3	7.3	7.3	100.0

d. (SASWD) Run `fsck` on all file systems

Value label	Value	Frequency	Percent	Valid percent	Cum percent
Yes	1	38	92.7	92.7	92.7
No data	9	3	7.3	7.3	100.0

e. (SASWE) Other

Value label	Value	Frequency	Percent	Valid percent	Cum percent
No	2	38	92.7	92.7	92.7
No data	9	3	7.3	7.3	100.0

22.(TMBK) How often do you implement your backup procedures?

Value label	Value	Frequency	Percent	Valid percent	Cum percent
Daily	1	36	87.8	87.8	87.8
Monthly	3	1	2.4	2.4	90.2
No data	9	4	9.8	9.8	100.0

23.(TMFSCK) How often do you run `fsck` on your systems?

Value label	Value	Frequency	Percent	Valid percent	Cum percent
Daily	1	15	36.6	36.6	36.6
Weekly	2	15	36.6	36.6	73.2
Monthly	3	1	2.4	2.4	75.6
As needed	4	5	12.2	12.2	87.8
Other	6	1	2.4	2.4	90.2
No data	9	4	9.8	9.8	100.0

The comment provided was: Two or three times weekly.

24. (TMDBST) How often do you check your database statistics?

Value label	Value	Frequency	Percent	Valid percent	Cum percent
Daily	1	1	2.4	2.4	2.4
Weekly	2	15	36.6	36.6	39.0
Monthly	3	15	36.6	36.6	75.6
As needed	4	6	14.6	14.6	90.2
Other	6	1	2.4	2.4	92.7
No data	9	3	7.3	7.3	100.0

The comment here was: Somewhere between weekly and monthly.

25. Have you established any automated procedures that include:

a. (SAAUTOA) Automated backups

Value label	Value	Frequency	Percent	Valid percent	Cum percent
Yes	1	30	73.2	73.2	73.2
No	2	8	19.5	19.5	92.7
No data	9	3	7.3	7.3	100.0

The other comments provided were: Running STD reports, activity logs, transaction logs, etc.; Monitor dial-in lines.

b. (SAAUTOB) Provide security checks (i.e., unauthorized logins, bad passwords).

Value label	Value	Frequency	Percent	Valid percent	Cum percent
Yes	1	16	39.0	39.0	39.0
No	2	22	53.7	53.7	92.7
No data	9	3	7.3	7.3	100.0

Appendices

c. (SAAUTOC) Logging off users after a specified time of inactivity.

Value label	Value	Frequency	Percent	Valid percent	Cum percent
Yes	1	22	53.7	53.7	53.7
No	2	16	39.0	39.0	92.7
No data	9	3	7.3	7.3	100.0

d. (SAAUTOD) Perform routine sys admin tasks.

Value label	Value	Frequency	Percent	Valid percent	Cum percent
Yes	1	30	73.2	73.2	73.2
No	2	8	19.5	19.5	92.7
No data	9	3	7.3	7.3	100.0

e. (SAAUTOE) Other

Value label	Value	Frequency	Percent	Valid percent	Cum percent
Yes	1	2	4.9	4.9	4.9
No	2	36	87.8	87.8	92.7
No data	9	3	7.3	7.3	100.0

26. (SHDOWN) How many hours of scheduled downtime do you experience each month? (Scheduled downtime should be interpreted as anytime your system is not in multi-user mode, such as init state 0 or 1, and regular user access to applications is denied.)

Value label	Value	Frequency	Percent	Valid percent	Cum percent
None	1	12	29.3	29.3	29.3
1–5 hours	2	14	34.1	34.1	63.4
6–10 hours	3	3	7.3	7.3	70.7
11–15 hours	4	2	4.9	4.9	75.6
16–20 hours	5	4	9.8	9.8	85.4
>20 hours	6	3	7.3	7.3	92.7
No data	9	3	7.3	7.3	100.0

27.(UNDOWN) How many hours of unscheduled downtime do you experience each month? (i.e., downtime resulting from system crashes, emergency maintenance, etc.).

Value label	Value	Frequency	Percent	Valid percent	Cum percent
None	1	17	41.5	41.5	41.5
1–5 hours	2	20	48.8	48.8	90.2
No data	9	4	9.8	9.8	100.0

28.(CRASH) What do you consider your average number of system crashes per year?

Value label	Value	Frequency	Percent	Valid percent	Cum percent
0	1	7	17.1	17.1	17.1
1	2	9	22.0	22.0	39.0
2	3	9	22.0	22.0	61.0
3	4	2	4.9	4.9	65.9
4	5	2	4.9	4.9	70.7
5	6	4	9.8	9.8	80.5
6–12	7	4	9.8	9.8	90.2
More than 12	8	1	2.4	2.4	92.7
No data	9	3	7.3	7.3	100.0

Appendices

29.(PERSREC) How many Personnel records do your automated systems
support?

Value	Freq	%	Cum %	Value	Freq	%	Cum %	Value	Freq	%	Cum %
0	1	3	3	600	2	6	39	1700	1	3	73
50	1	3	6	700	1	3	42	2200	1	3	76
150	1	3	9	716	1	3	45	2313	1	3	79
187	1	3	12	753	1	3	48	2500	1	3	82
200	1	3	15	1010	1	3	52	2551	1	3	85
250	1	3	18	1098	1	3	55	4600	1	3	88
300	1	3	21	1257	1	3	58	5000	1	3	91
350	1	3	24	1400	1	3	61	5200	1	3	94
375	1	3	27	1500	1	3	64	7000	1	3	97
425	1	3	30	1508	1	3	67	7115	1	3	100
500	1	3	33	1588	1	3	70				
Missing data								9999	8		

The following table provides descriptive statistics for the response to the number of
personnel records supported on automated systems.

Mean	1687.758	Median	1010.000	Mode	600.000
Range	7115.000	Minimum	0.0	Maximum	7115.000
Valid Cases		33	Missing Cases		8

30.(CUSREC) How many Customer Records do your automated systems support?

Value	Freq	%	Cum %	Value	Freq	%	Cum %	Value	Freq	%	Cum %
290	1	3	3	4204	1	3	37	13000	1	3	69
800	1	3	6	4384	1	3	40	13977	1	3	71
1100	1	3	9	5400	1	3	43	15270	1	3	74
1200	1	3	11	6000	1	3	46	16620	1	3	77
1500	1	3	14	7300	1	3	49	19500	1	3	80
2600	1	3	17	7700	1	3	51	24500	1	3	83
3000	1	3	20	8600	1	3	54	24800	1	3	86
3100	1	3	23	10000	1	3	57	28250	1	3	89
3500	2	6	29	10113	1	3	60	29741	1	3	91
3872	1	3	31	10437	1	3	63	30000	1	3	94
4100	1	3	34	10600	1	3	66	40000	2	6	100
Missing data								99999	6		

The following table provides descriptive statistics for the response to the number of customer records supported on automated systems.

Mean	11684.514	Median	7700.000	Mode	3500.000
Range	39710.000	Minimum	290.000	Maximum	40000.000
Valid Cases		35	Missing Cases		6

Appendices

31.(BUDGET) Do you participate in establishing your information systems budget?

Value label	Value	Frequency	Percent	Valid percent	Cum percent
Yes	1	31	75.6	75.6	75.6
No	2	7	17.1	17.1	92.7
No data	9	3	7.3	7.3	100.0

32.(PROCURE) Do you procure automation equipment and supplies for your location?

Value label	Value	Frequency	Percent	Valid percent	Cum percent
Yes	1	35	85.4	85.4	85.4
No	2	4	9.8	9.8	95.1
No data	9	2	4.9	4.9	100.0

33.In managing your computer resources please check all areas you are currently involved with:

a. (MANAGEA) Facility design

Value label	Value	Frequency	Percent	Valid percent	Cum percent
Yes	1	31	75.6	75.6	75.6
No	2	8	19.5	19.5	95.1
No data	9	2	4.9	4.9	100.0

b. (MANAGEB) Equipment installation

Value label	Value	Frequency	Percent	Valid percent	Cum percent
Yes	1	39	95.1	95.1	95.1
No data	9	2	4.9	4.9	100.0

c. (MANAGEC) Determining use of automation resources

Value label	Value	Frequency	Percent	Valid percent	Cum percent
Yes	1	38	92.7	92.7	92.7
No	2	1	2.4	2.4	95.1
No data	9	2	4.9	4.9	100.0

d. (MANAGED) Establishing automation operations procedures

Value label	Value	Frequency	Percent	Valid percent	Cum percent
Yes	1	39	95.1	95.1	95.1
No data	9	2	4.9	4.9	100.0

e. (MANAGEE) Other

Value label	Value	Frequency	Percent	Valid percent	Cum percent
Yes	1	2	4.9	4.9	4.9
No	2	37	90.2	90.2	95.1
No data	9	2	4.9	4.9	100.0

Other comments received were: Overseeing PC inventory with PC Admin; Many many other areas.

34. (AUTOSUP) From whom do you primarily receive automation support services?

Value label	Value	Frequency	Percent	Valid percent	Cum percent
Support center	1	2	4.9	4.9	4.9
HQ	2	26	63.4	63.4	68.3
Vendors	3	3	7.3	7.3	75.6
Other	4	2	4.9	4.9	80.5
No data	9	8	19.5	19.5	100.0

Another comment received was; We mostly rely on ourselves.

Appendices

35.(EXPER) How many years of systems administration experience do you have?

Value label	Value	Frequency	Percent	Valid percent	Cum percent
0–1 years	2	1	2.4	2.4	2.4
2–4 years	3	5	12.2	12.2	14.6
5–7 years	4	14	34.1	34.1	48.8
7–9 years	5	12	29.3	29.3	78.0
≥10 years	6	7	17.1	17.1	95.1
No data	9	2	4.9	4.9	100.0

36.(TMEMPLOY) How long have you been with the organization?

Value label	Value	Frequency	Percent	Valid percent	Cum percent
2–4 years	2	15	36.6	36.6	36.6
5–7 years	3	8	19.5	19.5	56.1
7–9 years	4	6	14.6	14.6	70.7
≥10 years	5	9	22.0	22.0	92.7
No data	9	3	7.3	7.3	100.0

37.(TITLE) What is your job title:

Value label	Value	Frequency	Percent	Valid percent	Cum percent
System Admin	SA	4	9.8	10.3	10.3
System Manager	SM	35	85.4	89.7	100.0

38. What is your educational background? (Check highest level attained.)

a. (EDA) High school

Value label	Value	Frequency	Percent	Valid percent	Cum percent
No	2	39	95.1	95.1	95.1
No data	9	2	4.9	4.9	100.0

b. (EDB) Some college

Value label	Value	Frequency	Percent	Valid percent	Cum percent
Yes	1	6	14.6	14.6	14.6
No	2	33	80.5	80.5	95.1
No data	9	2	4.9	4.9	100.0

c. (EDC) Associate degree

Value label	Value	Frequency	Percent	Valid percent	Cum percent
Yes	1	1	2.4	2.4	2.4
No	2	38	92.7	92.7	95.1
No data	9	2	4.9	4.9	100.0

d. (EDD) Bachelor's degree

Value label	Value	Frequency	Percent	Valid percent	Cum percent
Yes	1	27	65.9	65.9	65.9
No	2	12	29.3	29.3	95.1
No data	9	2	4.9	4.9	100.0

e. (EDE) Graduate degree

Value label	Value	Frequency	Percent	Valid percent	Cum percent
Yes	1	5	12.2	12.2	12.2
No	2	34	82.9	82.9	95.1
No data	9	2	4.9	4.9	100.0

f. (EDF) Other

Value label	Value	Frequency	Percent	Valid percent	Cum percent
No	2	39	95.1	95.1	95.1
No data	9	2	4.9	4.9	100.0

Appendices

39. If you attended college, what was your major?

(UNDER) Undergraduate major

Value label	Value	Frequency	Percent	Valid percent	Cum percent
CS/MIS	1	18	43.9	43.9	43.9
Technical	2	2	4.9	4.9	48.8
Other	3	16	39.0	39.0	87.8
No data	9	5	12.2	12.2	100.0

(GRAD) Graduate major

Value label	Value	Frequency	Percent	Valid percent	Cum percent
CS/MIS	1	1	2.4	2.4	2.4
Other	3	5	12.2	12.2	14.6
No data	9	35	85.4	85.4	100.0

The responses to undergraduate and graduate degree major were broken down into three categories. The first category was CS/MIS to indicate personnel who had a major in computer science, management information systems, or a related discipline. The second category was Technical to refer to technical degree majors that were not specifically CS/MIS, such as electrical engineering. The third category was Other and it included all degree majors that were not Technical or CS/MIS.

Comments

Closing comments, related to the survey, from respondents were as follows:

"Excellent survey questionnaire! Good luck!"

"This office would be very interested in getting a copy of the survey results, when available."

"Does your design account for the wishful thinking that may warp responses in favor of representing the systems team as godlike?"

"I hope the results of the survey are what you expected."

SPSS Data File and Associated Variables

The COMMENT lines are not part of the SPSS file.

COMMENT: This is the list of variables used:

data list / ux 1 uxser 3 uxnet 5 uxhda 7 uxhdb 9 uxhdc 11 uxhdd 13
uxhde 15 uxus 17 uxapa 19 uxapb 21 uxapc 23 uxapd 25 uxut 27
uxdb 29 ufyfna 31 ufyfnb 33 ufyfnc 35 ufyfnd 37 ufyfne 39 ufyfnf 41
ufyfng 43 ufyfnh 45 usneta 47 usnetb 49 usnetc 51 usnetd 53
usnete 55 usnetf 57 safna 59 safnb 61 safnc 63 safnd 65 safne 67
safnf 69 safng 71 safnh 73 safni 75 safnj 77 safnk 79 safnl 81 safnm
83 safnn 85 safno 87 safnp 89 safnq 91 safnr 93 safns 95 safnt 97
safnu 99 safnv 101 safnw 103 safnx 105 safny 107 safnz 109 safnaa 111
safnab 113 safnac 115 safnad 117 safnae 119 uxrs 121 uxmna 123 uxmnb
125 uxmnc 127 uxmnd 129 uxmne 131 tmmn 133 ustra 135 ustrb 137 ustrc
139 ustrd 141 uxtr 143
sctr 145 trdb 147 trsa 149 sahda 151 sahdb 153 sahdc 155 sahdd 157
sahde 159 sahdf 161 sahdg 163 saswa 165 saswb 167 saswc 169 saswd 171
saswe 173 tmbk 175 tmfsck 177 tmdbst 179 saautoa 181 saautob 183
saautoc 185 saautod 187 saautoe 189 shdown 191 undown 193 crash 195
tmdown 197 perrec 199-203 cusrec 205-209 budget 211 procure 213 managea 215 manageb 217 managec 219 managed 221 managee 223 autosup 225
exper 227

tmemploy 229 title 231-232 (a) eda 234 edb 236 edc 238 edd 240 ede 242
edf 244 under 246 grad 248 result 250.

COMMENT: Labels assigned to the variables.

variable labels
    ux 'UNIX Environment'
    uxser 'Number of UNIX Servers'
    uxnet "Are Servers Networked?"
    uxhda 'Intel 386'
    uxhdb 'Intel 486'
    uxhdc 'Pentium'
    uxhdd 'RISC'
    uxhde 'Other Hardware Platform'
    uxus 'Number of Unix Users'
    uxapa 'FMS'
    uxapb 'DSR'
    uxapc 'PUADS'
    uxapd 'Other UNIX Applications'
    uxut 'Primary Backup Utility'
    uxdb 'Primary Unix DBMS'
    ufyfna "Rebuild Unify hash tables & b-trees"
    ufyfnb 'Set up and register Unify execs'
    ufyfnc 'Use grpmnt'
    ufyfnd 'Set up menus'
    ufyfne 'Run appl'
    ufyfnf 'Run dbback'
    ufyfng 'Run restdb'
    ufyfnh 'Other DBMS Applications'
    usneta 'LAN Ethernet'
    usnetb 'UUCP'
    usnetc "modem (not UUCP)"
    usnetd "Null Modem/Direct Connect"
    usnete 'WAN'
    usnetf 'Other Network Services'
    safna 'Answer User System Questions'
    safnb 'Evaluate User Needs'
    safnc 'Provide User Training As Needed'
    safnd 'Troubleshoot Unix software'
    safne 'Connect User Offices to Unix'
    safnf 'Troubleshoot Unix hardware'
    safng 'Regularly do system backups'
    safnh 'Regularly do DBMS backups'
    safni 'Maintain OS backup media'
    safnj 'Set up User login accounts'

```
safnk 'Password Aging'
safnl 'Written Security Plan'
safnm 'Written Disaster Recovery Plan'
safnn 'Store backup media Offsite'
safno 'Store onsite in separate location'
safnp 'Maintain backup log'
safnq 'Maintain error log'
safnr 'Monitor System Permissions'
safns 'Monitor the passwd file'
safnt 'Automate using crontab'
safnu 'Monitor system date'
safnv 'Mount and Unmount file systems'
safnw 'Set up new file systems'
safnx 'Maintain inittab and gettydefs'
safny 'Set up and troubleshoot printers'
safnz "Do kernal reconfigurations?"
safnaa 'Install DBMS Software from HQ'
safnab 'Set up terminals'
safnac 'Set up data communications'
safnad "Have completed a risk analysis?"
safnae "Other SA functions"
uxrs 'Ever restore UNIX OS'
uxmna 'Monitor DBMS Size'
uxmnb 'Monitor User usage'
uxmnc 'Monitor file system size'
uxmnd 'Monitor CPU utilization'
uxmne 'Monitor other resources'
tmmn "How often are sys resources monitored?"
ustra 'Formal Training in UNIX'
ustrb 'Formal TRaining in security'
ustrc 'Formal TRaining in DBMS'
ustrd 'Other Formal Training'
uxtr "How Often - UNIX Training?"
sctr "How Often - Security Training?"
trdb "How Often - DBMS Training?"
trsa "Where Technical Training is received?"
sahda 'Clean tape drives'
sahdb 'Clean disk drives'
sahdc 'Check server performance'
sahdd 'Check network performance'
sahde 'Check for loose cabling'
sahdf 'Perform shutdowns and reboots'
sahdg 'Other hardware procedures'
saswa 'Check database statistics'
saswb 'Full system backups'
saswc 'Database backups'
```

Appendices

```
saswd 'Run fsck on file systems'
saswe 'Other Sys Admin procedures'
tmbk "How often are backups done?"
tmfsck "How often is fsck done?"
tmdbst "How often are DBMS stats checked?"
saautoa 'Automated Backups'
saautob 'Automate Security Checks'
saautoc 'Automate user logoffs'
saautod 'Automate routine SA tasks'
saautoe 'Automate other SA tasks'
shdown 'Scheduled downtime'
undown 'Unscheduled downtime'
crash 'Average Annual Crashes'
tmdown 'Average Crash Downtime'
persrec 'Number of Personnel Records'
cusrec 'Number of customer records'
budget 'Participate in automation budget'
procure 'Automation Procurement'
managea 'Involved in facility design'
manageb 'Involved in equipment installation'
managec 'Involved in resource allocation'
managed 'Involved in automation procedures'
managee 'Other Management resources'
autosup 'Received automation support'
exper "Year's Experience"
tmemploy "Year's with the Company"
title 'Job Title'
eda 'High School'
edb 'Some College'
edc 'Associate Degree'
edd 'Bachelor Degree'
ede 'Graduate Degree'
edf 'Other Education'
under 'Undergraduate major'
grad 'Graduate major'
result 'Send Results'.
```

COMMENT: Applicable Value for the Variables

value labels
```
ux 1 'Yes' 2 'No' 9 'No Data' /
uxser 1 '1' 2 '2' 3 '3' 4 '4' 5 '5' 6 'More than 5' 9 'No Data' /
uxnet 1 'Yes' 2 'No' 9 'No Data'/
uxhda 1 'Yes' 2 'No' 9 'No Data'/
uxhdb 1 'Yes' 2 'No' 9 'No Data'/
uxhdc 1 'Yes' 2 'No' 9 'No Data'/
```

```
uxhdd 1 'Yes' 2 'No' 9 'No Data'/
uxhde 1 'Yes' 2 'No' 9 'No Data'/
uxus 1 '1-20' 2 '20-40' 3 '40-60' 4 '60-80' 5 '80-100' 6 '100+'
     9 'No Data'/
uxapa 1 'Yes' 2 'No' 9 'No Data'/
uxapb 1 'Yes' 2 'No' 9 'No Data'/
uxapc 1 'Yes' 2 'No' 9 'No Data'/
uxapd 1 'Yes' 2 'No' 9 'No Data'/
uxut 1 'combkup' 2 'cpio' 3 'tar' 4 'other' 9 'No Data'/
uxdb 1 'BrandX' 2 'Informix' 3 'Oracle' 4 'Other' 9 'No Data'/
ufyfna 1 'Yes' 2 'No' 9 'No Data'/
ufyfnb 1 'Yes' 2 'No' 9 'No Data'/
ufyfnc 1 'Yes' 2 'No' 9 'No Data'/
ufyfnd 1 'Yes' 2 'No' 9 'No Data'/
ufyfne 1 'Yes' 2 'No' 9 'No Data'/
ufyfnf 1 'Yes' 2 'No' 9 'No Data'/
ufyfng 1 'Yes' 2 'No' 9 'No Data'/
ufyfnh 1 'Yes' 2 'No' 9 'No Data'/
usneta 1 'Yes' 2 'No' 9 'No Data'/
usnetb 1 'Yes' 2 'No' 9 'No Data'/
usnetc 1 'Yes' 2 'No' 9 'No Data'/
usnetd 1 'Yes' 2 'No' 9 'No Data'/
usnete 1 'Yes' 2 'No' 9 'No Data'/
usnetf 1 'Yes' 2 'No' 9 'No Data'/
safna 1 'Yes' 2 'No' 9 'No Data'/
safnb 1 'Yes' 2 'No' 9 'No Data'/
safnc 1 'Yes' 2 'No' 9 'No Data'/
safnd 1 'Yes' 2 'No' 9 'No Data'/
safne 1 'Yes' 2 'No' 9 'No Data'/
safnf 1 'Yes' 2 'No' 9 'No Data'/
safng 1 'Yes' 2 'No' 9 'No Data'/
safnh 1 'Yes' 2 'No' 9 'No Data'/
safni 1 'Yes' 2 'No' 9 'No Data'/
safnj 1 'Yes' 2 'No' 9 'No Data'/
safnk 1 'Yes' 2 'No' 9 'No Data'/
safnl 1 'Yes' 2 'No' 9 'No Data'/
safnm 1 'Yes' 2 'No' 9 'No Data'/
safnn 1 'Yes' 2 'No' 9 'No Data'/
safno 1 'Yes' 2 'No' 9 'No Data'/
safnp 1 'Yes' 2 'No' 9 'No Data'/
safnq 1 'Yes' 2 'No' 9 'No Data'/
safnr 1 'Yes' 2 'No' 9 'No Data'/
safns 1 'Yes' 2 'No' 9 'No Data'/
safnt 1 'Yes' 2 'No' 9 'No Data'/
safnu 1 'Yes' 2 'No' 9 'No Data'/
safnv 1 'Yes' 2 'No' 9 'No Data'/
```

```
safnw 1 'Yes' 2 'No' 9 'No Data'/
safnx 1 'Yes' 2 'No' 9 'No Data'/
safny 1 'Yes' 2 'No' 9 'No Data'/
safnz 1 'Yes' 2 'No' 9 'No Data'/
safnaa 1 'Yes' 2 'No' 9 'No Data'/
safnab 1 'Yes' 2 'No' 9 'No Data'/
safnac 1 'Yes' 2 'No' 9 'No Data'/
safnad 1 'Yes' 2 'No' 9 'No Data'/
safnae 1 'Yes' 2 'No' 9 'No Data'/
uxrs 1 'Yes' 2 'No' 9 'No Data'/
uxmna 1 'Yes' 2 'No' 9 'No Data'/
uxmnb 1 'Yes' 2 'No' 9 'No Data' /
uxmnc 1 'Yes' 2 'No' 9 'No Data'/
uxmnd 1 'Yes' 2 'No' 9 'No Data'/
uxmne 1 'Yes' 2 'No' 9 'No Data'/
tmmn  1 'Daily' 2 'Weekly' 3 'Monthly' 4 'As needed'
      5 'Do not monitor sys resources' 6 'Other' 9 'No Data' /
ustra 1 'Yes' 2 'No' 9 'No Data'/
ustrb 1 'Yes' 2 'No' 9 'No Data'/
ustrc 1 'Yes' 2 'No' 9 'No Data'/
ustrd 1 'Yes' 2 'No' 9 'No Data'/
uxtr  1 'Daily' 2 'Weekly' 3 'Monthly' 4 'Annually'
      5 'As needed' 6 'Do not provide UNIX training' 7 'Other'
      9 'No Data'/
sctr  1 'Daily' 2 'Weekly' 3 'Monthly' 4 'Annually'
      5 'As needed' 6 'Do not supply security training' 7 'Other'
      9 'No Data'/
trdb  1 'Daily' 2 'Weekly' 3 'Monthly' 4 'Annually'
      5 'As needed' 6 'Do not provide database application training'
      7 'Other' 9 'No Data'/
trsa  1 'AO' 2 'Prior Experience' 3 'Local Systems Staff'
      4 'Training vendors' 5 'Other' 9 'No Data'/
sahda 1 'Yes' 2 'No' 9 'No Data'/
sahdb 1 'Yes' 2 'No' 9 'No Data'/
sahdc 1 'Yes' 2 'No' 9 'No Data'/
sahdd 1 'Yes' 2 'No' 9 'No Data'/
sahde 1 'Yes' 2 'No' 9 'No Data'/
sahdf 1 'Yes' 2 'No' 9 'No Data'/
sahdg 1 'Yes' 2 'No' 9 'No Data'/
saswa 1 'Yes' 2 'No' 9 'No Data'/
saswb 1 'Yes' 2 'No' 9 'No Data'/
saswc 1 'Yes' 2 'No' 9 'No Data'/
saswd 1 'Yes' 2 'No' 9 'No Data'/
saswe 1 'Yes' 2 'No' 9 'No Data'/
tmbk  1 'Daily' 2 'Weekly' 3 'Monthly' 4 'As needed'
      5 'Do not implement' 6 'Other' 9 'No Data'/
```

```
tmfsck 1 'Daily' 2 'Weekly' 3 'Monthly' 4 'As needed'
       5 'Do not run' 6 'Other' 9 'No Data'/
tmdbst 1 'Daily' 2 'Weekly' 3 'Monthly' 4 'As needed'
        5 'Do not check' 6 'Other' 9 'No Data'/
saautoa 1 'Yes' 2 'No' 9 'No Data'/
saautob 1 'Yes' 2 'No' 9 'No Data'/
saautoc 1 'Yes' 2 'No' 9 'No Data'/
saautod 1 'Yes' 2 'No' 9 'No Data'/
saautoe 1 'Yes' 2 'No' 9 'No Data'/
shdown 1 'None' 2 '1-5 hours' 3 '6-10 hours' 4 '11-15 hours'
       5 '16-20 hours' 6 'More than 20 hours' 9 'No Data'/
undown 1 'None' 2 '1-5 hours' 3 '6-10 hours' 5 '11-15 hours'
       5 '16-20 hours' 6 'More than 20 hours' 9 'No Data'/
crash 1 '0' 2 '1' 3 '2' 4 '3' 5 '4' 6 '5' 7 '6-12' 8 'More than 12'
      9 'No Data'/
tmdown 1 '0-1 hours' 2 '1-3 hours' 3 '3-5 hours'
       4 '5-7 hours' 5 'More than 7 hours' 6 'No crashes'
       9 'No Data'/
budget 1 'Yes' 2 'No' 9 'No Data'/
procure 1 'Yes' 2 'No' 9 'No Data'/
managea 1 'Yes' 2 'No' 9 'No Data'/
manageb 1 'Yes' 2 'No' 9 'No Data'/
managec 1 'Yes' 2 'No' 9 'No Data'/
managed 1 'Yes' 2 'No' 9 'No Data'/
managee 1 'Yes' 2 'No' 9 'No Data'/
autosup 1 'Support Center' 2 'HQ' 3 'Vendors'
        4 'Other' 9 'No Data'/
exper 1 'None' 2 '0-1 Years' 3 '2-4 Years' 4 '5-7 Years'
      5 '7-9 Years' 6 '10 or more years' 9 'No Data'/
tmemploy 1 '0-1 Years' 2 '2-4 Years' 3 '5-7 Years'
         4 '7-9 Years' 5 '10 or more years' 9 'No Data' /
title 'SA' 'System Administrator' 'SM' 'System Manager' /
eda 1 'Yes' 2 'No' 9 'No Data'/
edb 1 'Yes' 2 'No' 9 'No Data'/
edc 1 'Yes' 2 'No' 9 'No Data'/
edd 1 'Yes' 2 'No' 9 'No Data'/
ede 1 'Yes' 2 'No' 9 'No Data'/
edf 1 'Yes' 2 'No' 9 'No Data'/
under 1 'CS/MIS' 2 'Technical' 3 'Other' 9 'No Data'/
grad 1 'CS/MIS' 2 'Technical' 3 'Other' 9 'No Data' /
result 1 'Yes' 2 'No' 9 'No Data'.

COMMENT: values for missing data or data not supplied

missing value
title ('99') / crmcase (9999) / civcase (99999).
```

COMMENT: Survey Data

begin data.
```
1 3 1 1 2 2 2 2 6 1 1 2 1 2 1 1 1 1 1 1 1 1 2 1 1 1 1 1 2 1 1 1 1 1 1
1 1 1 1 1 1 1 1 1 1 1 1 1 1 1 1 1 1 1 1 1 1 1 1 2 2 1 1 1 1 1 2 1 1 1 1
2 5 5 5 9 1 2 1 1 1 1 2 1 1 1 1 2 1 2 2 1 1 1 1 2 1 2 2 1  2551 13977
1 1 1 1 1 1 2 9 4 3 SM 2 1 2 2 2 2 3 9 1

1 3 1 1 1 1 2 2 4 1 1 1 1 4 1 1 1 1 1 1 1 1 2 1 1 1 1 2 2 1 1 1 1 1 1
1 1 1 1 1 2 2 1 2 1 1 2 1 1 1 1 1 1 1 1 1 1 2 2 1 1 1 1 1 2 1 2 2 1
2 5 6 5 1 1 2 1 1 1 1 2 1 1 1 1 2 1 1 2 2 1 1 2 2 6 2 5 2  7115 24500
1 1 2 1 1 1 2 2 3 2 SM 2 2 2 1 2 2 3 9 1

1 3 1 2 1 2 2 2 3 1 2 1 1 1 1 1 1 1 1 1 1 1 2 1 1 1 2 2 1 1 1 1 1 1
1 1 1 1 2 1 1 1 1 1 1 1 1 2 2 1 1 1 1 1 1 1 2 2 2 1 1 1 2 2 4 2 2 1
1 6 6 5 2 1 2 2 2 2 1 2 1 1 1 1 2 1 3 3 1 1 1 1 2 1 1 1 6   150  1500
1 1 1 1 1 1 2 2 4 2 SM 2 2 2 1 2 2 1 9 1

1 2 2 2 1 1 2 2 5 1 1 1 1 2 1 1 1 1 1 1 1 1 2 2 1 1 1 1 2 2 1 1 1 1 2 1
1 1 1 1 1 2 1 1 2 2 1 2 1 1 1 1 1 1 1 2 1 1 1 2 2 1 1 2 1 2 2 4 2 2 1
2 6 5 5 1 1 2 2 2 2 1 2 1 1 1 1 2 3 2 4 1 2 1 2 2 1 2 4 4   716 15270
1 1 1 1 1 1 2 9 5 4 SM 2 2 2 1 2 2 1 9 1

1 3 2 1 1 2 2 2 2 1 2 2 2 2 1 1 1 1 1 1 1 1 2 2 1 1 1 2 2 1 1 1 1 1 1
1 1 1 1 2 2 2 1 1 1 1 1 1 1 1 1 1 1 1 1 1 1 1 2 1 1 1 1 1 2 2 2 2 2
1 5 6 6 2 1 1 1 1 1 2 1 1 1 1 2 1 4 2 1 1 2 1 2 1 2 1 1 2 2  1010  4204
2 1 1 1 1 1 2 2 4 3 SM 2 2 2 2 1 2 3 3 1

1 3 1 2 1 1 2 2 6 1 1 1 2 2 1 2 1 1 1 1 1 1 1 2 1 1 1 1 2 2 1 1 1 1 2 1
1 1 1 1 1 1 2 1 2 1 1 1 1 1 1 1 2 1 1 1 1 1 1 2 2 2 1 1 1 2 2 1 2 1 1
2 5 5 5 3 2 2 2 2 2 1 2 1 1 1 1 2 1 6 2 1 2 1 1 2 5 1 1 6  2313 29741
2 1 1 1 1 1 2 2 4 5 SA 2 1 2 2 2 2 3 9 2

1 2 1 2 1 1 2 2 4 1 1 1 2 2 1 1 1 1 1 1 1 1 1 2 1 1 1 1 2 2 1 1 1 1 2 1
1 1 1 1 2 2 2 1 2 2 2 2 1 1 1 1 1 1 1 1 1 1 2 2 2 1 2 1 2 2 2 2 2 1
2 5 6 5 1 2 2 2 2 2 1 2 1 1 1 1 2 1 1 4 1 1 2 1 2 2 1 3 3  1500 10000
1 1 1 1 1 1 2 2 4 2 SM 2 2 2 1 2 2 1 9 1

1 2 1 2 1 2 2 2 3 1 2 2 1 2 1 1 1 1 1 1 1 1 1 2 2 1 1 1 2 2 1 1 1 1 1 1
1 1 1 1 1 1 1 1 2 1 1 1 1 1 1 1 2 1 1 1 1 1 1 2 2 1 1 1 1 1 2 2 1 1 1
2 5 5 5 1 1 1 1 1 1 1 2 1 1 1 1 2 1 1 3 2 2 2 2 6 1 2 4    50   290
1 1 1 1 1 1 2 2 5 3 SM 2 2 2 1 2 2 1 9 1
1 3 2 1 1 2 1 2 2 1 1 2 1 1 1 1 1 1 1 1 1 1 2 2 1 1 1 2 2 1 1 1 1 1 1
1 1 1 1 2 2 1 1 2 1 1 2 2 1 2 1 2 1 1 2 1 1 2 2 2 2 1 1 1 2 2 2 2 1
1 6 6 5 1 1 2 2 2 1 1 2 1 1 1 1 2 1 2 2 1 2 2 1 2 2 2 3 2   187  1100
1 1 2 1 1 1 2 2 4 2 SM 2 2 2 1 2 2 1 9 2
```

```
1 2 2 1 1 2 2 2 6 1 2 2 1 2 1 1 1 1 1 1 1 1 2 2 2 1 1 2 2 1 1 1 1 1 1
1 1 1 1 1 2 2 2 1 1 1 1 1 1 1 1 1 1 1 1 1 1 2 2 1 1 2 1 2 2 2 1 2 1
2 5 6 5 1 2 2 1 2 1 1 2 1 1 1 1 2 1 4 2 1 2 2 1 2 1 2 1 6  7000 13000
2 1 1 1 2 1 2 2 3 2 SA 2 2 2 1 2 2 1 9 1

1 3 1 2 1 2 2 2 3 1 1 1 1 2 1 1 1 1 1 1 1 1 1 1 1 1 1 1 2 1 1 1 1 1 1
1 1 1 1 1 1 1 1 1 1 1 1 1 1 1 1 1 1 1 1 1 1 2 2 1 1 1 1 1 2 4 2 2 1
1 5 5 5 3 1 1 1 1 1 2 1 1 1 1 2 1 2 4 1 1 1 1 2 1 2 7 2  1098 10437
1 1 1 1 1 1 2 2 5 3 SM 2 2 2 1 2 2 1 9 1

1 2 1 1 1 2 2 2 3 1 2 1 2 4 1 1 1 1 1 1 1 1 1 2 2 1 1 1 2 2 1 1 1 1 1 1
1 1 1 1 1 1 1 1 1 1 1 1 1 1 1 1 1 1 1 1 1 1 1 2 1 1 1 1 1 2 1 1 1 1
2 5 5 5 3 1 2 1 2 2 1 2 1 1 1 1 2 1 1 3 1 1 1 1 2 4 1 1 6   425 16620
2 1 1 1 1 1 2 2 4 5 SM 2 2 2 1 2 2 3 9 1

1 2 1 2 2 1 1 1 4 1 2 2 2 2 1 2 1 1 1 2 1 1 2 2 1 1 1 2 2 1 1 1 1 1 1
1 1 1 1 1 1 1 1 1 1 1 1 1 1 1 1 1 2 1 1 1 1 1 1 1 2 1 1 1 1 1 2 1 2 2 1
2 5 4 5 2 1 2 1 2 1 1 2 1 1 1 1 2 1 1 2 1 2 1 1 2 4 1 2 4   350  3500
1 2 2 1 1 1 2 2 5 3 SA 2 2 2 1 2 1 3 1

1 1 1 2 2 1 2 2 4 1 2 2 2 2 1 1 1 1 1 1 2 2 2 1 1 1 1 2 2 1 1 1 1 1 1
1 1 1 1 2 2 2 1 2 1 1 1 1 1 1 1 1 1 2 1 1 1 2 2 1 1 2 1 2 1 2 2 1 2 2 1
2 5 6 5 1 1 2 2 2 2 1 2 1 1 2 1 2 1 2 2 1 2 2 1 2 1 1 2 2   300  6000
1 1 1 1 1 1 2 9 3 2 SM 2 2 2 1 2 2 1 9 1

1 1 2 2 1 1 1 1 4 1 2 2 2 2 1 1 1 1 1 1 2 2 2 2 2 1 1 2 2 1 1 1 1 2 1
1 1 1 1 1 2 2 1 1 1 1 2 1 1 1 1 2 1 1 1 1 1 2 2 2 1 2 2 1 2 2 2 2 1
2 6 6 5 2 1 2 2 2 2 1 2 1 1 1 1 2 1 2 4 1 1 2 2 2 2 2 1 6   375 10113
1 1 2 1 1 1 2 2 4 2 SM 2 2 2 1 2 2 1 9 1

2 9 9 9 9 9 9 9 9 9 9 9 9 9 9 9 9 9 9 9 9 9 9 9 9 9 9 9 9 9 9 9 9 9 9
9 9 9 9 9 9 9 9 9 9 9 9 9 9 9 9 9 9 9 9 9 9 9 9 9 9 9 9 9 9 9 9 9 9 9
9 9 9 9 9 9 9 9 9 9 9 9 9 9 9 9 9 9 9 9 9 9 9 9 9 9 9 9 9  9999 99999
9 9 9 9 9 9 9 9 9 9 9 9 9 9 9 9 9 9 9 9 9

1 1 2 2 1 2 2 2 4 1 2 2 1 1 1 1 2 1 2 2 1 1 2 1 2 1 2 1 2 2 2 1 1 1 1 2 1
1 1 1 1 1 2 1 1 2 2 2 2 1 1 1 1 1 1 1 1 1 1 2 2 1 1 1 1 1 2 4 2 2 2
1 5 5 5 3 2 2 1 2 1 1 2 1 1 1 1 2 1 4 2 1 2 2 1 2 2 2 3 2  9999 99999
1 1 1 1 1 1 2 3 5 4 SM 2 1 2 2 2 2 9 9 2

1 2 1 1 1 2 2 2 2 1 2 2 2 4 1 1 1 1 1 1 1 1 2 1 1 1 1 2 2 9 9 9 9 9 9
9 9 9 9 9 9 9 9 9 9 9 9 9 9 9 9 9 9 9 9 9 9 9 9 9 9 9 9 9 9 9 9 9 9 9
9 9 5 5 1 1 1 1 1 1 1 2 1 1 1 1 2 1 2 2 1 1 1 1 2 2 1 1 6  1700 10600
1 1 1 1 1 1 2 2 6 3 SM 2 1 2 2 2 2 9 9 1
```

```
1 3 2 2 1 1 2 2 5 1 1 1 1 2 1 1 1 1 1 1 1 1 2 2 1 1 1 2 2 1 1 1 1 1 1 1
1 1 1 1 1 1 1 1 1 1 1 1 1 1 1 1 1 1 1 1 1 1 1 1 1 1 1 1 1 1 2 1 2 2 1
2 6 5 5 1 1 1 1 2 1 1 2 1 1 1 1 2 1 1 4 1 1 1 1 2 1 1 5 2   9999 99999
2 2 1 1 1 1 2 2 5 2 SA 2 2 2 1 2 2 3 9 1

1 4 2 1 1 1 2 2 6 1 1 1 1 4 1 1 1 1 1 1 1 1 2 2 1 1 1 2 2 1 1 1 1 1 1
1 1 1 1 1 1 1 1 2 1 1 1 1 1 1 1 1 1 1 1 1 1 2 2 1 1 2 1 2 2 4 2 2 1
2 5 5 5 3 1 2 2 2 2 1 2 1 1 1 1 2 1 1 3 1 2 1 1 2 2 2 3 2   1400 3000
1 1 1 1 1 1 2 2 6 5 SM 2 1 2 2 2 2 9 9 1

1 1 2 2 1 2 2 2 1 2 1 2 2 1 1 1 1 1 2 2 1 1 2 2 2 1 1 2 2 1 1 1 1 1 2 1
1 1 1 1 1 1 1 1 1 1 1 2 1 2 2 1 2 1 1 2 1 1 1 2 2 2 1 2 1 1 2 1 1 2 1
2 5 6 5 1 1 1 1 2 1 1 2 1 1 1 1 2 1 1 2 1 2 2 1 2 2 1 1 6   9999 99999
1 1 1 1 1 1 2 3 4 2 SM 2 2 2 1 2 2 1 9 2

1 1 2 2 1 2 2 2 3 1 2 2 2 2 1 1 1 1 1 2 2 2 1 1 1 1 2 2 1 1 1 1 1 1
1 1 1 1 1 1 1 1 2 1 1 1 2 1 1 1 2 1 1 1 1 1 2 2 1 1 1 1 2 2 1 1 2 1
2 5 6 5 1 1 2 1 1 2 1 2 1 1 1 1 2 1 1 2 1 1 1 2 3 1 2 5   500 7300
1 1 1 1 1 1 2 2 3 2 SM 2 2 1 2 2 2 2 9 1

1 3 1 1 1 2 2 2 4 1 2 1 1 2 1 1 1 1 1 1 1 1 1 1 1 1 1 1 2 1 1 1 1 1 1
1 1 1 1 2 1 1 1 1 1 1 1 1 1 1 1 1 1 1 1 1 1 2 2 1 1 1 1 1 1 2 2 2 1
2 6 7 5 3 1 2 1 1 1 1 1 1 1 1 2 1 2 3 1 1 1 1 2 2 3 1   1257 4384
1 1 1 1 1 1 2 2 4 2 SM 2 2 2 1 2 2 1 9 1

1 1 2 2 1 2 2 2 3 1 2 2 2 1 1 1 2 1 2 2 1 2 2 2 1 2 2 2 2 1 2 1 1 2 1
1 1 1 1 2 1 1 1 2 1 1 2 2 2 1 2 2 1 1 2 1 1 2 2 2 1 1 2 1 2 2 4 2 2 1
2 6 6 6 1 1 2 2 2 2 1 2 1 2 1 1 2 1 9 3 2 2 1 1 2 5 2 3 2   9999 8600
1 1 2 1 1 1 2 4 2 5 SM 2 2 2 2 1 2 3 3 1

1 3 2 2 1 1 2 2 6 1 1 1 2 2 1 1 1 1 1 1 1 1 2 1 1 1 1 2 2 1 1 1 1 1 1
1 1 1 1 1 2 1 1 1 1 1 1 1 1 1 1 1 1 1 1 1 1 2 2 2 1 1 1 1 2 1 2 2 1
2 6 5 5 1 1 1 1 1 1 1 2 1 1 1 1 2 1 2 2 1 1 1 1 2 2 2 4 5   600 4100
1 1 1 1 1 1 2 2 5 3 SM 2 2 2 1 2 2 1 9 1

1 3 1 2 1 1 2 2 6 1 1 1 1 2 1 1 1 1 1 1 1 1 1 1 1 1 1 1 2 2 1 1 1 1 2 1
1 1 1 1 2 1 1 1 1 1 1 1 1 2 1 1 1 1 1 1 1 1 1 1 2 2 1 1 1 1 1 2 2 2 1 1
1 5 5 5 3 1 2 2 2 1 1 2 1 1 1 1 2 1 1 3 1 2 1 1 2 1 1 3 4   1588 3872
2 2 1 1 1 1 2 2 6 5 SM 2 1 2 2 2 2 1 9 1

1 3 1 1 1 2 2 2 3 1 2 1 2 2 1 1 1 1 1 1 1 1 2 1 2 1 2 2 2 1 1 1 1 1 1
1 1 1 1 2 1 1 1 1 1 2 2 1 1 1 1 1 1 1 1 1 1 2 2 1 1 1 1 2 2 1 1 2 1
2 5 5 5 9 2 2 1 1 1 1 2 1 1 1 1 2 1 1 3 2 2 2 1 2 6 2 7 2   2200 7700
1 1 1 1 1 1 2 2 6 2 SM 2 2 2 1 2 2 3 9 1
```

```
1 2 1 2 1 2 2 2 4 1 1 1 2 9 1 1 1 1 1 1 1 1 2 1 1 1 1 2 1 1 1 1 1 1
1 1 1 1 1 1 1 1 1 1 1 1 1 1 1 1 1 1 1 1 1 1 2 2 2 1 1 1 1 2 9 1 2 1
2 5 4 5 9 1 2 1 2 1 1 2 1 1 1 2 9 2 3 2 2 1 2 1 3 1 7 1    700  5400
1 1 1 1 1 2 9 5 4 SM 2 2 2 1 2 2 3 1 1
```

```
1 2 1 2 1 1 1 2 2 1 1 2 2 2 1 1 1 1 1 1 1 1 2 1 1 1 1 2 2 1 1 1 1 1
1 1 1 1 2 2 2 2 1 2 1 2 2 1 1 1 1 1 2 1 1 1 2 2 1 1 2 1 2 2 4 2 1 1
2 5 5 5 1 1 2 2 2 2 1 2 1 1 1 1 2 1 2 2 1 2 2 1 2 2 6 2    250  1200
1 1 1 1 1 2 2 6 5 SM 2 2 2 1 2 2 3 9 2
```

```
1 1 2 2 1 2 2 2 3 1 2 2 2 4 1 1 1 1 1 1 1 1 2 2 1 1 2 2 2 1 1 1 1 1
1 1 1 1 1 2 2 1 2 1 1 1 1 1 1 1 1 1 1 1 1 1 2 2 2 1 1 1 1 2 4 2 2 1
2 5 6 5 1 1 2 1 1 1 1 2 1 1 1 1 2 1 2 2 2 2 2 2 2 2 1 8 1  5200  2600
1 1 1 1 1 2 2 3 2 SM 2 2 2 1 2 2 1 9 1
```

```
1 2 1 2 1 2 2 2 3 1 1 2 2 2 1 1 1 1 1 1 1 1 2 2 1 1 2 2 2 1 1 1 1 1
1 1 1 1 1 2 1 1 2 1 1 1 2 1 1 1 1 1 1 1 2 1 1 1 2 2 1 1 2 1 2 2 4 2 2 1
2 5 5 1 1 1 2 1 2 2 1 2 1 1 1 1 2 1 4 3 1 2 2 1 2 2 1 2 5  9999   800
1 1 2 1 1 1 2 9 6 2 SM 2 2 2 1 2 2 1 9 1
```

```
2 9 9 9 9 9 9 9 9 9 9 9 9 9 9 9 9 9 9 9 9 9 9 9 9 9 9 9 9 9 9 9 9 9
9 9 9 9 9 9 9 9 9 9 9 9 9 9 9 9 9 9 9 9 9 9 9 9 9 9 9 9 9 9 9 9 9 9
9 9 9 9 9 9 9 9 9 9 9 9 9 9 9 9 9 9 9 9 9 9 9 9 9 9 9 9  9999 99999
9 1 2 1 1 1 2 3 4 3 SM 2 2 2 1 2 2 1 9 2
```

```
1 3 1 2 1 1 2 2 5 1 1 1 2 2 1 1 1 1 1 1 1 1 2 1 1 1 1 2 2 1 1 1 1 1
1 1 1 1 1 2 2 1 1 2 2 1 1 1 1 1 1 1 1 1 1 1 2 1 1 1 1 1 2 2 6 2 2 1
2 6 6 5 1 1 2 2 2 1 1 2 1 1 1 1 2 1 1 6 1 2 1 1 2 1 2 6 3  2500 40000
1 1 1 1 1 2 2 5 4 SM 2 2 2 1 2 2 3 9 1
```

```
1 3 2 1 1 1 2 2 6 1 1 1 2 2 1 1 1 1 1 1 1 1 1 2 2 1 1 1 2 2 1 1 1 1 1 1
1 1 1 1 1 1 1 2 1 1 1 1 1 1 1 1 1 1 1 1 1 1 2 2 1 1 1 1 1 2 2 1 2 1
1 5 5 5 1 1 2 2 2 2 1 1 1 1 1 1 2 1 1 3 2 1 1 2 2 2 6 3    753 24800
1 1 1 1 1 1 1 1 5 5 SM 2 2 2 1 2 3 3 1
```

```
1 3 2 1 1 2 2 2 6 1 2 1 1 2 1 1 1 1 1 1 1 1 1 1 2 1 1 1 1 1 2 1 1 1 1 2 1
1 1 1 1 1 1 1 1 1 1 1 1 2 1 1 1 1 1 1 1 1 1 1 1 2 1 1 1 1 2 2 4 2 1 1
1 9 5 3 1 1 2 1 1 2 1 1 1 1 1 1 1 2 1 2 3 1 1 2 2 2 2 1 2 2   200  3100
1 1 1 1 1 1 1 2 6 4 SM 2 2 2 1 2 2 3 9 1
```

```
1 3 9 2 1 1 2 2 5 1 1 2 1 2 1 1 1 1 1 1 1 1 1 1 1 2 1 2 1 1 1 2 1 1 1
1 1 1 1 1 2 1 1 1 1 1 1 1 1 1 1 1 1 1 1 1 1 1 1 1 2 2 1 2 1 2 1 1 2 4 2 2 1
2 5 5 5 2 1 2 2 2 2 1 2 1 1 1 1 2 1 4 4 1 2 1 1 2 1 9 2 4  5000 30000
1 1 1 1 1 1 2 2 5 9 SM 2 2 2 1 2 2 3 9 2
```

```
1 1 2 2 1 2 2 2 4 1 2 1 1 2 1 1 1 1 1 1 1 1 2 2 1 1 1 2 2 1 1 1 1 1 1
1 1 1 1 1 2 1 1 2 1 1 2 2 1 1 1 1 1 1 1 1 1 1 2 2 1 1 1 1 2 2 1 2 2 1
2 6 6 5 3 2 2 2 2 2 1 2 1 1 1 1 2 1 1 1 2 2 1 1 2 5 2 3 2    0 40000
1 2 1 1 1 1 2 1 4 5 SM 2 2 2 1 2 2 3 9 2

9 9 9 9 9 9 9 9 9 9 9 9 9 9 9 9 9 9 9 9 9 9 9 9 9 9 9 9 9 9 9 9 9 9 9
9 9 9 9 9 9 9 9 9 9 9 9 9 9 9 9 9 9 9 9 9 9 9 9 9 9 9 9 9 9 9 9 9 9 9
9 9 9 9 9 9 9 9 9 9 9 9 9 9 9 9 9 9 9 9 9 9 9 9 9 9 9 9 9  9999 99999
9 9 9 9 9 9 9 9 9 9 9 99 9 9 9 9 9 9 9 9 9

1 3 1 1 1 2 2 2 2 1 1 2 1 2 1 1 1 1 1 1 1 2 1 1 1 1 1 2 1 1 1 1 1 1
1 1 1 1 1 2 2 1 2 1 1 2 1 1 1 1 2 1 1 2 1 1 1 2 2 1 1 2 1 2 2 3 2 2 1
2 5 5 5 2 1 2 1 1 2 1 2 1 1 1 1 2 1 2 3 1 2 2 1 2 5 2 7 2   600  3500
2 1 1 1 1 1 2 9 5 2 SM 2 2 2 1 2 2 1 9 1

1 2 2 2 1 1 2 2 6 1 1 1 2 2 1 1 1 1 1 1 1 1 2 1 1 1 1 2 2 1 1 1 1 1 1
1 1 1 1 1 1 1 2 1 1 1 1 1 1 1 1 1 2 1 1 1 2 2 1 1 1 1 1 2 4 2 2 1
2 5 5 5 1 1 2 2 2 2 1 2 1 1 1 1 2 1 1 3 1 1 1 1 2 3 2 3 2  1508 28250
1 1 2 1 1 1 2 2 4 5 SM 2 2 2 1 2 2 3 9 2

1 2 1 2 1 1 2 2 6 1 1 2 1 2 1 1 1 1 1 1 1 1 1 2 1 1 2 1 1 2 1 1 1 1
1 1 1 1 1 2 2 1 1 1 2 2 2 1 2 1 1 1 1 2 1 1 1 2 2 1 1 2 1 2 1 2 2 4 2 2 1
1 6 6 5 1 1 1 2 2 2 1 2 1 1 1 1 2 1 2 3 1 2 2 2 1 2 6 2   4600 19500
1 1 1 1 1 1 2 4 4 4 SM 2 2 2 1 2 2 3 1
```

end data.

SPSS t-Test Results

The raw data or transformation pass is proceeding
 41 cases are written to the uncompressed active file.

LEGEND:
COMP = Composite Variable
GE = Greater than and Equal to
LT = Less Than

Independent samples of COMP

Group 1: COMP GE   .781   Group 2: COMP LT   .781

t-test for: TOTPROC (Total Number of Incorrect Practices Per Case)

	Number of Cases	Mean	Standard Deviation	Standard Error
Group 1	19	27.2105	8.404	1.928
Group 2	18	55.8333	10.182	2.400

Pooled Variance Estimate   Separate Variance Est.

Appendices

F Value	2-Tail Prob.	t Value	Degrees of Freedom	2-Tail Prob.	t Value	Degrees of Freedom	2-Tail Prob.
1.47	.427	-9.35	35	.000	-9.30	33.03	.000

Independent samples of COMP
Group 1: COMP GE .781   Group 2: COMP LT .781

t-test for: UNDOWN (Hours of Unscheduled Downtime)

	Number of Cases	Mean	Standard Deviation	Standard Error
Group 1	19	1.4737	.513	.118
Group 2	17	1.6471	.493	.119

Pooled Variance Estimate   Separate Variance Est.

F Value	2-Tail Prob.	t Value	Degrees of Freedom	2-Tail Prob.	t Value	Degrees of Freedom	2-Tail Prob.
1.08	.877	-1.03	34	.310	-1.03	33.81	.309

Independent samples of COMP
Group 1: COMP GE .781   Group 2: COMP LT .781

t-test for: CRASH (Number of System Crashes)

	Number of Cases	Mean	Standard Deviation	Standard Error
Group 1	19	3.8421	2.115	.485
Group 2	18	3.1111	2.083	.491

Pooled Variance Estimate   Separate Variance Est.

F Value	2-Tail Prob.	t Value	Degrees of Freedom	2-Tail Prob.	t Value	Degrees of Freedom	2-Tail Prob.
1.03	.954	1.06	35	.297	1.06	34.94	.297

Independent samples of COMP

Group 1: COURT GE .781   Group 2: COURT LT .781

t-test for: TMDOWN (Average Downtime Per Crash)

	Number of Cases	Mean	Standard Deviation	Standard Error
Group 1	19	2.7368	1.522	.349
Group 2	18	3.5556	1.790	.422

Pooled Variance Estimate   Separate Variance Est.

F Value	2-Tail Prob.	t Value	Degrees of Freedom	2-Tail Prob.	t Value	Degrees of Freedom	2-Tail Prob.
1.38	.501	-1.50	35	.142	-1.50	33.45	.144

Independent samples of COMP

Group 1: COMP GE   .781   Group 2: COMP LT   .781

t-test for: SHDOWN (Hours of Scheduled Downtime)

	Number of Cases	Mean	Standard Deviation	Standard Error
Group 1	19	2.4737	1.577	.362
Group 2	18	2.5556	1.756	.414

Pooled Variance Estimate   Separate Variance Est.

F Value	2-Tail Prob.	t Value	Degrees of Freedom	2-Tail Prob.	t Value	Degrees of Freedom	2-Tail Prob.
1.24	.653	-.15	35	.882	-.15	34.10	.882

Independent samples of COMP

Group 1: COMP GE   .781   Group 2: COMP LT   .781

t-test for: PERSREC (Number of Personnel Records on system)

Appendices

	Number of Cases	Mean	Standard Deviation	Standard Error
Group 1	18	1600.2778	1829.481	431.213
Group 2	14	1799.3571	2210.040	590.658

		Pooled Variance Estimate			Separate Variance Est.		
F Value	2-Tail Prob.	t Value	Degrees of Freedom	2-Tail Prob.	t Value	Degrees of Freedom	2-Tail Prob.
1.46	.459	-.28	30	.782	-.27	25.10	.788

Independent samples of COMP

Group 1: COMP   GE   .781   Group 2: COMP   LT   .781

t-test for: CUSREC (Number of Customer Records on System)

	Number of Cases	Mean	Standard Deviation	Standard Error
Group 1	18	11130.7778	11254.222	2652.645
Group 2	16	12376.5000	11847.415	2961.854

		Pooled Variance Estimate			Separate Variance Est.		
F Value	2-Tail Prob.	t Value	Degrees of Freedom	2-Tail Prob.	t Value	Degrees of Freedom	2-Tail Prob.
1.11	.832	-.31	32	.755	-.31	31.07	.756

Independent samples of SA   Software Admin Module

Group 1: SA GE   .838   Group 2: SA LT   .838

t-test for: SWPROC (Number of incorrect SA procedures)

	Number of Cases	Mean	Standard Deviation	Standard Error
Group 1	18	2.9444	1.259	.297
Group 2	19	8.2105	2.699	.619

	Pooled Variance Estimate			Separate Variance Est.		
F Value	2-Tail Prob.	t Value	Degrees of Freedom	2-Tail Prob.	t Value	Degrees of Freedom	2-Tail Prob.
4.60	.003	-7.53	35	.000	-7.67	25.78	.000

Independent samples of HA   Hardware Admin Module

Group 1: HA GE   .754   Group 2: HA LT   .754

t-test for: HWPROC (Number of incorrect HA procedures per case)

	Number of Cases	Mean	Standard Deviation	Standard Error
Group 1	20	3.2000	2.526	.565
Group 2	17	4.4706	2.004	.486

	Pooled Variance Estimate			Separate Variance Est.		
F Value	2-Tail Prob.	t Value	Degrees of Freedom	2-Tail Prob.	t Value	Degrees of Freedom	2-Tail Prob.
1.59	.354	-1.67	35	.103	-1.71	34.86	.097

Independent samples of CA   Security Admin Module

Group 1: CA GE   .773   Group 2: CA LT   .773

t-test for: SA (Number of incorrect security procedures per case)

	Number of Cases	Mean	Standard Deviation	Standard Error
Group 1	18	8.6667	2.808	.662
Group 2	19	18.2632	3.724	.854

	Pooled Variance Estimate			Separate Variance Est.		
F Value	2-Tail Prob.	t Value	Degrees of Freedom	2-Tail Prob.	t Value	Degrees of Freedom	2-Tail Prob.
1.76	.250	-8.81	35	.000	-8.88	33.36	.000

Independent samples of NA   Network Admin Module

Group 1: NA GE   .745   Group 2: NA LT   .745

t-test for: NETPROC (Number of incorrect network procedures per case)

	Number of Cases	Mean	Standard Deviation	Standard Error
Group 1	19	2.3158	1.293	.297
Group 2	18	5.8889	.963	.227

	Pooled Variance Estimate			Separate Variance Est.		
F Value	2-Tail Prob.	t Value	Degrees of Freedom	2-Tail Prob.	t Value	Degrees of Freedom	2-Tail Prob.
1.80	.231	-9.49	35	.000	-9.56	33.20	.000

Independent samples of OA   Operations Admin Module

Group 1: OA GE   .795   Group 2: OA LT   .795

t-test for: OPSPROC (Number of Incorrect Operations Procedures per case)

	Number of Cases	Mean	Standard Deviation	Standard Error
Group 1	19	9.4211	3.061	.702
Group 2	18	18.9444	3.556	.838

		Pooled Variance Estimate			Separate Variance Est.		
F Value	2-Tail Prob.	t Value	Degrees of Freedom	2-Tail Prob.	t Value	Degrees of Freedom	2-Tail Prob.
1.35	.534	-8.75	35	.000	-8.71	33.60	.000

FREQUENCY LIST AND STATISTICS OF INCORRECT PROCEDURES

SWPROC

VALUE	FREQ	PCT	CUM PCT	VALUE	FREQ	PCT	CUM PCT	VALUE	FREQ	PCT	CUM PCT
0	1	3	3	5	2	5	49	9	3	8	89
2	6	16	19	6	5	14	62	10	1	3	92
3	5	14	32	7	6	16	78	11	2	5	97
4	4	11	43	8	1	3	81	17	1	3	100

M I S S I N G   D A T A

VALUE	FREQ	VALUE	FREQ	VALUE	FREQ
99	4				

SWPROC

Mean	5.649	Std Err	.558	Median	6.000
Mode	2.000	Std Dev	3.393	Variance	11.512
Kurtosis	2.030	S E Kurt	.759	Skewness	1.060
S E Skew	.388	Range	17.000	Minimum	0.0
Maximum	17.000	Sum	209.000		

Valid Cases   37   Missing Cases   4

Appendices

HWPROC

VALUE	FREQ	PCT	CUM PCT	VALUE	FREQ	PCT	CUM PCT	VALUE	FREQ	PCT	CUM PCT
0	1	3	3	4	8	22	68	8	1	3	97
1	5	14	16	5	6	16	84	12	1	3	100
2	6	16	32	6	2	5	89				
3	5	14	46	7	2	5	95				

MISSING DATA

VALUE	FREQ		VALUE	FREQ		VALUE	FREQ
99	4						

HWPROC

Mean	3.784	Std Err	.388	Median	4.000
Mode	4.000	Std Dev	2.359	Variance	5.563
Kurtosis	2.795	S E Kurt	.759	Skewness	1.187
S E Skew	.388	Range	12.000	Minimum	0.0
Maximum	12.000	Sum	140.000		

Valid Cases   37   Missing Cases   4

SECPROC

VALUE	FREQ	PCT	CUM PCT	VALUE	FREQ	PCT	CUM PCT	VALUE	FREQ	PCT	CUM PCT
3	1	3	3	11	5	14	43	18	1	3	78
4	1	3	5	12	1	3	46	20	3	8	86
6	2	5	11	13	1	3	49	21	3	8	95
7	2	5	16	14	3	8	57	22	1	3	97
8	3	8	24	15	1	3	59	29	1	3	100
9	1	3	27	16	4	11	70				
10	1	3	30	17	2	5	76				

MISSING DATA

VALUE	FREQ		VALUE	FREQ		VALUE	FREQ
99	4						

SPSS t-Test Results — 283

SECPROC

Mean	13.595	Std Err	.963	Median	14.000
Mode	11.000	Std Dev	5.857	Variance	34.303
Kurtosis	-.158	S E Kurt	.759	Skewness	.321
S E Skew	.388	Range	26.000	Minimum	3.000
Maximum	29.000	Sum	503.000		

Valid Cases   37   Missing Cases   4

NETPROC

VALUE	FREQ	PCT	CUM PCT	VALUE	FREQ	PCT	CUM PCT	VALUE	FREQ	PCT	CUM PCT
0	2	5	5	3	5	14	41	6	8	22	89
1	3	8	14	4	5	14	54	7	3	8	97
2	5	14	27	5	5	14	68	8	1	3	100

M I S S I N G   D A T A

VALUE	FREQ	VALUE	FREQ	VALUE	FREQ
99	4				

NETPROC

Mean	4.054	Std Err	.351	Median	4.000
Mode	6.000	Std Dev	2.134	Variance	4.553
Kurtosis	-.918	S E Kurt	.759	Skewness	-.201
S E Skew	.388	Range	8.000	Minimum	0.0
Maximum	8.000	Sum	150.000		

Valid Cases   37   Missing Cases   4

OPSPROC

VALUE	FREQ	PCT	CUM PCT	VALUE	FREQ	PCT	CUM PCT	VALUE	FREQ	PCT	CUM PCT
3	1	3	3	11	3	8	35	18	1	3	76
5	1	3	5	12	3	8	43	19	1	3	78
6	1	3	8	13	2	5	49	20	3	8	86
7	3	8	16	14	2	5	54	21	1	3	89
8	2	5	22	15	1	3	57	22	3	8	97
9	1	3	24	16	3	8	65	29	1	3	100
10	1	3	27	17	3	8	73				

```
                         M I S S I N G   D A T A
      VALUE    FREQ           VALUE    FREQ              VALUE    FREQ
       99       4

OPSPROC

Mean      14.054    Std Err       .958    Median     14.000
Mode       7.000    Std Dev      5.826    Variance   33.941
Kurtosis  -.240     S E Kurt      .759    Skewness     .248
S E Skew   .388     Range       26.000    Minimum     3.000
Maximum   29.000    Sum        520.000


Valid Cases      37     Missing Cases      4
-----------------------------------------------------------------
```

Using the vi Editor

Introduction

vi is an editor commonly used in UNIX environments. Its commands are easy to use once learned. Unfortunately, by word processor standards, vi can be archaic and difficult because it is not intuitive. Nonetheless, it is an extremely valuable tool for the UNIX system administrator.

Modes of Operation

vi operates in two different modes: command mode and insert mode. Command mode is used for cursor control and file operations. Insert mode is used for entering and manipulating text. Executing commands in the wrong mode will result in no action taken by vi followed by beeps to indicate an invalid command.

vi is in command mode at startup. To enter insert mode, press the a, i, or o key (explained in *Insert Mode* later in this chapter). To return to command mode, press the Esc key. You will toggle between insert and command modes often while entering text and moving about the screen.

Appendices

Command Mode

vi is in command mode at startup. When in insert mode, enter command mode by pressing Esc. The following commands are case sensitive. Commands with the same letter but a different case perform different tasks.

Exit Commands

Esc followed by a : (colon) allows you to exit vi and perform certain file operations. The exit commands are:

:wq	write file and quit
:w	write file (do not quit)
:q	quit
:q!	quit and do not save changes
:w <*filename*>	write to the file named <*filename*>
:w! <*filename*>	overwrite the file named <*filename*>
:r <*filename*>	read in <*filename*> (and append at the point of the cursor)

Cursor Control

These commands move the cursor.

j	move down one line
k	move up one line
h	move left one character
l	move right one character
w	move forward one word
W	move forward one word, punctuation ignored
b	move back one word
B	move back one word, punctuation ignored
$	move to the end of line
^	move to the beginning of line
{	go to previous paragraph
}	go to next paragraph
G	go to last line in the file

*nn*G	go to the *n*th line in the file, where *nn* is the line number
H	move to top of screen (home)
M	move to middle of screen
L	move to bottom of screen
Cntl-F	move forward one screen
Cntl-B	move backward one screen
Cntl-D	move forward a half screen
Cntl-U	move backward a half screen
Return key	move cursor to start of next line
+	(plus) move cursor to start of next line
	(dash) move cursor to start of previous line
^	(carat) move to start of the current line
e	move to the end of a word
E	move to the end of a word, ignore punctuation
{	move to start of previous paragraph
}	move to start of next paragraph
(	move to start of previous sentence
)	move to start of next sentence

Search Commands

Search commands are used to locate specific text (indicated below by the term *textcriteria*) while in command mode. These commands allow you to find text based on the search criteria provided. vi stores the search pattern until a new search pattern is specified. Note that a space is not entered after the command.

/*textcriteria*	a forward text search
?*textcriteria*	a backward text search
n*textcriteria*	repeat search in same direction
N*textcriteria*	repeat search in opposite direction
;*textcriteria*	repeat previous find command
f*xtextcriteria*	go to the next occurrence of the value, where x is any character

Text Commands

One or more characters can be deleted while in command mode where [n] is the number of characters or lines for command interpretation. The commands can be used without an n value, giving an n default of 1. For example, 7x (i.e., [n]x) deletes seven characters, but using just x deletes only one character.

x	delete character(s)
dd	delete line(s)
D	delete the remainder of a line from the cursor

Cut and Paste Commands

Command mode also has commands that allow text to be copied into and from buffers, commonly known as cut and paste. Also, the [n] option is available to specify the number of lines to be used by the command.

yy	yank a line
"ay	yank line into a specified buffer (the buffer is labeled a)
p	place a yanked line after the current line
"ap	place the contents of buffer a after the current line
P	place a yanked line before the current line
"aP	place the contents of buffer a before the current line

Insert Mode

The following commands allows you to enter insert mode and enter and manipulate text. Notice that these commands are case sensitive. Commands with the same letter but a different case perform different tasks.

i	insert text at the cursor location
I	insert text at the beginning of the line
a	append text after the cursor
A	append text at the end of the current line
o	open a new line below the cursor
O	open a lew line above the cursor
J	join two lines
u	undo the last change or command (U can be used too)

r	replace character under the cursor
R	replace a string of text (overstrike)
.	(dot) use the previous command
u	undo your last command (U can be used too)

More on vi

Start practicing on the vi editor with these commands. More functionality is available, but this overview gives you the basics needed to use vi to create, modify, and save your files.

UNIX Shell Script Construction

Introduction

The UNIX shell interprets commands that are entered on a command line or through a program called a script. Shell scripts are text files created with an editor. Because the text in a shell script is filled with commands and program controls, it becomes an executable that is interpreted by the shell. Shell scripts that work in one shell, such as Bourne, may not be executable in another, such as Korn unless you make modifications. Remember, each shell is its own interpreter and requires its own syntax. This tutorial focuses on Bourne shell scripts.

This appendix is intended to give the user an overview of shell scripting, which provides very robust system utilities that can automate tasks, improve system utilization, and support applications. It is very similar to C programming. Note that shell scripts are not compiled but are interpreted by the operating system at run time. Critical shell scripts should be assigned the proper permissions to prevent unauthorized users from changing script contents.

Appendices

Creating a Simple Script

This section describes how to create a simple shell script that finds files that begin with the letters a–i (note the lowercase; it will not find files beginning with A–I), with the otherwise similar name `plane`. The script begins its search at the root (/) directory.

Create the script below using vi by entering **vi** *filename* at the prompt and typing:

```
#This shell script is a sample to
#illustrate the creation of an executable
#!/bin/sh
find / -name [a-i]plane -print
```

Commands in a shell do not execute if they are not in the search path. The explicit path for a command can also be specified. Put a PATH statement in the script as follows:

```
#This shell script is a sample to
#illustrate the creation of an executable
#!/bin/sh
PATH=/usr/bin:/bin; export PATH        #The search path
find / -name [a-i]plane -print
```

To exit vi and save the file, enter :wq

By convention, #!/bin/sh indicates that this is a Bourne shell program by specifying the interpreter being used. Specifying the interpreter is not required but improves readability and understanding of the content of the script in terms of how it will be executed. The PATH statement sets a path variable and is then exported to the shell interpreter. The semicolon (;) is used to delimit commands on the same line, so PATH=/usr/bin:/bin; export PATH is actually two command statements. The first statement PATH=/usr/bin:/bin assigns the path, and the second statement, export PATH, obviously does the export function.

Checking Inputs and Exit Status

A shell script should always validate arguments being passed, if any. Arguments passed can include parameters such as options and filenames. For instance, the command **ls** -l fun* actually contains three arguments. The first is ls, the filename of the command to execute. The second is -l. The third is fun*, checking for words beginning with *fun* followed by any characters.

```
if [ 'echo $argmnt cut -c1' = '#' ];
    then
      echo "The $argument passed is not valid"
    exit 51
fi
```

In the above sample script, an argument label is passed with the variable $argmnt. The first character is cut from the argument and compared to see if it is equal to the pound sign (#). If true the script reports that the argument passed is invalid and exits. An exit value of 0 is normal termination. Exit codes that are non-zero indicate an error condition.

It is possible for the script to continue and exit properly without an exit. However, it is good practice to end scripts with an exit status. Exit status codes are sometimes referred to as signal interrupts and are important because they can handle unwanted control signals, such as those sent by users.

Some common signals are:

1	Hangup
2	Break
3	Quit
4	Illegal instruction
12	System call error
14	Alarm
15	Kill
18	Child process is dead
19	Power failure

Program Control

As in any programming language, there are control statements:

• Conditional statements

```
if condition; then
    do something
fi
```

This statement makes a decision in an if construct based on the condition specified. If the condition is met, then an action is taken. The command fi closes out the if construct. For example:

```
if ls -l; then
     echo listing directory \^D
fi
```

- If–then–else construct

```
if condition
then
     execute_statement1
[ else
     command ]
fi
```

For example:

```
if command; then command; [ else command; ] fi
```

- While/until looping structure
  Continue in loop until the condition is no longer valid

```
{while | until} command
do
     command
done
```

For example:

```
# for each argument mentioned, remove that directory
while [ $# -ge 1 ]; do
          rm $1
          shift
done
```

- stdin, stdout, stderr
  Standard input, output, and error files use descriptors 0, 1, and 2. Each has a particular role and should be used accordingly.

```
# out of range year
if [ $year -lt 1901 -o $year -gt 1999 ]; then
     echo 1>&2 Year \"$year\" out of range for system
```

```
        exit 127
fi
```

Be sure to include error messages in stderr. Output should appear on stdout. For example:

```
# ability to exit on specified condition
if tty -s ; then
     echo Rremove files in $* since
     echo $n Ok to procede? $c;        read res
     case "$res" in
         n*|N*)
echo File delete stopped;
exit 0  ;;
     esac
     REMV="rm -rfi"
else
     REMV="rm -rf"
fi
```

Note that this code behaves differently if there's a user to communicate with (i.e., if the standard input is a TTY rather than a pipe, file, etc.

- Language constructs for loop iteration

Values are substituted:

```
do
     command
done
```

For example:

```
for i in `cat $SYSLOGS`
do
        mv $i $i.$OLD
        cp /dev/null $i
        chmod 664 $i
done
```

Variables

Variables include letters, digits, or other valid characters and begin with a letter or underscore. To get the contents of a variable, you must prefix the name with $.

- Variable assignment:

  Assign a value to a variable by *variable=value*. For example:

  ```
  PATH=/usr/ucb:/usr/bin:/bin; export PATH
  ```

  or

  ```
  SOMEDAY=`(set \`date\`; echo $1)`
  ```

  To use variables in a script, they must be exported. Use the **export** command (i.e., **export** SOMEDAY)

- Referencing variables

  Use $*variable* (or, if necessary, ${*variable*}) to reference the value.

  ```
  # Using an assigned PATH
  if [ "$USER" != "root" ]; then
          PATH=$HOME/bin:$PATH
  else
          PATH=/etc:/usr/etc:$PATH
  fi
  ```

  This gives the user a path assigned to HOME (i.e., /usr/wetsch/bin) and a system-specified path determined by and reassigned to PATH.

- Double quotes

  Double quotes allow variable substitution (i.e., the dollar sign is interpreted), but the filename is not created (i.e., * and ? are quoted). The result is one word.

  ```
  if [ ! "${parent}" ]; then
    parent=${people}/${group}/${user}
  fi
  ```

- Back quotes

  Back quotes allow you to run a command and provide a substitution for the output.

```
if [ "`echo -n`" = "-n" ]; then
  n=""
  d="\d"
else
  n="-n"
  d=""
fi
```

and

```
SOMEDAY=`(set \`date\`; echo $1)`
```

Functions

Functions can be used in shell scripts. Just as in any programming language, they are a potent means of programming and are similar to C constructs.

```
funcname ()
{
      shell commands
}
```

For example:

```
# Function to Determine the Existence of a Directory
dirchk()
{
      # check for the existence of a directory
      if [ ! -d $1 ]; then
         echo $1: No such directory 1>&2
         return
      fi
}
```

SAmatrix User Guide

Contents

Appendices

1. Introduction

1.1. Technical Support

Questions, feedback, and helpful input can be directed to the author via e-mail at DR_WETSCH@prodigy.net.

1.2. Disclaimer

Use of this software or any results from an analysis performed by this program is at the sole discretion of the user. The author or publisher assumes no liability for its use or interpretation of the results by a user.

1.3. System Requirements

SAmatrix requires Windows 3.1 or higher.

1.4. SAmatrix Overview

SAmatrix is a tool for assessing system administration and system management practices. SAmatrix provides a framework on which a user can build an assessment tool customized for a specific system. Using the information provided in the book and from other system management sources, a user can develop a comprehensive set of assessment questions that pertain to a particular computing environment.

The program is based on a robust statistical application of system administration practices using a statistical analysis package to analyze data gathered from a manual survey. The simplification of the analysis in SAmatrix reduces the statistical analysis to a set of rules that can be applied to data provided. The analysis of the data can then provide feedback to the user on whether or not the system is at risk. That is, as the risk to a system increases, the integrity and reliability of a system decreases. The methodology used in SAmatrix was successfully applied to a distributed system of national scope.

SAmatrix contains five modules that assess major areas of system administration: Software, Hardware, Network, Security, and Operations. A database of more than 100 assessment questions that relate to each module is supplied with this program. In addition, refinements and enhancements are being planned for future releases of SAmatrix to improve the system interface and the expert analysis of the data. User input is important to improving this software and comments are appreciated.

No system is free of risk. The best risk assessment this program can provide is LOW risk. A result showing moderate risk, substantial risk, or high risk may justify a review of the system administration policies and procedures of the organization. If a result shows low data reliability or questions the reliability of the data, individual assessment modules should be checked to make sure they are comprehensive.

2. Installation

The disk contains the files:

`samatrix.exe//`	The SAmatrix program
`samatrix.adm//`	The SAmatrix database
`sauser.txt//`	The SAmatrix User Guide (this document)

To install SAmatrix, create a directory on the drive of choice; for example, `C:\samatrix`. Copy the contents of the disk to the new directory.

3. Basic Operation

3.1. Starting the Program

Start SAmatrix from the File or Start menu. Select Run and enter the drive, directory, and executable file `samatrix.exe`, for example, `C:\samatrix\samatrix`, to start the program. The main screen displays the main screen, which contains a menu bar, a scrollable list of the assessment questions, the name of the currently loaded database file, and Edit and Cancel keys.

3.2. Loading a Database

To load a database into SAmatrix for analysis, select File/Open, then the name of the database file. SAmatrix recognizes files with the extension `adm`. A template database file called `samatrix.adm` is provided with this program.

To learn how to create or customize a database, see Section 4 of this document, *Creating/Customizing a Database*.

3.3. Analyzing Data

When the program is loaded, you can immediately conduct an analysis of the data by clicking on the Analysis menu and selecting either the module to analyze or by selecting System to analyze the entire system. If you are using the `samatrix.adm` file, note that all numerical fields in the database contain zeros (0), so all data analysis comes back as 0 percent compliant.

Appendices

Module assessment will only show compliance of the prime module assessments. A system assessment will show compliance of the entire system, including prime assessment areas and related compliance modules.

The analysis is completely dependent on the quality of the input provided. Fair assessment and common sense should be provided. A document should be developed giving background information on the assessment questions, such as the objective of the question, examples of compliance, or a sample response. The background document provides a system administrator or system manager with a common reference. It helps them to understand the meaning of a question and whether or not the system complies. It also helps to identify associated areas in which the system does or does not comply. This can vary between environments, so it is up to the organization to implement a standardized assessment. If assessment and risk analysis is already in place, you can break your assessment down into the appropriate data format for SAmatrix.

3.4. Printing a Matrix Listing

SAmatrix can print a listing of the current database. Select File/Print on the menu bar. Here is an example of the output:

```
Matrix Listing

Module: S
Assessment:    Do you have a software configuration management
plan?
SW:            0
HW:            0
NET:           0
SEC:           0
OPS:           0
```

Only the complete database can be printed.

3.5. Exiting SAmatrix

To exit SAmatrix, select Cancel on the main screen. If changes have been made since the last cancel, SAmatrix will ask if you want to save the changes. Choose Yes or No. The program then closes. Alternatively, you can choose File/Exit or the exit icon in the corner of the screen. All methods prompt you to save changes.

4. Creating/Customizing a Database

The information gathered by your survey must be added to a database filein order for SAmatrix to analyze it. (See Chapter 11, *Implementing a Systems Administration Matrix,* for more information on designing a survey.) You can use the file samatrix.adm provided as a template or create your own.

An SAmatrix database file must be ASCII text. Use any editor to create the file, but the data must be in the record format described in the section that follows. Keep each database file to a maximum of 200 assessment questions. Consider making additional assessment files if you exceed this amount.

It is possible to maintain more than one database file. For instance, in an enterprise system you can maintain assessments for specific systems at specific locations as well as an enterprise system file to measure the overall enterprise. However, only one file at a time is loaded into the system.

4.1. Record Format

A record contains seven data elements separated by a line break. The fields in each record must be in the following order:

Assessment
Module
Software Compliance
Hardware Compliance
Network Compliance
Security Compliance
Operations Compliance

The values that can be assigned to these data elements are:

Assessment	A text string of an assessment question.
Module	The character values S (software), H (hardware), N (network), C (security), and O (operations).
Compliance Data	Either a 0 or a 1, where 1 = TRUE and 0 = FALSE

For example, the last record in the sample is:

```
Do you provide security training to new users? (Assessment)
C (Module)
0 (Software compliance)
0 (Hardware Compliance)
0 (Network Compliance)
0 (Security Compliance)
0 (Operations Compliance)
```

Here is a three-question sample from `samatrix.adm`. In this example, all compliance values equal zero.

```
-------Sample records from samatrix.adm--------
Do you provide security training to new users?
C
0
0
0
0
0
Do you provide annual security training to all users?
C
0
0
0
0
0
Are server resources monitored periodically and often?
H
0
0
0
0
0
--------------------End Data File Records-------------------
```

Each assessment question must include a module. This makes the assessment question a "prime" question for the module. In the last example above, the module assessment is for hardware. The hardware compliance value is 0, indicating that the administration of this resource is not in compliance. If this assessment were in compliance, the database record would read:

```
------------Hardware Assessment Record in Compliance----------
Are server resources monitored periodically and often?
H
0
1
0
0
0
----------------------------------------------------------------
```

The above record now indicates that the system complies with the assessment question.

An assessment may affect areas other than its primary module. When the assessment affects more than one module, the person doing the assessment may want to assign a value to the record to indicate that a procedure for the additional module(s) is in place and enforced. In the above example, the question is also an operations issue. To show compliance in both the hardware and operations modules, the record would look like:

```
---Data Record Showing Hardware and Operations Compliance----
Are server resources monitored periodically and often?
H
0
1
0
0
1
-------------------------------------------------------------
```

4.2. Adding a Record

On the menu bar, select Edit/Add Entry. SAmatrix displays the Module Edit screen.

In the field labeled Assessment, enter the assessment question. The length is limited to the field provided. Longer questions must be reworded or possibly broken up into two or more assessment questions. Assessment questions should be written to indicate that a 1 shows compliance and a 0 shows noncompliance. Negatives should be avoided. For more information on formulating an assessment question, see Chapter 11.

Press the Tab key to advance to the next field or click on the field labeled Module Data. Enter the module to which the assessment question is assigned, usually the module on which it has the greatest impact. In general, questions relating to administering applications, databases, operating systems are assigned to the Software Module (S); installing hardware, hardware maintenance, etc., are assigned to the Hardware Module (H); network operating systems, protocols, and network administration are assigned to the Network Module (N); access, passwords, physical security, and other security issues are assigned to the Security Module (C); and general procedures, enforcement of procedures, system administration operations issues, and user satisfaction are assigned to the Operations Module (O). The Module Data field will only accept the letters shown in the legend.

Press the Tab key or click on the first Admin Data field. Enter a 1 for Compliance or a 0 for Noncompliance. Press Tab to advance or click on the next box and enter the appropriate number until all Admin Data fields are complete. Admin Data fields, also called compliance data or assessment data, will only accept 1 or 0.

Appendices

When all fields are complete, select OK to add to the database without saving. The new record will be included in the next analysis whether you save the database or not.

4.3. Editing a Record

On the main screen, scroll the question list to the question/record that needs editing. Click on the question to highlight.

Select Edit, or on the menu bar select Edit/Edit Entry and edit as needed.

When finished, click OK to add the changes to the database without saving. The changes will be included in the next analysis whether you save the database or not.

4.4. Deleting a Record

On the main screen, scroll the question list to the question/record that needs editing. Click on the question to highlight.

On the menu bar, select Edit/Delete Entry. SAmatrix will prompt for confirmation. Select Yes or No as desired.

4.5. Adding a Database File

To add a new database file, select File/New on the menu bar. SAmatrix displays the Module Edit screen. Add record(s) as described previously. The filename area displays New File.

When the desired records are added, select File/Save on the menu bar. Enter the correct drive, subdirectories, and filename.

4.6. Saving a Database File

To save the current database file, select File/Save on the menu.

Index

N

naming conventions 70–72
    file system 77
National Computer Security
    Association. *See* NCSA.
National Institute of Standards and
    Technology. *See* NIST.
National Science Foundation 128
NCSA 154, 156
netstat command 119, 120
network
    access 104–105
    architecture 102–114
    assessing 123
    bottleneck 125
    cables 102–103
    connections
        logical 107–114
        physical 102–104
    connectors 102–103
    load 125
    models 102, 107–108
    optimizing 125
    peer-to-peer 102
    protocol 108
    server-based 102
    services
        basic communications
          119–120
        configuring network interface
          118–119
        debugging 122–123
        file sharing 120–122
        file transfer 119–120
        managing 115–118
        modem communications
          123–125
        routing 118–119
        TCP/IP 119–120
    topology 104–105
    traffic congestion 125
    troubleshooting 125
    types 101–102
Network File System. *See* NFS.
network interface card 108
newfs command 32
newgrp command 142
NFS 120–122, 159
NIC card 103, 108
nice command 52, 65
nice number 52
NIST 146, 154, 156
node 102
noglob option 82
NSFNET 128
null file 73
nulladm command 61
numbering conventions 70–72

O

octal numbers 11, 13
operating system
    maintaining 54–65
    tuning 54–65
operations
    administration standards,
      developing 188
    administration, overview 187–188
    role of system administrator
      188–189
Orange Book 154, 155, 156, 158
OSI model 107, 108

P

packet
    addressing 108
    filter 149
paging 57, 58, 76
parent process 4

R

S